The Rise and Relapse of European Human Rights in Turkey

# The Rise and Relapse of European Human Rights in Turkey

*The AKP Era, 2002–2024*

*Tuğba Bayar*

CEU PRESS

Central European University Press
Budapest–Vienna–New York

The publication of this book is made possible by a grant from the European Commission under the Jean Monnet Module for the project entitled *International and European Protection of Human Rig.*

Cover illustration: iStock

Cover design: Coördesign, Leiden
Lay-out: Crius Group, Hulshout

| | |
|---|---|
| ISBN | 978 90 4857 381 3 |
| e-ISBN | 978 90 4857 459 9 (pdf) |
| e-ISBN | 978 90 4857 460 5 (accessible ePub) |
| DOI | 10.5117/9789048573813 |
| NUR | 697 |




Central European University Press is an imprint of Amsterdam University Press.

*For Selin,*
*in the hope of a world where human rights need no defence.*

# Table of Contents

# List of Figures

# Abbreviations

| | |
|---|---|
| AFAD | Disaster and Emergency Management Presidency (Afet ve Acil Durum Yönetimi Başkanlığı) |
| AKP | Justice and Development Party (Adalet ve Kalkınma Partisi) |
| AKUT | Search and Rescue Association (Arama Kurtarma Derneği) |
| ANAP | Motherland Party (Anavatan Partisi) |
| AP | Justice Party (Adalet Partisi) |
| ATL | Anti-Terror Law |
| AYM | Anayasa Mahkemesi (Constitutional Court of Turkey) |
| BTK | Information and Communication Technologies Authority (Bilgi Teknolojileri ve İletişim Kurumu) |
| CAT | Convention against Torture and Other Cruel, Inhuman or Degrading Treatment or Punishment |
| CEAS | Common European Asylum System |
| CEDAW | Convention on the Elimination of All Forms of Discrimination against Women |
| CHP | Republican People's Party (Cumhuriyet Halk Partisi) |
| CM | Committee of Ministers of the Council of Europe |
| COE | Council of Europe |
| CPI | Corruption Perception Index |
| CPT | European Committee for the Prevention of Torture and Inhuman or Degrading Treatment or Punishment |
| CRC | Convention on the Rights of the Child |
| CSO | civil society organization |
| CU | Customs Union |
| DDP | Party for Democratic Change (Demokratik Değişim Partisi) |
| DEP | Democracy Party (Demokrasi Partisi) |
| DG HOME | Directorate-General for Migration and Home Affairs |
| DGM | State Security Court (Devlet Güvenlik Mahkemesi) |
| DGMM | Directorate General of Migration Management |
| DHKP/C | Revolutionary People's Liberation Party/Front (Devrimci Halk Kurtuluş Partisi-Cephesi) |
| DKP | Democratic Mass Party (Demokratik Kitle Partisi) |
| DP | Democrat Party (Demokrat Parti) |
| DPRK | Democratic People's Republic of Korea (North Korea) |
| DSP | Democratic Left Party (Demokratik Sol Parti) |
| DTP | Democratic Society Party (Demokratik Toplum Partisi) |
| DYP | True Path Party (Doğru Yol Partisi) |

| | |
|---|---|
| EAEC | European Atomic Energy Community (Euratom) |
| EASO | European Asylum Support Office |
| EC | European Commission/European Community |
| ECHR | European Convention on Human Rights |
| ECOSOC | Economic and Social Council |
| ECSC | European Coal and Steel Community |
| ECtHR | European Court of Human Rights |
| EEC | European Economic Community |
| EMEP | Labour Party (Emek Partisi) |
| EP | European Parliament |
| ETIAS | European Travel Information and Authorisation System |
| EU | European Union |
| EUAA | European Union Agency for Asylum |
| eu-LISA | EU Agency for the Operational Management of Large-Scale IT Systems |
| Euratom | European Atomic Energy Community (EAEC) |
| Eurodac | European Dactyloscopy (the EU fingerprint database) |
| Eurosur | European Border Surveillance System |
| FDI | Foreign Direct Investment |
| FETÖ | Fethullah Terrorist Organization (Fetullahçı Terör Örgütü) |
| FIDH | International Federation for Human Rights |
| FP | Virtue Party (Fazilet Partisi) |
| Frontex | European Border and Coast Guard Agency |
| GİB | Göç İdaresi Başkanlığı (Presidency for Migration Management) |
| GREVIO | Group of Experts on Action against Violence against Women and Domestic Violence |
| HADEP | People's Democracy Party (Halkın Demokrasi Partisi) |
| HDP | People's Democratic Party (Halkların Demokrasi Partisi) |
| HEP | People's Labour Party (Halkların Emek Partisi) |
| HREI | Human Rights and Equality Institution of Turkey (Türkiye İnsan Hakları ve Eşitlik Kurumu) |
| HRW | Human Rights Watch |
| HSK | Council of Judges and Prosecutors (Hakimler Savcılar Kurulu) |
| HSYK | High Council of Judges and Prosecutors (Hakimler Savcılar Yüksek Kurulu) |
| İBDA-C | Islamic Raiders of the Great East–Front (İslamî Büyük Doğu Akıncılar Cephesi) |
| ICC | International Criminal Court |

| | |
|---|---|
| İCCB | Union of Islamic Communities and Congregations (İslamî Cemiyetler ve Cemaatler Birliği) |
| ICCPR | International Covenant on Civil and Political Rights |
| ICERD | International Convention on the Elimination of All Forms of Racial Discrimination |
| ICESCR | International Covenant on Economic, Social and Cultural Rights |
| ICJ | International Commission of Jurists |
| ICT | Intra-Corporate Transferee |
| İHÖ | Islamic Movement Organization (İslami Hareket Örgütü) |
| ILO | International Labour Organization |
| INGO | international non-governmental organization |
| IOM | International Organization for Migration |
| IO | international organization |
| İP | Good Party (İyi Parti) |
| KCK | Kurdistan Communities Union (Koma Civakên Kurdistan) |
| LFIP | Law on Foreigners and International Protection |
| LGBTIQ | lesbian, gay, bisexual, transgender, intersex, and queer |
| MASAK | Financial Crimes Investigation Board (Mali Suçları Araştırma Kurulu) |
| METU | Middle East Technical University |
| MGK | National Security Council (Milli Güvenlik Kurulu) |
| MHP | Nationalist Movement Party (Milliyetçi Hareket Partisi) |
| MNC | multinational corporation |
| NGO | non-governmental organization |
| NPAA | National Programme for the Adoption of the Acquis |
| NPE | normative power Europe |
| OAS | Organization of American States |
| OECD | Organisation for Economic Co-operation and Development |
| OPEC | Organization of the Petroleum Exporting Countries |
| OSCE | Organization for Security and Co-operation in Europe |
| ÖZDEP | Freedom and Democracy Party (Özgürlük ve Demokrasi Partisi) |
| PACE | Parliamentary Assembly of the Council of Europe |
| PKK | Kurdistan Workers' Party (Partiya Karkerên Kurdistanê) |
| PYD | Democratic Union Party (Partiya Yekîtiya Demokrat) |
| RİG | Reform İzleme Grubu (Reform Monitoring Group) |
| RP | Welfare Party (Refah Partisi) |
| RSD | refugee status determination |

| | |
|---|---|
| RTÜK | Radio and Television Supreme Council (Radyo ve Televizyon Üst Kurulu) |
| SBP | Socialist Unity Party (Sosyalist Birlik Partisi) |
| SCIFA | Strategic Committee on Immigration, Frontiers and Asylum |
| SIS | Schengen Information System |
| TBKP | United Communist Party of Turkey (Türkiye Birleşik Komünist Partisi) |
| TBMM | Turkish Grand National Assembly (Türkiye Büyük Millet Meclisi) |
| TCP | Progressive Republican Party (Terakkiperver Cumhuriyet Fırkası) |
| TEU | Treaty on European Union |
| TI | Transparency International |
| TİKKO | Turkish Workers and Peasants Liberation Army (Türkiye İşçi Köylü Kurtuluş Ordusu) |
| TL | Turkish lira |
| TLSP | Turkey Human Rights Litigation Support Project |
| TMSF | Savings Deposit Insurance Fund (Tasarruf Mevduatı Sigorta Fonu) |
| TPC | Turkish Penal Code |
| TSP | Socialist Party of Turkey (Türkiye Sosyalist Partisi) |
| UDHR | Universal Declaration of Human Rights |
| UN | United Nations |
| UNGA | United Nations General Assembly |
| UNHCR | United Nations High Commissioner for Refugees |
| USOM | National Cyber Incident Response Centre (Ulusal Siber Olaylara Müdahale Merkezi) |
| USSR | Union of Soviet Socialist Republics |
| VCLT | Vienna Convention on the Law of Treaties |
| WEU | Western European Union |
| YAŞ | Supreme Military Council (Yüksek Askeri Şura) |
| YÖK | Higher Education Council (Yüksek Öğrenim Kurulu) |
| YSK | Supreme Electoral Council (Yüksek Seçim Kurulu) |
| ZP | Victory Party (Zafer Partisi) |

# Preface

This book examines Turkey's human rights trajectory through the lens of international relations, situating domestic developments within the evolving dynamics of EU–Turkey relations. Between 2002 and 2024, human rights reforms initially advanced under the influence of European Union conditionality, as Turkey sought to meet the Copenhagen criteria and secure accession prospects. Yet, following the opening of accession negotiations in 2005, the transformative power of the EU began to diminish. By 2013, and especially after 2016, Turkey's human rights record sharply deteriorated, despite the continued formal ties to the EU framework. This shifting trajectory reveals the complex interplay between external incentives and internal political dynamics, prompting a deeper inquiry into the conditions under which international actors can successfully promote domestic change, and the limits of normative influence over time.

As this book goes to print, Turkey's human rights situation has reached a critical point. Democracy and fundamental freedoms are facing their gravest threats to date. The arrest of Istanbul mayor Ekrem İmamoğlu on 19 March 2025, widely condemned by the opposition as the '19 March Coup', represents a profound escalation in political repression. İmamoğlu's detention is not an isolated event; it forms part of a broader strategy to silence dissent. Alongside him, Ümit Özdağ, leader of a far-right opposition party, and Selahattin Demirtaş, the former pro-Kurdish leader who has been imprisoned since 2016, have also been targeted. These high-profile arrests illustrate an increasingly deliberate effort to dismantle political opposition and entrench authoritarian rule.

The 19 March Coup triggered the largest wave of anti-government protests in a decade. The state's response was swift and severe: hundreds of demonstrators were detained, and credible allegations of ill-treatment and torture, particularly against student protesters, surfaced. In a society marked by deep polarization, opposition-led boycotts of cafés and bookstores were met with visible counter-mobilization by government supporters. Meanwhile, the government's broadcasting regulator, the Radio and Television Supreme

Bayar, Tuğba. *The Rise and Relapse of European Human Rights in Turkey: The AKP Era, 2002–2024*. Amsterdam University Press/Central European University Press, 2025.
DOI 10.5117/9789048573813_PREF

Council (Radyo ve Televizyon Üst Kurulu, RTÜK), imposed a ten-day blackout on television channels critical of the regime, further restricting the flow of independent information.

Against this backdrop of democratic backsliding, the European Union's collective response has been characterized by striking silence. Prioritizing strategic interests over normative commitments, the EU has largely refrained from condemning the crackdown. The recalibration of EU–Turkey relations reflects a broader shift: as the EU grapples with its security vulnerabilities, particularly in light of Russian aggression, Turkey has re-emerged as a valuable geopolitical partner. This transaction-oriented approach, anchored in security imperatives rather than democratic values, highlights the limits of the EU's normative power and underscores the deepening gap between its rhetoric and its strategic behaviour.

This book is driven by scientific curiosity, but its motivation extends beyond academic inquiry. As a professor teaching numerous classes and regularly engaging with young people, I have witnessed first-hand the profound impact of rights violations and limitations on their aspirations. Many of my students have increasingly lost hope for their future, disheartened by the erosion of state institutions and their diminishing belief that a promising future awaits them. Discussions in my human rights courses, particularly those under the Jean Monnet Module on International and European Protection of Human Rights (EUHR) funded by the European Commission, have mirrored this shift. Students who once actively engaged in debates on human rights have become more reserved, reluctant to express critical views out of fear that doing so could jeopardize their career prospects after graduation. Their growing silence in the classroom and reluctance to voice concerns are symptomatic of a broader climate of fear and repression, a climate now made even more oppressive by the government's latest actions.

Beyond these personal observations, this book primarily motivated by an intellectual inquiry into a critical paradox: How and why did the human rights dimension of EU–Turkey relations evolve over the past two decades? It witnessed progress in the early years of AKP rule, only to deteriorate sharply later, a paradox made even more striking by the apparent continuity of both actors and their formal obligations.

This study seeks to unravel these questions by examining Turkey's responsiveness to external human rights expectations and assessing the EU's capacity to effect changes within Turkey. Utilizing a neo-Gramscian hegemony framework, this analysis sheds light on Turkey's inconsistent readiness and capacity to embrace human rights reforms. Simultaneously, the framework also illuminates the European Union's much-vaunted normative power as a capacity and willingness to influence Turkey's human rights practices. This work equally criticizes AKP for its repression of human rights and the European Union for revealing that their approach to human rights was never purely normative, but deeply transactional

The catalysts for this study include the ongoing deterioration of human rights in Turkey, such as the rising rates of femicide, pervasive impunity, and a sharp decline in public trust towards the judiciary's fairness and objectivity. Particularly troubling are instances where the Turkish government disregarded verdicts from key institutions such as the European Court of Human Rights, exemplified by the case of Osman Kavala, and Turkey's own Constitutional Court (Anayasa Mahkemesi, AYM), as seen in the case of Can Atalay. Legislative initiatives such as the 'agents of influence' law and new media regulations under the Information and Communication Technologies Authority (Bilgi Teknolojileri ve İletişim Kurumu, BTK) further threaten freedom of expression and media independence. The latest political arrests and repression confirm that these concerns are not hypothetical but represent an escalating reality. Democracy in Turkey is nearly down, but not yet out.

Equally alarming is the muted response from the Western world, particularly the European Union. Despite Turkey's increasingly authoritarian trajectory, neither the EU nor its member states have raised a sufficiently strong voice against Erdoğan's crackdown. Instead of exercising its normative power to promote democratic reforms, the EU has engaged with Turkey on a largely transactional basis, prioritizing security concerns, particularly migration management, over human rights. The EU's securitized approach characterized by entry-prevention policies, deceptive practices against migrants, illegal detentions, and the construction of physical barriers starkly contradicts the human rights standards it claims to uphold. The containment of refugees on isolated islands like Lampedusa in Italy and Lesvos in Greece, and the Union's reliance on Turkey to block migration flows, expose the troubling gap between European rhetoric and reality.

This book is a product of both my research and my teaching activities, supported by the Jean Monnet Module grant. It is designed to engage a broad audience, including policymakers, students, and scholars from the fields of international relations, political science, and the law, as well as human rights advocates and concerned citizens. At this crucial moment, as Turkey stands at a crossroads between deeper authoritarian consolidation and the possibility of democratic resilience, I hope this work will serve as a timely and critical contribution to the understanding of how national governance and international human rights standards intersect.

Tuğba Bayar
Ankara
22 April 2025

# 1. Introduction

**Abstract:** This introductory chapter outlines the trajectory of Turkey's human rights landscape under AKP rule, from its early alignment with European Union norms to its subsequent democratic backsliding. It presents the central puzzle of the book: Why and how did Turkey's initial reformist momentum, encouraged by EU accession prospects, gradually gave way to authoritarian entrenchment? The chapter frames this shift through the lens of international regime theory, later reinterpreted with a neo-Gramscian approach, to account for evolving power dynamics between domestic actors and external institutions. It also sets out the book's structure and methodological choices, and it argues that the EU's inconsistent conditionality and strategic interests contributed to the erosion of human rights norms in Turkey rather than their consolidation.

**Keywords:** AKP, EU–Turkey relations, human rights conditionality, neo-Gramscianism

This book scrutinizes the interplay between the European Union and Turkey with respect to human rights from 2002 onwards, a period predominantly under the governance of the Justice and Development Party (Adalet ve Kalkınma Partisi, AKP). The analysis chronicles the evolution of human rights within Turkey during this era, contextualizing it within the broader EU–Turkey relations. It posits that the trajectory of human rights in Turkey during this time exhibits a complex pattern: initial improvements until 2006, a stable yet stagnant phase up to 2013, followed by a marked regression post-2013, especially after the failed coup attempt in 2016. This decline has reached a nadir in recent years, where fundamental rights are routinely violated, judicial independence is severely eroded, and state mechanisms increasingly suppress dissent.

The core argument of this work is that while both the Turkish government and the EU remained constant stakeholders, their dynamics evolved significantly, influenced by both internal policies and external pressures.

Bayar, Tuğba. *The Rise and Relapse of European Human Rights in Turkey: The AKP Era, 2002–2024.* Amsterdam University Press/Central European University Press, 2025.
DOI 10.5117/9789048573813_CH01

The book critically assesses the EU's dual role, initially as a promoter of democratic reforms in Turkey, and subsequently, post-2016, as a pragmatic actor prioritizing migration control over democratic standards. This shift is epitomized by the 2016 EU–Turkey deal designed to restrict the flow of irregular migrants to Europe, thus sidelining broader human rights concerns in favour of geopolitical and security interests.

This book benefits from neo-Gramscian theory to offer a critical perspective on the structures of power and domination shaping both domestic and international landscapes. Neo-Gramscianism, building on the work of the Italian Marxist thinker Antonio Gramsci, moves beyond classical economic explanations of power by emphasizing the role of ideas, institutions, and cultural practices in maintaining social and political order. Gramsci's concept of cultural hegemony provides a crucial foundation, illustrating how ruling classes secure consent and reproduce their dominance not only through coercive mechanisms, but by establishing a sense of common sense and moral leadership within civil society. Extending these insights to the global sphere, neo-Gramscian scholars analyse how dominant social forces construct and uphold international hegemonies by forging alliances, as historic blocs, around prevailing modes of production and governance. This framework is particularly attentive to the subtle, often hidden, ways in which global consent is manufactured and contested. The contemporary relevance of neo-Gramscianism is clear: in a world marked by economic instability, political disaffection, and the rise of reactionary nationalist movements, it offers a powerful lens to understand the fractures within the existing global order. By emphasizing the interplay of material interests, discursive strategies, and institutional dynamics, this theoretical approach allows for a more nuanced examination of how power is structured, challenged, and potentially transformed. Throughout this study, neo-Gramscian concepts guide the analysis of how dominant projects are sustained, how counter-hegemonic forces emerge, and how struggles over consent and authority unfold within and across national borders.

Accordingly, through a neo-Gramscian lens, the European Union can be seen as having initially operated as a hegemonic actor in Turkey's candidacy process by projecting its norms and values, particularly regarding human rights, democracy, and the rule of law, as the common sense of a modern, legitimate political order. Through the conditionalities embedded in the accession process, the EU successfully exercised moral and intellectual leadership, encouraging a historic bloc within Turkey, including the AKP, to align national reforms with the broader European project. This period witnessed significant transformations within Turkey's civil and political structures, as European norms were internalized to a considerable extent. However, the EU's subsequent retreat from its full membership promise, evidenced by proposals for a privileged partnership and the politicization of the Cyprus issue as a definitive obstacle, undermined the hegemonic consensus it had painstakingly built. The perception that Turkey was being permanently excluded, despite its compliance efforts and in light of the EU's different treatment of Greece and the Greek Cypriot administration, exposed the contradictions within the EU's hegemonic project and fractured the ideological link between European norms and Turkish reform ambitions. As a result, the AKP's initial historic bloc, which had formed in alliance with EU-driven reforms, entered a plateau phase marked by reform stagnation, selective norm adoption, and growing scepticism towards external leadership. In the ensuing organic crisis, the AKP, drawing on its strengthened position within Turkish society and state institutions, embarked on a counter-hegemonic project. By repositioning itself as the authentic representative of national will and cultural identity, and by exploiting grievances rooted in perceived external humiliation, the AKP gradually displaced the EU's normative influence, constructing an alternative hegemonic vision centred on majoritarianism, sovereignty, and a redefined moral order within Turkish civil society.

The historical evolution of EU–Turkey relations and human rights in Turkey reveals a complex chemistry between domestic political dynamics and external pressures, particularly from the European Union. Following the establishment of the Republic, Turkey's human rights trajectory has been marked by significant fluctuations, with periods of progressive reform often overshadowed by authoritarian setbacks, military interventions, and socio-political turbulence. The post-1980 era witnessed a politically repressive environment that hindered civil society and delayed the adoption of international human rights standards. However, the EU's increasing emphasis on human rights, particularly through its conditionality based on the Copenhagen criteria and accession negotiations, introduced external incentives that catalysed legal and institutional reforms in Turkey. These efforts aimed at aligning Turkey's legal framework with European norms, addressing issues such as freedom of expression, gender equality, and the eradication of the death penalty.

From the 1999 Helsinki Summit to the early 2000s, Turkey's human rights reforms gained momentum, influenced heavily by its EU candidacy and the promise of integration. Significant milestones included the abolition of the death penalty, enhanced minority rights, and judicial reforms, reflecting the EU's transformative influence. However, Turkey's progress was consistently hindered by enduring political challenges, such as the Kurdish question, counterterrorism measures, and rising authoritarian tendencies. While the early 2000s marked a peak in EU–Turkey cooperation on human rights, subsequent years saw growing tensions, particularly as domestic political shifts under the Justice and Development Party led to stagnation and eventual regression in reforms. These dynamics underscored the delicate balance between Turkey's domestic priorities and its aspirations for European integration, highlighting the EU's critical but contested role as a normative power in shaping Turkey's human rights trajectory.

During its formative years in power, the Justice and Development Party embarked on what can be seen as a passive revolution, initiating a series of top-down reforms designed to realign Turkey with the dominant European historic bloc and its hegemonic articulation of human rights and democratic norms. By curtailing the entrenched power of the military in civilian politics, promoting gender equality, abolishing the death penalty, and advancing minority rights, the AKP sought to embed Turkey more deeply within the neoliberal and democratic consensus that the European Union projected as universal common sense. These reforms were building (both domestic and international) legitimacy and recognition of Erdoğan's AKP, too. The reforms initially reinforced a broad societal acceptance of the EU-oriented modernization project, functioning as both a source of moral leadership and a strategy to secure the consent of key segments of Turkish civil society. The dismantling of tutelary democracy removed a key check on political authority, enabling the AKP to consolidate power with fewer constraints. Yet, by 2013, the fragile historic bloc between the AKP's project and European hegemony began to unravel. The Gezi Park protests marked a turning point, as peaceful demonstrations were met with severe police violence, arbitrary restrictions on assembly, and a hostile narrative from then–prime minister Erdoğan, who portrayed the protests as foreign-orchestrated conspiracies. This response signalled a shift towards autocratic governance, undermining pluralism and the rule of law. The reaction to the protests and then the 2016 coup attempt and its consequences revealed the deep contradictions embedded within the earlier hegemonic alignment. As organic crises multiplied, reflected in growing societal unrest, declining trust in institutions, and intensified nationalist discourses the AKP gradually abandoned its initial war of position towards liberal-democratic hegemony. Instead, it began constructing a counter-hegemonic project grounded in a sovereigntist, majoritarian, and increasingly authoritarian redefinition of political legitimacy, using both coercive measures and a rearticulated ideological narrative that sought to neutralize and delegitimize liberal opposition forces within civil society.

The erosion of democratic institutions continued with the state of emergency during which transition to a presidential system happened in 2017. This new system, presented as a 'Turkish type' presidential system, concentrates executive power, diminishes legislative oversight, and weakens judicial independence. Subsequent actions, such as appointing trustees to replace elected officials in south-eastern provinces and withdrawing from the Istanbul Convention, further highlighted the deepening democracy deficit. While Turkey experienced peak democratization between 2004 and 2006, its trajectory since has been one of significant regression, culminating in its classification as a hybrid or electoral autocracy, a departure from its earlier aspirations of Europeanization and democratic consolidation.

The rule of law in Turkey under the Justice and Development Party has undergone significant shifts, shaped by both external pressures, such as the European Union's Copenhagen criteria conditionality, and domestic challenges. Early AKP reforms focused on judicial independence and alignment with EU standards, introducing critical measures like limiting the military influence on civilian politics, abolishing the State Security Courts, and enhancing legal transparency. These reforms demonstrated a commitment to democratization, as evidenced by judicial packages that sought to harmonize Turkey's judiciary with European norms.

However, since 2013, Turkey has experienced a marked deterioration in its rule of law, with systemic issues such as the politicization of the judiciary, executive overreach, and the erosion of judicial independence. Executive influence over judicial bodies like the Council of Judges and Prosecutors (HSK) has undermined impartiality, while constitutional changes under the presidential system have diluted legislative oversight and weakened democratic checks and balances.

Turkey's non-compliance with European Court of Human Rights (ECtHR) rulings, including high-profile cases like those of Osman Kavala and Selahattin Demirtaş, underscores its declining adherence to international judicial norms. This trend has strained relations with the EU and Council of Europe (COE), with the latter initiating rare infringement proceedings against Turkey for defying ECtHR judgements.

The periodic revival of death penalty discussions further exemplify Turkey's departure from European values to establish its counter-hegemony. Although abolished in 2004 as part of its EU accession process, the AKP has reignited these debates as a populist tool, often in response to domestic crises. Reinstatement would contravene Turkey's commitments under the

European Convention on Human Rights and jeopardize its COE membership and EU aspirations.

In summary, the AKP's initial reforms aimed at bolstering the rule of law have been overshadowed by significant regression. The judiciary has become a tool for political consolidation, and the rule of law remains compromised, hindering Turkey's alignment with European legal standards and eroding its democratic institutions.

Freedom of expression in Turkey under AKP rule has been marked by a duality of progress and regression. Early reforms, driven by Turkey's EU accession process, abolished the state monopoly on broadcasting, lifted bans on publications in languages other than Turkish, and enacted legal amendments to safeguard press freedoms. These measures aligned Turkey with European standards, fostering a more pluralistic media environment. However, their implementation has been inconsistent, often undermined by political motivations and the selective use of restrictive laws.

Key limitations have persisted throughout the AKP era. The Radio and Television Supreme Council (RTÜK) law, while aimed at harmonizing media regulations with democratic principles, has imposed stringent penalties and fostered self-censorship, particularly on sensitive topics such as Kurdish rights. Legal mechanisms, such as article 301 (prohibiting 'insulting Turkishness') and article 299 (criminalizing insults to the president) have been weaponized to suppress dissent, targeting journalists, authors, and ordinary citizens. Prosecutions for perceived criticism have surged, especially during President Erdoğan's tenure, with a marked increase following the transition to the presidential system in 2018.

The AKP government has also concentrated media ownership among pro-government entities, stifling pluralism and enabling direct influence over media narratives. These entities, often lacking media experience, have shaped public discourse to align with government priorities, further eroding press independence.

Digital expression has faced similar challenges. The government has imposed frequent closures of websites, social media accounts, and platforms critical of its policies. High-profile cases of individuals detained for social media posts or stickers criticizing economic conditions exemplify the government's intolerance of dissent in digital spaces.

Turkey's commitments under international treaties, such as the European Convention on Human Rights, provide a legal framework for safeguarding freedom of expression. However, the government's selective adherence to these obligations highlights systemic governance issues. While judicial reforms initially addressed some concerns, the AKP's focus on political survival has led to authoritarian practices that suppress dissenting voices.

In summary, despite early advancements in press and media freedoms, Turkey's trajectory under the AKP reflects a troubling pattern of regression. The selective application of reforms, legal restrictions on dissent, and consolidation of media control underscore the erosion of freedom of expression. To align with democratic norms and international obligations, Turkey must implement reforms consistently, remove restrictive measures, and foster a genuinely pluralistic and open public sphere.

Migration has emerged as a pivotal aspect of the EU's engagement with Turkey, reflecting the EU's use of its normative power to advance its hegemony and own material interests, particularly migration management and security. Through its accession process and agreements, the EU has influenced Turkey to align its migration laws and regulations with EU standards. This alignment includes legislative reforms that enhance migration control, border security, and the establishment of institutional frameworks to manage irregular migration flows. However, significant differences persist in the international commitments of the EU and Turkey. While the EU adheres to international refugee protections, Turkey maintains geographic reservations under the Refugee Convention (1951) and the Refugee Protocol (1967), limiting its obligations to refugees originating from Europe. This discrepancy has allowed Turkey to adopt policies that trap irregular migrants within its borders, effectively serving as a buffer zone to prevent their entry into the EU.

The EU–Turkey deal of 2016 epitomizes this dynamic, linking financial aid to Turkey with its role in stemming irregular migration to Europe. Subsequent agreements have reinforced this trend, further entrenching Turkey as a key actor in the EU's migration securitization strategy. While this approach serves EU interests, it has also led to widespread human rights violations and abuses. Policies aimed at preventing migrant entry, including pushbacks and the confinement of migrants in Turkey, often undermine the EU's self-portrayal as a champion of human rights and dignity.

Hence, the EU–Turkey migration framework illustrates the EU's prioritization of security over human rights in its external migration policies. While the alignment of Turkish legislation with EU standards have enhanced migration management, the broader consequences include human rights challenges that highlight the tension between normative commitments and material interests.

The book concludes with a reflection on the future prospects of EU–Turkey relations and the trajectory of human rights in Turkey. It offers a critical analysis of potential scenarios that could unfold based on current trends and international dynamics, providing a thoughtful examination of how Turkey and the EU might navigate their complex relationship moving forward.

By providing this detailed exploration, the introduction sets the stage for a nuanced discussion of human rights within the geopolitical context of EU–Turkey relations, offering readers a comprehensive understanding of the multifaceted issues at play. To this end, the first chapter introduces the broader themes and central issues that underpin this book, including EU–Turkey relations, human rights, and migration under the AKP's governance. The second chapter explores the theoretical frameworks that illuminate Turkey's initial receptiveness to European human rights norms, as well as the EU's capacity and structural limitations in transferring these norms, drawing on a neo-Gramscian hegemony framework. Building on this theoretical foundation, the third chapter examines the architecture of the European human rights regime, offering a detailed analysis of its development and the roles of key institutions. The fourth chapter provides a comprehensive overview of Turkey's human rights trajectory prior to 2002, setting the historical context for understanding later developments. The fifth chapter presents an in-depth analysis of human rights under the AKP, structured around three distinct phases: the Reform Era (2002–5), the Plateau Era (2005–13), and the Retrenchment of Human Rights (2013–24). Within this chapter, key themes such as the emerging democracy deficit, the politicization of the judiciary and erosion of the rule of law, the shrinking space for fundamental freedoms, and the evolving migration relationship between Turkey and the EU are critically examined. The sixth chapter turns to the current challenges facing human rights in Turkey, assessing the interplay between domestic political transformations and the EU's shifting priorities. Finally, the seventh chapter concludes by reflecting on the broader implications of Turkey's human rights trajectory, highlighting the decline of European hegemonic influence and the rise of a domestic counter-hegemony.

# 2. Theoretical Approaches to the Puzzle of EU–Turkey Relations

**Abstract:** This chapter lays the theoretical foundation of the book by drawing on neo-Gramscian approaches to international relations and global governance. It conceptualizes the EU–Turkey human rights dialogue not merely as a legal or normative exercise, but as a hegemonic project embedded in asymmetrical power relations. The chapter revisits key neo-Gramscian concepts such as hegemony, passive revolution, and the role of civil society, in order to frame the EU's human rights discourse as a mechanism of soft power and conditionality. It also critically examines how Turkish domestic actors selectively internalize, resist, or reframe EU norms in ways that reflect broader struggles over legitimacy, sovereignty, and modernization. The chapter positions human rights as a terrain of contestation rather than a universal normative good.

**Keywords:** neo-Gramscianism, hegemony, EU–Turkey relations, human rights, conditionality, passive revolution

Turkey's trajectory in human rights and democracy presents an apparent paradox. The same ruling party, the Justice and Development Party (AKP), was once celebrated for advancing democratic reforms in line with the accession criteria of the European Union (EU), only to later preside over a period of severe democratic backsliding. Conventional explanations, such as democratization theories or rationalist accounts of EU conditionality, fail to fully capture this transformation. While early analyses viewed Turkey's alignment with EU norms as a success story of external incentives and norm diffusion, these frameworks struggle to explain the EU's shifting stance as Turkey's authoritarian turn became more pronounced. Why did the EU initially support Turkey's reforms but later deprioritize democracy promotion in favour of geopolitical stability? This chapter argues that a neo-Gramscian perspective, which situates power struggles within the broader structures

Bayar, Tuğba. *The Rise and Relapse of European Human Rights in Turkey: The AKP Era, 2002–2024.* Amsterdam University Press/Central European University Press, 2025.
DOI 10.5117/9789048573813_CH02

of hegemony and resistance, offers a more comprehensive explanation of both Turkey's domestic transformation and the EU's evolving response.

In this book, the theoretical framework is grounded in the tradition of neo-Gramscianism, a critical approach to international relations that extends the Marxist analysis of class and production relations into the study of global power structures. Rooted in the thought of Antonio Gramsci, neo-Gramscian theory emphasizes the centrality of cultural hegemony, the ways in which ruling classes secure and maintain dominance not only through coercive means, but also through the consensual reproduction of ideas, norms, and institutions that appear as 'common sense' to subordinate groups. This understanding challenges classical Marxist formulations of power as purely based on economic exploitation or coercive domination, instead highlighting the complex, dialectical relationships within civil society and between state and society, where ideological leadership plays a fundamental role. Gramsci's insights into the extended nature of the state, where civil society institutions like the media, education systems, and religious organizations serve as key sites of ideological reproduction, offer critical tools for examining how global hegemonies are constructed, maintained, and challenged. In international relations, neo-Gramscianism applies these concepts to explore how historic blocs at the global level form around dominant modes of production, articulating a hegemonic order that is upheld through both material power and ideological leadership. Particularly significant is the idea of a 'global organic crisis', a term neo-Gramscians use to describe the systemic instability that arises when hegemonic orders, such as the neoliberal project after the 2008 financial crisis, begin to fracture under the weight of their internal contradictions.[1] The growing disconnect between political elites and popular classes, the rise of reactionary nationalist movements, widespread political disaffection, financial speculation, and mounting geopolitical tensions all signal the unravelling of existing hegemonic structures. Neo-Gramscian scholars provide nuanced insights into these processes, drawing attention to how counter-hegemonic movements form and contest dominant ideologies through a 'war of position' within civil society. Thus, neo-Gramscianism furnishes this book with a sophisticated and historically sensitive lens to critically analyse the dynamics of power, consent, and resistance in both

1 Jonathan Pass, 'What Neo-Gramscians Get Right (and Wrong) about the World', *Medium*, 23 January 2024, https://medium.com/international-affairs-blog/what-neo-gramscians-get-right-and-wrong-about-the-world-74c8349a8bb9.

national and international contexts, emphasizing the contingent, contested, and deeply ideational nature of political domination and social change.

Building on the work of Robert W. Cox and other critical theorists, a neo-Gramscian approach does not situate the EU as a neutral promoter of liberal norms, but as a hegemonic bloc that maintains its dominance through a combination of material power, ideational leadership, and institutional structures. Turkey's initial alignment with EU norms can be understood as a strategic integration into this hegemonic order, where the AKP positioned itself as a reformist actor benefiting from Europeanization. However, as global and regional power configurations shifted, particularly with the EU's growing prioritization of migration control and security over democratization, Turkey's role within this hegemonic structure also changed. The AKP, no longer dependent on EU support, consolidated an alternative power bloc domestically, resisting liberal-democratic norms while maintaining transactional relations with the EU. This perspective reframes EU–Turkey relations not as a simple case of compliance or non-compliance, but as a dynamic contestation of hegemonic structures, shaped by shifting material and ideological interests.

This book seeks to answer the research question: How has the AKP government both advanced and later deteriorated human rights in Turkey, and what role has the EU played in this transformation? Existing theoretical approaches attempting to explain this dynamic are predominantly grounded in the rationalist school, encompassing realist, institutionalist, and intergovernmentalist perspectives. These approaches conceptualize the EU's normative power as a distinct form of influence. However, from a rationalist standpoint, EU–Turkey relations are primarily transactional, functioning as a strategic cost–benefit game.

Accordingly, this book departs from the rationalist orthodoxy that reduces EU–Turkey relations to a strategic interplay of preferences and incentives, and instead advances a neo-Gramscian critique that reconceptualises these interactions as embedded within broader configurations of power, ideology, and historical material forces. Rationalist approaches, whether realist, liberal institutionalist, or intergovernmentalist, reify the EU's normative agency as an autonomous, strategic instrument, neglecting the ways in which norms themselves are historically contingent constructs serving particular hegemonic projects. In contrast, this study conceptualises the EU not as a neutral conveyor of universal values, but as a historically specific hegemonic bloc whose normative authority is dialectically produced and contested. The trajectory of human rights in Turkey under AKP rule is thus analysed not as a linear function of compliance or defection, but as an articulation of shifting hegemonic alignments, wherein ideational, material, and institutional structures are mutually constitutive. This framework foregrounds the contestation over the terms of 'common sense' within both domestic and international civil society, situating EU–Turkey relations within the global organic crisis of neoliberal order. In tracing the contradictory evolution of Turkey's engagement with EU norms, this book offers a critical intervention into the study of international relations, emphasizing the historicity, partiality, and ideological embeddedness of normative discourses, and illuminating the dynamics of consent, coercion, and counter-hegemonic struggle at the heart of contemporary world order.

## Existing Theoretical Approaches

Neorealist scholars challenge the notion of the EU as an independent actor in international affairs, arguing that it lacks hard power and functions at best as a secondary player in global politics. In contrast, neoliberal institutionalists view the EU as a regulatory institution that reduces transaction costs, facilitating cooperation through rules and norms. However, they do not see the EU as a dominant force over sovereign states. Under this logic, Turkey complies with EU norms only when the perceived benefits outweigh the costs. Another key factor in compliance is credibility. Turkey's commitment to EU norms declined as the EU itself lost institutional credibility. This decline became evident when EU leaders openly expressed reluctance towards Turkey's full membership, instead proposing a privileged partnership, which diminished the incentives for compliance.

From the perspective of rational choice institutionalism, the EU functions as a bargaining arena where states pursue their strategic interests rather than internalizing shared norms and identities. The AKP's early compliance with EU-led reforms, such as curbing military influence in politics, was not primarily driven by democratization but rather by the party's goal of consolidating its own power. The Erdoğan government has since demonstrated a selective approach to EU conditionality: reforms are implemented when they serve to enhance the government's authority, but they are disregarded when they do not align with the regime's political survival and dominance, a distinction that prioritizes the government's interests over those of the Turkish state.

This pattern of strategic, interest-driven engagement with the EU highlights the limits of institutionalist and rationalist frameworks in fully capturing the dynamics of EU–Turkey relations. Accordingly, an understanding of hegemony, not merely as material dominance but as the construction and contestation of consent, becomes essential to explain the deeper transformations in Turkey's trajectory and the evolving nature of its relationship with the European Union. Thus, to move beyond the explanatory limits of materialist and institutionalist approaches, it becomes necessary to foreground the concept of hegemony.

## Theoretical Foundations: Hegemony in Traditional Approaches

In the most common sense, hegemony in the international relations discipline indicates the ability of an actor to shape the international system.[2] The concept is mostly mentioned together with concepts like dominance and hard power, such as economic and military capabilities. This emphasis on material capabilities directs us to the most predominant school in international relations, which is rationalism. A rationalist framework is marked by the states' interests and their rational strategies to pursue their motives. In this regard, neorealism and neoliberalism are worthy of mention.

Neorealism, also known as structural realism, marks a departure from classical realism by emphasizing the structure of the international system rather than the nature of states. The founding figures of this school, Kenneth N. Waltz and John J. Mearsheimer, argue that both the international structure (the system) and the distribution of capabilities among states determine outcomes in world politics.[3] The international system is anarchic, meaning there is no overarching authority above states, and this compels them to rely on self-help strategies to ensure survival. In this framework, hegemony emerges from the concentration of material capabilities, primarily military and economic power, in a single state.[4] Unlike liberal or ideational approaches, neorealism considers domestic variables, such as regime type, to be largely irrelevant. States compete with one another in a zero-sum game for international (regional or global) hegemony, as this is seen as the most

2 Carla Norrlof, 'Hegemony', in *Oxford Bibliographies in International Relations*, 2015, https://www.oxfordbibliographies.com/display/document/obo-9780199743292/obo-9780199743292-0122.xml.

3 Kenneth N. Waltz, 'Realist Thought and Neorealist Theory', in *The Realism Reader*, ed. Colin Elman and Michael Jensen (London: Routledge, 2014), 124–28; John J. Mearsheimer, 'Structural Realism', in *International Relations Theories: Discipline and Diversity*, ed. Tim Dunne, Milja Kurki, and Steve Smith, 5th ed. (Oxford: Oxford University Press, 2021), 51–67; John J. Mearsheimer, *The Tragedy of Great Power Politics*, updated ed. (New York: W.W. Norton & Company, 2003).

4 Kenneth N. Waltz, *Theory of International Politics* (Long Grove, IL: Waveland Press, 2010).

effective way to ensure security in an anarchic environment.[5] Maximization of power and elimination of other competitors assures security and establishes hegemony.[6] The hegemon, as the most powerful actor, becomes the rule maker, shaping the international order to its advantage. It is the role of the rule maker in the system to maintain international stability by controlling the less powerful.[7] However, this stability is contingent on the hegemon's ability to maintain dominance; once its relative power declines, systemic instability and conflict are likely to follow.[8]

Neoliberal institutionalism, while sharing neorealism's basic assumption of an anarchic international system, diverges by emphasizing the possibility and significance of cooperation through institutions. This approach, associated with scholars like Robert O. Keohane and Joseph S. Nye, posits that even in an international environment lacking central authority, states can and do cooperate through rules, norms, and international institutions that reduce uncertainty, promote transparency, and lower transaction costs. On the issue of hegemony, neoliberals adopt and expand the hegemonic stability theory, which argues that a dominant power is necessary to initiate and establish international order, particularly in the economic realm. As Charles P. Kindleberger famously stated, 'for the world economy to be stabilized, there has to be a stabilizer, one stabilizer'.[9] However, neoliberals differ from neorealists in arguing that once hegemonic order is institutionalized, it can outlive the hegemon. Institutions, once created under hegemonic leadership, can become self-sustaining mechanisms that serve the interests of multiple actors, not just the dominant power. They create a framework in which cooperation becomes the rational strategy even in the absence of coercion. Thus, while hegemony is instrumental in the creation of order, it is not necessarily required for its maintenance. The liberal view holds a more optimistic outlook on global governance: institutions can develop their own legitimacy and functionality, stabilizing international politics beyond shifts in material power. In this framework, the EU can be seen as both a product and a promoter of such institutionalized hegemony, sustaining

5 Waltz, *Theory of International Politics*; Mearsheimer, *The Tragedy of Great Power Politics*; Mearsheimer, 'Structural Realism'.

6 Mearsheimer, *The Tragedy of Great Power Politics*.

7 Robert Gilpin, *War and Change in World Politics* (Cambridge: Cambridge University Press, 1981), 29.

8 Robert O. Keohane, *After Hegemony: Cooperation and Discord in the World Political Economy* (Princeton: Princeton University Press, 2005).

9 Charles P. Kindleberger, *The World in Depression, 1929–1939* (Berkeley: University of California Press, 1986), 304.

liberal norms like human rights, democracy, and market openness, even as global hegemonic power becomes more fragmented.

## Neo-Gramscian Hegemony in International Relations

The neo-Gramscian framework offers a critical and interdisciplinary approach to understanding international relations, drawing from historical materialism, critical theory, and the legacy of Antonio Gramsci's thought. Gramsci's approach is consistent with Marxist historicism. Gramscian historical materialism builds upon the Marxist critique of political economy. Central to this perspective is the concept of 'hegemony', understood not merely as 'dominance' through 'coercive' power, but as a form of leadership sustained by the manufacture of consent. In this view, global neoliberal hegemony expands not solely through material capabilities, but through the dissemination of the moral, political, and cultural values of dominant social groups, particularly those representing transnational capitalist interests. These values are institutionalized and normalized via a dense network of civil society actors, including media, think tanks, educational institutions, and NGOs, that function to legitimize the existing order.

Unlike neoliberal theories, which emphasize cooperation through international institutions for mutual gain, the neo-Gramscian approach stresses the interplay between structure and agency, particularly how social forces, class relations, and historical blocs shape and reproduce global order. Hegemony in this framework is not static or purely coercive; it is constructed and contested in the ideological and institutional arenas where elites seek to secure both material advantage and ideological leadership. Thus, the hegemon emerges not only as a material power but also as an intellectual and moral authority, shaping the rules of the game and the very terms of legitimacy. This allows for a more nuanced understanding of how international institutions function as instruments of hegemonic reproduction, embedding the interests of dominant powers within seemingly neutral legal and normative frameworks.

The Gramscian concept of hegemony differs from the hegemony conception of the realist school. According to orthodox realism, hegemony is the dominance of one state over another one. The dominance connoted coercion to a large extent. In the neo-Gramscian tradition, hegemony is understood as a historically contingent configuration of material power, ideology, and institutional structures, which together generate both 'dominance' and 'consent' on a global scale. The hegemonic leadership is essentially based on the consent of the led. Such consent is achieved through the dissemination and normalization (popularization) of the ruling class's world view across society. The consent enables subaltern classes subjecting themselves to the rule of the hegemon. As Robert W. Cox eloquently puts it, hegemony is not simply the exercise of coercion, but the result of a 'fit' between material capabilities, legitimating ideologies, and institutional arrangements that stabilize and reproduce a particular world order.[10] Unlike neorealist approaches that treat power as a fixed attribute derived from accumulated capabilities, a tendency Cox critiques as the 'fetishism of power',[11] paraphrasing Karl Marx, the neo-Gramscian view situates power within social processes and class relations, emphasizing that it emerges through struggles over ideas, norms, and institutional configurations.

Post–World War II global hegemony, for instance, was deeply institutionalized through the Bretton Woods system and other global governance mechanisms, which functioned to reconcile the imperatives of global capitalism with domestic political pressures in the core countries.[12] These institutions not only codified the norms of neoliberal order but also incorporated mechanisms of discipline, particularly for peripheral states, by conditioning economic assistance on adherence to hegemonic norms, such as fiscal austerity, trade liberalization, and structural reform.

Crucially, Cox underscores the internationalization of the state, a process by which national policy agendas, especially in weaker or dependent countries, are shaped not primarily by domestic social contracts but by the strategic interests embedded in transnational capitalist institutions.[13] Countries like Turkey have been subject to this logic, with external institutions (e.g., the IMF, World Bank, EU) dictating domestic policy in exchange for financial support, thereby enabling a coalition of conservative forces to implement and sustain externally defined reform agendas.[14] This dynamic illustrates how hegemony is not solely a coercive order imposed from above, but a deeply embedded, structural condition, legitimated through institutions that naturalize capitalist discipline and reproduce inequality on a global scale. The expansion of international production thus goes hand in hand with the expansion of hegemonic power, as states and societies

10 Robert W. Cox, 'Social Forces, States and World Orders: Beyond International Relations Theory', *Millennium* 10, no. 2 (1981): 126–55, at 141.

11 Ibid., 141.

12 Ibid., 145.

13 Ibid.

14 Ibid., 146.

are integrated into a global order that reflects and serves the interests of dominant social forces.[15]

In contrast to conventional usages that conflate 'hegemony' with mere state dominance or imperialism, Cox insists on preserving the Gramscian sense of hegemony as a multifaceted order in which coercion and consent are dialectically interwoven, and where legitimacy is produced through the alignment of material capabilities, ideational structures, and institutional practices. While 'dominance' may denote the overt power of one state over others, 'hegemony' in the neo-Gramscian lexicon refers to a broader historical bloc, a configuration of class forces that universalizes its particular interests by embedding them in the fabric of global governance, thus rendering them common sense.[16] Cox states that this was most evident in the post–World War II period, when the United States, drawing from the British imperial template, constructed a hegemonic world order tailored to the exigencies of an increasingly integrated and crisis-prone global capitalist economy. But unlike earlier forms of dominance, this new hegemony was more deeply institutionalized, more ideologically refined, and more adept at absorbing resistance. Dominance hides an enforcement potential that the dominant force can use against the weaker one, when necessary. In the institutionalized form of hegemony, the ideological, normative dimension of the hegemon creates a hierarchy that the weak accepts the dominance of the hegemon without the stick of enforcement.[17]

Institutionalization and neo-Gramscian hegemony are closely linked.[18] International institutions occupy a central position within this hegemonic project, not as neutral arenas of cooperation, but as mechanisms for reproducing and expanding the dominant social order. They perform both functional and ideological roles: they codify rules that facilitate the global expansion of capitalism while permitting marginal adjustments for subordinated actors to minimize systemic friction. These institutions, such as the Bretton Woods system, the OECD, or the ILO, do not simply reflect the balance of power among states, but rather serve the dominant configuration of social and economic forces, shaping national policies in line with the interests of transnational capital. Their apparent flexibility – as seen in mechanisms like floating exchange rates or social safety clauses – is

15 Ibid.

16 Robert W. Cox, 'Gramsci, Hegemony and International Relations: An Essay in Method', in *Gramsci, Historical Materialism and International Relations*, ed. Stephen Gill (Cambridge: Cambridge University Press, 1993), 49–66, at 59–60, https://doi.org/10.1017/CBO9780511558993.003.

17 Cox, 'Social Forces, States and World Orders', 137.

18 Ibid.

not a departure from neoliberal orthodoxy, but its adaptive strength: they allow the world order to survive crisis and contradiction by selectively accommodating peripheral interests, so long as these do not threaten the core logic of capital accumulation.[19]

Moreover, these institutions operate as vehicles of ideological incorporation, legitimizing neoliberal policy paradigms at the national level and constructing normative consensus around the institutions of core capitalist societies. For instance, the OECD's endorsement of monetarism did not merely reflect economic theory. It rather empowered political forces aligned with anti-inflationary, pro-market agendas while marginalizing alternative voices concerned with employment and social protection. The ILO's promotion of tripartism, similarly, normalizes labour–capital–state relations as structured in the Global North, projecting them as universally desirable.[20]

A critical feature of hegemonic consolidation is the passive revolution that can be pursued in different forms. '*Transformismo*' is one of those strategies. It is about the co-optation of peripheral elites and ideas into the hegemonic project. It can be understood as a way of gaining popular consent and support. Literature also refers to it as 'hegemonic process'. The process indicates the practice of the hegemon to receive the consent of the ruled classes. The *transformismo* is not a formal consent received procedure but rather about letting society absorb the ideologies of the hegemon, accepting it, not rebelling against it, following their daily routines, embodying the hegemon's values in everyday common sense. The hegemon does not coerce their norms to the subaltern classes. Moreover, the passive revolution (or *transformismo,* or hegemonic process) is an everlasting process. The hegemon remains as the hegemon as long as it achieves to reproduce this practise.

Robert W. Cox played a pivotal role in adapting Gramscian theory to the study of world politics, providing a critical reinterpretation that emphasized the dynamic interrelation between ideas, institutions, and material capabilities in the constitution of international orders. Through his Gramscian approach, Cox challenged dominant theories of international relations and international political economy, arguing instead for a historicist and critical perspective that exposes how hegemonies are constructed, maintained, and contested over time.

Cox developed an alternative framework for analysing world politics, famously encapsulated in his assertion that 'theory is always *for* someone

19 Cox, 'Gramsci, Hegemony and International Relations', 62.
20 Ibid., 63.

and *for* some purpose'.[21] Cox's statement reflects a Marxist, and a Gramscian, reasoning, which posits that specific social relations appoint purpose to the values and ideas. These social relations transform the very nature of knowledge. Thus, knowledge is a product of its historical context. It is not an ever enduring, independent, neutral phenomenon. The knowledge is biased, subjective, and dependent. It is rolled together with ideas, values, and interests. In this context, it can be asserted that theories reflect the values and interests of their formulators. As Cox suggests, theories reflect the perspective of their (political) time, society, and space. Social and political theory are history bound to serve certain people and purposes.[22] In essence, Cox offers a critique of the rationalist school, particularly realism, on these grounds. He argues that rationalist approaches serve the interests of those who benefit from the prevailing global order, notably the elites in the developed states. Their underlying purpose, whether intentionally or not, is to consolidate and legitimize the status quo by presenting the existing configuration of international relations as natural. In this sense, realism functions to perpetuate the hegemonic structures of the global order.

The production process of knowledge is a process not only for the hegemon. Simultaneously, counter knowledge, values, and norms are produced. The success of counter-hegemonic values is up to their dissemination and silent absorption by lower levels of society.

According to the neo-Gramscianism of Robert W. Cox, international institutions actively absorb counter-hegemonic energies by incorporating individuals from subordinate societies into their ranks, thereby diluting their oppositional potential. These individuals, despite entering global governance structures with reformist aspirations, are often constrained to operate within the parameters of hegemonic ideology. The case of 'self-reliance' is illustrative: originally a call for autonomous, endogenous development against dependency, the term has been repurposed within hegemonic discourse to mean locally managed welfare under the aegis of global capitalism, programmes designed to stabilize populations that the global economy cannot absorb, rather than to transform structural inequalities.[23]

Cox offers a brilliant metaphor for this process: hegemony is like a pillow; it absorbs blows.[24] Potential challengers are not violently suppressed, but

21 Cox, 'Social Forces, States and World Orders', 128.

22 Ibid., 128–30.

23 Cox, 'Gramsci, Hegemony and International Relations', 63–64.

24 Ibid., 63.

gently assimilated, rendered inert through comfort and compromise. In this way, hegemony maintains its dominance not by crushing opposition, but by neutralizing it through institutionalization, ideological framing, and elite co-optation. Only the formation of a counter-hegemonic historic bloc, grounded in articulated social forces and capable of confronting global capital both ideologically and materially, holds the potential to rupture the existing order. Until then, hegemonic institutions will continue to sustain a global system that reproduces inequality under the guise of consensus, legitimacy, and governance.[25]

Karl Marx conceptualized the arena of class struggle as embedded within the mode of production, wherein the bourgeoisie secures its dominant position by controlling economic processes, thus anchoring societal conflict fundamentally in the capitalist economic system. Robert W. Cox reinterpreted this approach by replacing the conflict zone from the economic system to ideology. Hegemony is achieved by the social group whose ideas are more effectively disseminated and internalized across society. The clashing social powers, ideologies, and norms represent the counter-hegemony, in neo-Gramscian terms. Gramsci contends that the struggle between hegemonic and counter-hegemonic forces is perpetual, as no single ideology can achieve absolute and uncontested dominance over all alternative world views.

Building upon the neo-Gramscian understanding of hegemony as a historically contingent synthesis of material capabilities, ideational dominance, and institutional consolidation, the book is now equipped to examine how these dynamics manifest in contemporary global politics. This framework is particularly instructive for analysing the European Union, not merely as a constellation of states or a sui generis polity, but as a hegemonic actor that seeks to universalize its normative agenda while simultaneously navigating the strategic imperatives of global capitalism and geopolitical competition. The question thus arises: does the EU function primarily as a normative power, diffusing values such as human rights, democracy, and the rule of law through consensual institutional means? Or does its external action reflect a deeper logic of strategic pragmatism, whereby the projection of norms serves to legitimize economic and geopolitical interests? The following chapter interrogates this tension, situating the EU's external policies within the neo-Gramscian conception of hegemony and asking whether its normative discourse masks the reproduction of a particular world order aligned with its own structural interests.

25 Ibid., 63–64.

Cox argues that the presiding hegemonic idea is free trade.[26] The hegemons (the UK and the US for Cox) spread the idea that free trade is beneficial for all states and their inhabitants, which found a silent acceptance to gain common sense eminence. As the hegemon is also the most efficient actor in the production, it is the one that benefits most from this system. Marx criticizes capitalism for being instable thus economic crises are inevitable. It is then expected that each time the neoliberal system stumbles counter-hegemonic movements will emerge. This approach helps us to comprehend the EU's hegemony to attract Turkey as well as the Turkish government's broadening and consolidating its legitimacy among the Turkish society via embedding the European values that improve human rights. However, after the first disengagement when the unwillingness of the EU to progress Turkey's accession surfaced, the 2007–8 sovereign debt crisis became a catalyst to lead the AKP government to build its contra-hegemony, moving away from European norms.

The EU's hegemony is constructed through a system of conditionality that interweaves neoliberal economic imperatives with normative commitments to democracy, human rights, and the rule of law. This dual foundation has allowed the EU to exert influence beyond its borders, shaping the preferences and institutional trajectories of candidate and neighbouring states. In the early years of the AKP government, Turkey appeared highly receptive to this hegemonic configuration. The alignment between EU conditionality and the AKP's reformist agenda facilitated a convergence in both discourse and policy, as accession negotiations and domestic political objectives were mutually reinforcing. However, this alignment proved historically contingent rather than structurally embedded. Following the Gezi Park protests and the failed coup attempt in 2016, the Erdoğan government recalibrated its priorities and increasingly viewed EU norms as constraints on its consolidation of power. While rationalist accounts may interpret this shift as a reassessment of cost–benefit calculations, neo-Gramscian analysis directs attention to deeper structural contestations. From this perspective, Erdoğan's initial compliance can be seen as a strategic manoeuvre to dismantle domestic opposition and consolidate a hegemonic bloc. Once internal obstacles were neutralized, the government began to assert its own counter-hegemonic project, rejecting EU norms not merely for pragmatic reasons but as part of a broader ideological reconfiguration. Thus, the transformation of EU–Turkey relations reflects not simply a failure of conditionality but an unfolding hegemonic struggle, in which the EU's

26 Ibid., 60.

role as a normative power is challenged by competing articulations of order. As Frank Schimmelfennig and others have emphasized, EU conditionality can be effective in promoting institutional convergence; yet, from a neo-Gramscian lens, such convergence is sustainable only when it aligns with the broader configuration of social forces and material interests. The erosion of EU influence in Turkey, therefore, marks not only a geopolitical divergence but the emergence of an alternative hegemonic vision shaped by authoritarian populism and state-led capitalism.

## The EU as a Hegemonic Actor: Normative Power or Strategic Pragmatism?

Ian Manners's influential concept of 'normative power Europe' (NPE) builds upon the English school tradition, particularly Hedley Bull's critical engagement with the earlier notion of 'civilian power'.[27] In the early 1970s, François Duchêne famously characterized the European Community as a 'civilian power', an *idée force* with formidable economic resources but limited military capabilities.[28] Bull, however, challenged the viability of this vision, arguing that Europe's civilian influence remained contingent upon the military power of states, thus casting doubt on its capacity for autonomous international agency. Subsequent thinkers contributed to the evolving conceptualization of Europe's global role: Christopher Hill reframed the EU as a 'soft power'[29], Johan Galtung depicted it as a 'non-military superpower'[30], a force anchored in the appeal of its ideas rather than coercion, and Ian Manners eventually advanced the NPE framework, arguing that the EU's identity rested on its ability to shape international norms.[31] These conceptual developments collectively position the Union as a distinct international actor, not merely a collection of states. In a complementary line of thought,

27 Hedley Bull, 'Civilian power Europe: a contradiction in terms', Journal of Common Market Studies. 1982: 21-149.

28 François Duchêne, 'The European Community and the uncertainties of interdependence', in *A nation writ large? Foreign-policy problems before the European community* eds. M. Kohnstamm and W. Hagner (London: Routledge, 1973), 1-21.

29 Christopher Hill, 'Cheques and Balances: The European Union's soft power strategy' in *Soft power and hegemony in US foreign affairs*. eds. M. Cox and I. Parmar (London: Routledge, 2010), 194-210.

30 Johan Galtung, *The European Community: A Superpower in the Making* (London: George Allen & Unwin, 1973).

31 Ian Manners, 'Normative Power Europe: A Contradiction in Terms?', *JCMS: Journal of Common Market Studies* 40, no. 2 (2002): 235–58.

Kenneth J. Twitchett[32] and Hanns W. Maull[33] highlighted three defining features of the EU's external identity: (i) the use of economic power to pursue strategic objectives; (ii) a commitment to resolving international disputes through diplomatic means; and (iii) the promotion of global progress via legally binding supranational institutions. Together, these dimensions illustrate how the EU has sought to construct a unique form of influence that transcends traditional realist paradigms.

In formulating his concept of normative power Europe, Ian Manners deliberately sought to distinguish it from earlier notions of civilian power, which he regarded as rooted in a fundamentally Westphalian understanding of statehood, akin to the traditional concept of military power. Whereas civilian power emphasizes the instrumental use of economic means and diplomatic tools within a state-centric framework, 'normative power' articulates a post-Westphalian vision of influence grounded in the diffusion of norms, values, and principles. Manners was particularly critical of how the civilian power concept often perpetuated neocolonial discourses, implicitly privileging Western modes of governance and modernization. In contrast, his normative approach foregrounded the constitutive role of ideas and the centrality of principles such as democracy, human rights, and the rule of law, not only in the EU's internal order but as foundational to its entire external engagement. Furthermore, unlike the civilian power model, which presumes the fixity of the international state system, Manners's normative power framework challenged the ontological permanence of the Westphalian order, envisioning the EU as an actor capable of reshaping the structures and practices of global governance. By reframing power not merely as a function of inter-agent relations but as the capacity to shape what is considered normal or legitimate in international politics, Manners opened conceptual space for a more reflexive, post-positivist analysis of the EU's global role. His intervention thus moved the scholarly debate beyond instrumental and Cold War era interpretations of European influence, towards a critical engagement with how norms themselves are constructed, circulated, and contested.

This research situates the concept of NPE within a neo-Gramscian framework of hegemony, challenging the assumption that the EU's diffusion of values is neutral or purely altruistic. From this perspective, the Union's

32 Kenneth J. Twitchett, *Europe and the World: The External Relations of the Common Market*, (New York: St. Martin's Press,1976).

33 Hanns W. Maull, 'Germany and Japan: The New Civilian Powers', *Foreign Affairs* 69, no. 5 (1990): 91-106.

promotion of norms such as democracy, human rights, and the rule of law is not merely idealistic but serves to legitimize and stabilize a particular liberal international order. As a hegemonic actor in the neo-Gramscian sense, the EU privileges consent over coercion, seeking to secure the active assent of partner states through ideational leadership rather than through material force. The EU's normative influence is thus embedded in the institutionalization of values that align with its broader economic and political interests.

Lacking a unified military force and operating with only above-average economic clout, the EU has constructed its international role primarily through the projection of norms and values rather than through traditional instruments of hard power. Its supranational structure emerged from a peace project rooted in the post-war desire to institutionalize cooperation and eliminate intra-European conflict. In this regard, Robert W. Cox identifies the EU as a post-Westphalian political formation, characterized by multilayered authority that transcends the nation-state paradigm. He further describes the Union as a post-globalization entity, offering an alternative model of governance that aspires to address the broader needs of humanity. By effectively eliminating war among its members and fostering an integrated regional order, the EU has established itself as one of the most institutionalized and normatively driven actors in the international system. In a similar vein, Zbigniew Brzezinski has observed that the liberal-democratic framework promoted by the EU provides a potential foundation for a global political consensus.[34]

Within a neo-Gramscian framework, the European Union emerges not as a neutral purveyor of universal values, but as a hegemonic actor whose normative project is intrinsically tied to broader structures of power. The diffusion of norms such as democracy, human rights, and the rule of law, often framed as benign or altruistic, is in fact a central component of the EU's ideological leadership. These norms are not external to power; rather, they constitute the ideational dimension of hegemony, working in tandem with material interests and institutional mechanisms to secure consent and stabilize a particular liberal-capitalist world order. The EU's external engagement, especially through conditionality in accession and neighbourhood policies, operates as a form of passive revolution, facilitating structural transformations in peripheral states that align with the dominant bloc's vision of order. In this light, normative power is not an alternative to realpolitik but an instrument of hegemony that legitimates and reproduces

34 Zbigniew Brzezinski, *Out of Control: Global Turmoil on the Eve of the 21st Century* (New York: Simon and Schuster, 2010).

prevailing relations of dominance. The EU's strength lies in its ability to naturalize its own preferences as universal norms, thereby depoliticizing contestation and anchoring consent within the very fabric of international governance.

Despite its self-image as a normative power, the European Union's external actions often reveal a persistent and structural tension between its rhetorical commitment to universal values and its strategic pursuit of material interests. While the EU projects itself as a promoter of democracy, human rights, and the rule of law, its external engagements frequently betray selective applications of these principles, shaped by geopolitical calculations and economic imperatives. For instance, in the realm of energy policy, the EU has long maintained strategic alliances with authoritarian regimes, such as Azerbaijan, Algeria, and, previously, Russia, whose human rights records starkly contradict the values the Union purports to champion. Similarly, its approach to migration governance illustrates a pragmatic, and at times ethically ambivalent, logic: by externalizing border control through deals with countries like Turkey and Libya, the EU has effectively outsourced human rights violations, shielding itself from legal responsibility while benefiting from the containment of irregular migration. In the security and defence domain, the EU's tolerance of arms exports to conflict-ridden or repressive regimes further undermines the credibility of its normative posture, especially when such transactions directly contravene its own export control standards and conflict prevention objectives. These contradictions reveal that the EU functions not as a disinterested moral actor, but rather as a 'selective norm entrepreneur', which is invoking values when they align with its strategic interests and sidelining them when they do not. This selective invocation of norms is not incidental but constitutive of the EU's external identity: it reflects the embeddedness of normative claims within broader structures of global political economy and hegemonic contestation. Far from transcending power politics, the EU's normative agenda is deeply enmeshed in them, operating as both a discursive legitimization and a regulatory mechanism for the preservation of its geopolitical and economic preferences.

A particularly telling example of the EU's selective application of norms lies in its approach to minority rights. Throughout Turkey's accession process, the EU has consistently emphasized the protection and recognition of minorities as a benchmark for democratic reform. However, this insistence is not matched by a coherent or uniform policy on minority rights within the Union itself. Several member states either lack formal recognition of their own national minorities or apply minority rights inconsistently, such as Germany's reluctance to recognize its Turkish population as a national minority, France's enduring resistance to ethno-cultural categorization in the name of republican universalism, or the marginalization of South Asian communities in the United Kingdom. This asymmetry illustrates how the EU engages in what may be termed 'normative externalization', which means applying its values stringently to candidate countries while avoiding equivalent commitments internally. From a neo-Gramscian perspective, such discrepancies underscore the fact that norms are not autonomous moral imperatives but rather integral to ideological leadership. They serve to legitimize and stabilize a liberal hegemonic order that privileges certain interests and actors while marginalizing others. In this sense, the EU's invocation of minority rights becomes not merely a reflection of normative commitment, but a strategic instrument within a broader hegemonic project, employed selectively and often in service of maintaining hierarchical relations between the Union and its periphery.

There are also empirical contradictions considering norms vs. pragmatism. Although the European Union depicts itself as normative power committed to the diffusion of democracy, human rights, and the rule of law, its external actions often reveal a disjuncture between its proclaimed values and its strategic interests. Nowhere is this more evident than in the EU's engagement with its southern neighbours, particularly in the Middle East and North Africa (MENA) region. In the aftermath of the Arab uprisings, the EU rhetorically endorsed democratization while simultaneously deepening security and migration cooperation with authoritarian regimes. Partnerships with countries such as Egypt, Tunisia, and Morocco were often maintained, or even intensified, despite well-documented human rights violations, in the name of regional stability and counterterrorism. These tendencies suggest that the EU has prioritized geopolitical imperatives, such as curbing irregular migration and preserving energy security, over supporting substantive democratic reform. From a neo-Gramscian standpoint, this reflects a broader hegemonic logic that norms are not upheld for their intrinsic moral worth but mobilized selectively to sustain a liberal order that serves dominant interests.

A similar pattern of contradiction emerges within the Union's own borders. The EU has been notably restrained in addressing democratic backsliding among its member states, particularly Hungary and Poland. While both governments have systematically undermined judicial independence, media freedom, and civil society, the EU's institutional response has often been delayed, fragmented, or ineffectual. This ambivalence is further accentuated in the EU's external relations with countries like Turkey, where democratic erosion has been tolerated in exchange for cooperation on migration management and regional security. Such inconsistencies have led many scholars to critique the concept of normative power Europe as ideologically overstated and empirically underwhelming. Rather than a purely altruistic actor, the EU is increasingly viewed as a 'selective norm entrepreneur' that instrumentalizes values discourse to legitimize its strategic preferences. As critics argue, the normative rhetoric serves as a veil for realpolitik, masking the pragmatic calculations that underpin much of the Union's foreign policy. Thus, the EU's normative identity appears less as a fixed ontological trait and more as a discursive strategy embedded within the hegemonic structures it seeks to maintain.

From a neo-Gramscian perspective, the apparent contradiction between the EU's normative discourse and its pragmatic actions should not be read simply as a failure of policy coherence or a lapse in ethical commitment. Rather, it constitutes a fundamental feature of hegemonic practice. The European Union's external governance projects a particular model of capitalist modernity, institutionalized through market liberalization, legal-rational authority, and democratic formalism. This model is not neutral but deeply embedded in specific historical and material power relations. Norms such as human rights, the rule of law, and democratic governance function as legitimating tools within a broader strategy of stabilizing a liberal order favourable to the EU's geopolitical and economic interests. They mask asymmetries in global governance by presenting the European project as universally desirable, even while reinforcing a hierarchy in which the EU acts as both norm setter and gatekeeper. Within this configuration, the EU's normative power becomes a mechanism of consent making that is crucial for establishing legitimacy among subordinate actors, yet always intertwined with material imperatives.

Concepts such as 'passive revolution' and '*transformismo*' further illuminate how peripheral actors like Turkey are drawn into the EU-led hegemonic project not as equal participants, but as selectively integrated components. Through instruments like accession negotiations, trade liberalization agreements, and migration compacts, the EU seeks to align the domestic trajectories of non-member states with its own institutional norms and market logics. However, this absorption is partial and contingent. The process often neutralizes more radical political alternatives in these peripheral contexts while sustaining their structural subordination. Turkey's early AKP era reforms, for instance, reflected a Gramscian-style passive revolution, whereby a domestic political bloc advanced transformative claims under the aegis of EU norms, only to later diverge once its own counter-hegemonic capacity had been consolidated. In this sense, the EU's normative outreach does not aim at the realization of universal values per se, but at producing manageable forms of order that reproduce its geopolitical and ideological leadership. Seen through this lens, norm diffusion is less about ethical consistency than about hegemonic resilience.

The tension between normative idealism and strategic pragmatism places the European Union at a critical juncture in its international identity. As this study has shown, the EU's projection of values related to human rights, democracy, and the rule of law has often served not only as a moral compass but as a mechanism to legitimize and stabilize a particular liberal order in line with its geopolitical interests. However, the increasing visibility of contradictions between rhetoric and practice, such as tacit support for authoritarian allies, migration management deals with regimes of questionable legitimacy, or the strategic tolerance of democratic erosion within its borders, raises pressing questions about the coherence and credibility of the EU as a normative actor. If the Union's values are selectively applied and subordinated to material or geopolitical imperatives, its normative claims risk being perceived as instrumental rather than principled, thus eroding the soft power and legitimacy that once distinguished it in global affairs.

While the European Union consistently positions itself as a promoter of normative values on the global stage, the diffusion of these norms has proven to be far more complex and contentious than the EU's discourse suggests. The EU's normative framework, grounded in principles like democracy, human rights, and the rule of law, assumes a capacity for seamless transmission to non-member states, particularly in its neighbourhood and enlargement processes. However, the reality reveals numerous failures in the successful diffusion of these values. In cases such as Turkey, compliance with EU norms has often been partial, inconsistent, or reversed as the dynamics of power, both internal and external, challenge the very foundations of normative transfer. The neo-Gramscian lens demonstrates to us that these failures underscore not merely a lack of enforcement or coherence in policy, but deeper structural contradictions inherent in the EU's own hegemonic practices. Rather than promoting genuine transformation, EU norms often operate as instruments of power, entangled with strategic interests that ultimately limit their efficacy and foster resistance from peripheral states. This phenomenon of norm diffusion failure highlights the challenges of imposing a normative framework in a global order where material interests frequently overshadow ideals.

Situating the EU's normative power within the neo-Gramscian hegemonic framework, such contradictions are not aberrations but constitutive features of hegemonic practice. Hegemony is always contested, never total, and depends on a tenuous balance between consent and coercion, ideas and material power. The EU's normative hegemony is therefore inherently unstable, especially as it is increasingly challenged by external actors offering alternative governance models (e.g., China, Russia), and as internal fragmentation such as political polarization, democratic backsliding, and populist nationalism, that weakens its normative unity from within. In this context, the EU must confront a fundamental dilemma: whether to recalibrate its identity as a more openly pragmatic geopolitical actor or to revitalize its normative project with genuine commitment and consistency. Either path entails significant costs and strategic recalculations, but maintaining the illusion of moral superiority while acting otherwise may prove the most damaging in the long term both for the EU's global role and the internal legitimacy of its integration project.

The relationship between the European Union and Turkey can be understood through various lenses, with neo-Gramscianism offering a distinctive framework that contrasts sharply with more transactional, rationalist approaches. While rationalist theories tend to explain state behaviour as a simple calculus of costs and benefits, where compliance with EU norms is seen as a strategic decision made when the benefits outweigh the costs, neo-Gramscianism frames the relationship as a hegemonic struggle. From this perspective, Turkey's evolving stance towards the EU is not merely a response to shifting incentives or material advantages. Instead, it reflects deeper structural power dynamics. Initially, Turkey aligned with EU norms as the EU's hegemonic influence seemed to serve the AKP government's objectives, particularly in terms of economic development and integration into the European political system. However, as Turkey's political landscape evolved, particularly with the rise of Erdoğan's more autocratic policies, a significant shift occurred. Under neo-Gramscian theory, this shift is not simply a matter of rational calculation but represents a deliberate move towards building a counter-hegemony, a rejection of the EU's normative power in favour of an alternative vision of governance, sovereignty, and regional influence.

Where rationalist approaches might focus on the apparent costs of non-compliance or the tangible benefits of cooperation, neo-Gramscian hegemony approach highlights the deeper ideological and structural forces at play. For Erdoğan, rejecting EU norms was not solely a tactical decision but part of a broader effort to assert Turkey's independence from EU influence and to establish an alternative vision of power within the region. In this context, the EU–Turkey relationship becomes a reflection of broader global power struggles, with each side attempting to shape the rules of the international system to suit its own strategic objectives. Turkey's move away from EU norms, thus, embodies not just a break in compliance but an attempt to challenge the EU's hegemonic influence and establish an autonomous counter-hegemonic order.

## Neo-Gramscian Hegemony Framework: A Way to Understand Both Domestic Political Transformations in Turkey and the EU's Shifting Priorities

To answer the research question, this study adopts a neo-Gramscian hegemony framework to analyse Turkey's initial compliance and subsequent diversion from European human rights. This study situates the EU as a hegemonic power seeking to expand its hegemony by using its economic capabilities and normative potential. In this sense, the human rights approach of the EU is not a pure one but a tool of hegemonic expansion. The Erdoğan government's initial compliance with European human rights was (i) to consolidate its domestic power via eradicating the military elements that were obstacles to achieving that power and (ii) to act as a periphery state in the global neoliberal (capitalist) economy because nations embracing pro-market economic strategies attract foreign direct investment and can gain access to international credit. The subsequent deviation of the AKP government from the EU norms began as soon as Erdoğan faced the Gezi Park protests and then the failed coup d'état attempt by FETÖ. He started to perceive liberal democracy as a Western trap to weaken his governance. Thus, he attempted to build a counter-hegemony by the use of authoritarianism.

Domestically, repression, arrests, and media control grew immediately, and an Islamist–nationalist discourse was followed with the establishment of the People's Alliance (Cumhur İttifakı). Simultaneously, an anti-Western foreign policy was formulated. As an alternative to ties with the EU and the US, closer relations were built with Russia, China, and the Gulf. The new ties were designed to bolster both military strength (for example, the S-400 missile system purchase from Russia) and economic strength (new monetary sources in the Gulf). As the AKP government deviated from European norms, the EU did not try to offer incentives or implement enforcement to encourage the reversal of the backsliding in democracy, human rights, and the rule of law. The new priority of the EU was to securitize against increased migration flows. Thus, the EU offered Turkey a migration deal, which also undermined human rights in many ways. The AKP government accepted the deal and started to use it as leverage against the EU. In the final analysis, the alternative economic model Turkey tried to build failed to a large extent and proved its structural dependency on the EU. This work concludes that human rights regimes are flexible tools, applied only when they align with hegemonic interests. The book criticizes Turkey's authoritarianism not only through the AKP policies but also through the selective human rights commitment of the EU, which engaged pragmatically with Erdoğan despite his democratic backsliding.

## Methodology

The methodology employed in this study integrates process tracing within a critical-historical analysis of hegemonic shifts, offering a nuanced examination of the EU–Turkey relationship through human rights. Rather than merely tracking policy responses and assessing cause-and-effect relationships, this approach seeks to delve deeper into the underlying hegemonic dynamics at play. Process tracing will be utilized to explore not only the specific policy decisions made by the European Union and Turkey, but also the broader reconfiguration of hegemony throughout the course of their engagement. In this regard, the study will investigate how the AKP's shifting alliances with different elite groups within Turkey have impacted domestic politics and foreign policy, as well as how these changes have intersected with the EU's evolving strategic priorities.

Furthermore, the methodology will focus on the historical contingency of hegemony, considering how it has fluctuated over time in response to a variety of global trends. Process tracing will map the trajectory of EU–Turkey relations, particularly during pivotal moments such as the early 2000s, when Turkey's potential integration into the EU seemed promising, and the later shifts in the 2010s, when this trajectory began to fracture. These periods reflect key hegemonic transformations. First, the early 2000s, when Turkey was embraced by the liberal bloc, followed by a phase of growing tension and fragmentation in the late 2000s to 2010s. In this time, Turkey's alignment with the EU faltered as domestic political changes, most notably Erdoğan's growing authoritarianism, led to a diminishing willingness to adopt EU norms. Finally, the study will explore the post-2016 phase, when the EU, despite ongoing ideological tensions, has passively accommodated Turkey due to the strategic geopolitical importance of its relationship with the country.

By embedding hegemonic analysis within the process-tracing methodology, this approach allows for a broader understanding of how the EU's norms, once presented as a model for regional governance, are shaped by global geopolitical trends such as the 2008 economic crisis, the migration crisis, and the rise of authoritarian populism across Europe. This enables the study to examine the shifting dynamics within the EU–Turkey relationship not just as a series of discrete policy decisions, but as a historically contingent process shaped by both internal and external forces. The focus is not solely on formal policy change but on the reconfiguration of hegemonic structures, providing a rich, multifaceted analysis of EU–Turkey relations over time.

## Comprehending Turkey's Behaviour through the Neo-Gramscian Hegemony Lens

From Turkey's declaration of its EU candidacy in 1999 to the start of formal negotiations in 2005, Turkey's government initially demonstrated a willingness to align with European human rights standards. The reforms during this period were seen as part of Turkey's integration into a broader liberal international order led by the EU, which exerted its hegemonic influence through normative power. However, by 2006, reforms began to plateau. While reforms continued in some areas, they lacked the momentum of earlier years. From 2013 onwards, and particularly after 2016, Turkey witnessed a significant backslide in human rights as the government embraced increasingly authoritarian practices. To understand this trajectory, it is essential to examine the dynamics behind Turkey's initial alignment with EU human rights norms in the early 2000s, viewed through the lens of neo-Gramscian hegemony. Subsequently, we must explore the factors that contributed to the diminishing intensity of these reforms. Importantly, we need to ask why, after more than a decade of aligning with EU criteria, Turkey began to reject these norms. Finally, the role of the EU as both a normative power and a hegemonic actor in this process must be considered to see how the EU initially promoted human rights reforms in Turkey, and how its influence may have contributed to the stagnation and eventual erosion of these reforms.

A neo-Gramscian hegemony perspective highlights the role of power struggles in shaping the EU–Turkey relationship, where norms are not merely abstract ideals but part of a broader hegemonic project. Neo-Gramscianism suggests that Turkey's initial embrace of EU norms can be understood not just as a rational calculation for benefits, but as part of its incorporation into a European-led liberal order, facilitated by EU hegemony. However, as Turkey's own hegemonic ambitions grew under the AKP government, it began to challenge these norms in a bid to create its own counter-hegemony. The EU's initial role in promoting human rights reforms in Turkey can thus be seen as a process of hegemonic embedding, where Turkey was encouraged to adopt norms that aligned with the EU's liberal framework. But the decline in the momentum of the reform and the eventual backslide in human rights are not merely the result of Turkey's cost–benefit analysis; they reflect a deeper structural shift. From a neo-Gramscian standpoint, these changes signal a struggle between competing hegemons, with Turkey increasingly asserting its sovereignty and challenging the EU's normative framework.

To fully understand the dynamics of Turkey's human rights trajectory in relation to the European human rights regime, it is necessary to shift focus from conventional regime theory to the neo-Gramscian hegemony perspective on international regimes. Neo-Gramscianism provides a framework for understanding how Turkey's engagement with international human rights regimes is not merely about compliance with external rules, but a reflection of hegemonic power struggles. Regimes, defined as 'sets of implicit or explicit principles, norms, rules, and decision-making procedures',[35] are not neutral actors. They are shaped by power dynamics, with hegemonic states influencing weaker ones. International regimes typically function horizontally, adjusting state behaviour in the interstate sphere, fostering cooperation, and providing mechanisms for monitoring compliance. However, human rights regimes differ from other international regimes due to their verticality.[36] Accordingly, they do not govern interstate affairs.[37] They are designed to impose obligations on states in relation to their citizens, which challenges traditional state sovereignty.[38]

Under neo-Gramscian theory, human rights represent a tool to conceal unacceptable geopolitical goals and military actions. Accordingly, human rights discourse facilitates the new Western imperialism, as put forward by

35 Stephen D. Krasner, 'Structural Causes and Regime Consequences: Regimes as Intervening Variables', *International Organization* 36, no. 2 (1982): 185–205, at 186.

36 They often hit coordination problems. See: Duncan Snidal, 'Coordination versus Prisoners' Dilemma: Implications for International Cooperation and Regimes', *American Political Science Review* 79, no. 4 (1985): 923–42.

37 Andrew Moravcsik, 'The Origins of Human Rights Regimes: Democratic Delegation in Postwar Europe', *International Organization* 54, no. 2 (2000): 217–52, at 217.

38 Robert O. Keohane and Joseph S. Nye, *Power and Independence* (Boston: Little, Brown, 1977), 19.

David Harvey.[39] In the same vein, the verticality of human rights regimes becomes an expression of hegemonic power: the EU, as the leading liberal power, uses international human rights law not only to govern interstate behaviour[40] but to exert influence over domestic affairs, holding states accountable to international norms.[41] Human rights treaties, unlike other international agreements, are not based on reciprocity;[42] they are enforced through the state's responsibility to protect its citizens. This creates a tension, as states like Turkey are required to balance their own sovereignty with the demands of international human rights law. In the context of EU–Turkey relations, the EU's normative power was initially successful in drawing Turkey into its liberal framework. But as Turkey sought to challenge the EU's hegemonic order, particularly after the AKP's rise to power, the EU's ability to influence Turkey's human rights practices diminished. The dynamics of this shift reflect a broader struggle between competing hegemonic projects: the EU's liberal order versus Turkey's emerging counter-hegemony.

In the structure of international law, states bear the obligations created by these treaties, while the rights enshrined therein are conferred upon individuals. This arrangement necessitates a synergistic interaction between international public law and national legal systems to fulfil these objectives effectively. Consequently, these treaties empower individuals to assert their rights not only through domestic judicial systems but also in international forums, thereby reinforcing the global governance of human rights.

In the field of international relations, the nature and function of international human rights regimes have often been debated in terms of their effectiveness and impact. Mainstream theories,[43] particularly realist and

39 David Harvey, 'The "New" Imperialism: Accumulation by Dispossession', in *Karl Marx*, ed. Bertell Ollman and Kevin B. Anderson (London: Routledge, 2017), 213–37, at 219.

40 Moravcsik, 'The Origins of Human Rights Regimes', 217.

41 Andrew Moravcsik, 'Explaining the Emergence of Human Rights Regimes: Liberal Democracy and Political Uncertainty in Postwar Europe', Working Paper Series 98-17, Weatherhead Center for International Affairs, Harvard University, 1998.

42 Ibid.

43 Mainstream theories' approach to human rights regimes: Unlike other international regimes that are horizontally devised to regulate interstate affairs and whose effects are primarily visible in the interstate sphere (such as environmental or trade regimes), human rights regimes are devised vertically to intervene directly in the domestic realm. They mediate the relationship between the state and its subjects by diffusing norms that, while universal in appearance, are historically rooted in specific ideological and material contexts. The complexities of international human rights regimes cannot be reduced to collective action difficulties (Ryan Goodman and Derek Jinks, 'How to Influence States: Socialization and International Human Rights Law', *Duke Law Journal* 54, no. 3 (2004): 621–703, at 628). This vertical reach of human rights norms, reaching into national legal and political orders, is precisely what makes them instruments of

rationalist approaches, have typically dismissed these regimes as inconsequential, viewing them as symbolic gestures rather than drivers of real political change.[44] From this perspective, human rights discourse is often portrayed as rhetorical cover, a normative language that lacks enforcement and is selectively applied. However, such interpretations fail to capture the deeper structural function that human rights regimes play within the international order.

A neo-Gramscian approach reframes these regimes not as neutral or benign mechanisms for cooperation, but as part of a broader hegemonic project. Human rights regimes are embedded within a historical bloc of ideas, institutions, and material power relations that reflect the dominant interests of leading global actors, such as the EU. In this sense, the international human rights regimes should not be seen merely as a set of legal instruments designed to constrain state behaviour, but as a key

hegemonic power. The sovereignty concerns they provoke are not simply about legal jurisdiction, but about the legitimacy of competing world views. In this light, the international human rights regime is not just about protecting individuals, it is also about reproducing a global order that privileges certain modes of governance, economy, and authority over others. Notably, the realist school does not foresee any reason states would cooperate to promote human rights. This approach pays attention to the cost of sovereignty as the primary reason for deterring cooperation. Liberal approaches hold that democratizing states are more prone to commit to international human rights regimes as the external gain of demonstrating compliance ability overrides the sovereignty cost and as they leave some space for domestic will. For example, in the literature, Spain's dedication to incorporate the European Convention on Human Rights and the jurisprudence of the European Court of Human Rights is evaluated as a result of the transition from Franco's dictatorship towards well-established Western democracies (Nico Krisch, 'The Open Architecture of European Human Rights Law', *The Modern Law Review* 71, no. 2 (2008): 183–216, at 187–88). On the other hand, as a state with well-established domestic institutions, French ratification of the ECHR took place in 1974 and the recognition of the individual complaint right was in 1981. France was not as rapid as democratizing states to adopt and implement the treaty. In time, the French system digested the convention as an international convention status, which is above the national legislation, as a source. Moreover, the international human rights regime cannot be fully understood through a framework that limits state behaviour to material self-interest or cost–benefit analyses, where the literature mostly piles (Jack Donnelly, 'International Human Rights: A Regime Analysis', *International Organization* 40, no. 3 (1986): 599–642, at 616). Rather than being marginal to 'high politics' such as security or the economy, human rights play a strategic role in shaping the ideological foundations of modern governance. From a neo-Gramscian standpoint, these regimes are not neutral instruments; they are part of the hegemonic order constructed by dominant global actors to universalize particular liberal-democratic norms and capitalist logics of state–society relations. The uneven adoption of human rights treaties across states does not simply reflect varying levels of interest or institutional capacity, but points to differing degrees of alignment, or resistance, to this broader hegemonic project.

44 Donnelly, 'International Human Rights', 616.

component in the projection and stabilization of a particular vision of modernity. This vision – liberal, capitalist, and individualistic – seeks to shape the relationship between states and citizens in ways that align with the normative and institutional preferences of hegemonic powers. As such, the tensions that arise around sovereignty, domestic legal traditions, and cultural particularities are not merely implementation issues; they are manifestations of deeper political contestations over whose model of order will prevail.

Commitments to human rights regimes, therefore, are not merely about demonstrating compliance or legitimacy in rational terms, but are deeply embedded in the dynamics of hegemonic incorporation. For instance, Spain's swift embrace of the European Convention on Human Rights during its transition from authoritarianism can be interpreted not only as a desire for democratization, but also as a strategic move to align with the liberal Western bloc and gain inclusion in its normative and material structures. Conversely, France's slower ratification process, despite being a consolidated democracy, reflects its negotiation with the hegemonic order, resisting some supranational impositions while eventually absorbing them into its legal architecture. In both cases, the international human rights regime functioned not just as a legal framework, but as an ideological and institutional mechanism for constructing and stabilizing a particular form of state legitimacy within the liberal hegemonic order.

The mainstream literature has explanations about the motivation of a state to enter and to comply or non-comply with human rights regimes. Considering Turkey's willingness to enter, adopt, and conform with European human rights, the first phase of accelerated human rights reforms can be seen from the liberal approach to the international human rights regimes that discuss that newly established democracies and democratizing countries are 'the primary proponents of reciprocally binding human rights obligations'. This is explicable when we include the domestic political self-interest in the equation.[45] As the human rights regime started to grow and spread at global and regional levels, the interest of the international relations discipline grew. This interest is mostly owing to the challenge regimes pose against the traditional supremacy of realist approaches. Their evolution, their attractiveness for governments, compliance, enforcement, effectiveness to shape state behaviour, and the regime complex they create with other international regimes, as well as with national systems, are the main spheres of examination for international relations scholars. The realist

45 Moravcsik, 'The Origins of Human Rights Regimes', 220.

strand does not expect states cooperating with each other under a treaty and implementing the rules of the treaty, unless it reflects the interests of the party state. Another factor can also be the fear of sanctions or coercion that makes a state cooperate.[46] Yet, those actors that implement human rights domestically are not always willing or able to implement coercive measures on those that violate human rights domestically.

From a neo-Gramscian perspective, the EU's (human rights) conditionality does not represent natural incentives but a prolongation of the global hegemony. Moreover, domestic actors also benefit from the conditionality, whose implementation generates internal legitimacy, besides the opportunity to reshape internal structures. Thus, Turkey's initial willingness to access the EU and implement the human rights norms was not merely a rational calculation of material benefits, but rather a strategic attempt by the government to align with the prevailing liberal international order. In the early 2000s, the Justice and Development Party and allied reformist coalitions among bureaucratic, business, and civil society elites viewed EU accession as a means to restructure the domestic hegemonic configuration. Embracing EU-promoted norms, particularly in human rights and democratization, provided these actors with a powerful ideological and institutional framework to challenge the entrenched Kemalist-nationalist state apparatus and to consolidate a new bloc of social and political forces. Thus, Turkey's early reform period can be seen as a process of 'hegemonic re-articulation', wherein the adoption of European human rights standards served both to legitimize internal power shifts and to embed Turkey more deeply within the transnational liberal order.

The adoption of international legal instruments is determined by the consent of the given state. At this stage, the discipline of international relations questions the reasons that persuade the state to be bound by human rights treaties. The rationalist school holds that participation in human rights agreements requires special attention due to the fact that, unlike other international treaties, they 'constitute the paradigmatic hard case'.[47] This is because when states join financial, trade, or security agreements (involving arms control or environmental concerns, for example), they do so for mutual benefit. Under the Gramscian approach, state sovereignty

46 Chris Brown and Kirsten Ainley, *Understanding International Relations* (Springer, 2009), 97–98; also see Paul W. Kahn, 'Lessons for International Law from the Gulf War', *Stanford Law Review* 45 (1992): 425–41. Kahn uses the anecdotal evidence of Saddam's withdrawal from Kuwait as a result of the coercion of the UNSC coalition.

47 Oona A. Hathaway, 'Why Do Countries Commit to Human Rights Treaties?', *Journal of Conflict Resolution* 51, no. 4 (2007): 588–621, at 589.

is reinforced through integration in the international political economy, which establishes classes in the system.

Human rights agreements are horizontal in that the provisions regulate the relations in the given issue area among the party members. As for human rights agreements, instead of presenting reciprocal benefits, the provisions predominantly regulate the relations among the state and subjects under its jurisdiction by creating obligations over the state. The higher the obligations, the greater the cost to a state's sovereignty. Some human rights regimes even delegate enforcement of human rights to international bodies, such as the European Court of Human Rights (ECtHR). This system establishes a direct connection between the micro level of individuals and the macro level of supranational organizations. In a sense, human rights treaties open the gates to the interference of foreign states into a state's domestic affairs between the state and the individual. This relationship was kept strictly intimate until the internationalization of human rights. Hence, while assessing international human rights regimes, we have to consider the sovereignty costs of joining human rights agreements,[48] to question why and to what extent this relationship is tolerable for the state. Yet, the right to interfere in a state's domestic arrangements is given to all the other states participating in a human rights treaty. The participant is not only giving up one portion of its own sovereignty, but it also gains the right to monitor another state, equally. This makes participation plausible to a regime.

The answer given in mainstream literature as to why states commit to international human rights conventions vary among the rationalist and non-rationalist schools. The rationalist school, pioneered by Keohane, holds that states join in international cooperation when their self-interest is entrenched in the regime/treaty and preserved by organizations.[49] Accordingly, states commit to international regimes for utility maximization. This strand ponders the sovereignty costs of joining a human rights convention. These theories, such as neorealism and liberal theorizing, are predominantly utility oriented.[50] A state party will remain within a regime only as long as doing so serves the state party's interests. The interests can be international as well

48 The cost of joining a treaty depends upon the design of the given regime. The costs are composed of the limitations the treaty bring, the obligations over the member state, such as implementation, trainings, monitoring, in addition to the enforcement costs.

49 Robert O. Keohane, 'The Demand for International Regimes', *International Organization* 36, no. 2 (1982): 325–55; Robert O. Keohane, 'International Institutions: Can Interdependence Work?', *Foreign Policy* 110 (1998): 82–194; Robert O. Keohane, *International Institutions and State Power: Essays in International Relations Theory* (New York: Routledge, 2008).

50 Moravcsik, 'Explaining the Emergence of Human Rights Regimes'.

as domestic. From the classical realist perspective, avoiding causing harm to its own citizens does not represent a particular material interest for any state. For this reason, the formation of human rights regimes is unlikely. If a state joins a human rights regime, the regime must be promising direct or concealed material interests. Moreover, the state will deviate from the regime as soon as these interests vanish. A human rights regime changes the behaviour of a state either by coercion or by persuasion (offering benefits).[51]

Regarding material interests, scholars have posited that enhanced human rights records may attract greater foreign direct investment (FDI). This correlation is exemplified in the period from 2002 to 2006 in Turkey, during which notable improvements in human rights were accompanied by a significant increase in foreign direct investment. However, there is also evidence that high human rights scores increase the probability of attracting foreign direct investment. Formerly, multinational corporations (MNCs) perceived states that used repressive measures as those capable of 'maintaining order and guaranteeing the maintenance of operations'[52] by guaranteeing low labour costs and high profits. Today, we know that 'investors pay attention to human rights treaties as part of the host country's legal framework' and they avoid violators of human rights.[53] In the following years, studies found that violator states are prone to social conflict and those government who respect human rights are able to maintain political stability. For this reason, investors opt to invest in states with high human rights scores.

There is no strong, widely cited neo-Gramscian literature directly focusing on the exact question, 'Why would states accept human rights regimes despite sovereignty costs, in neo-Gramscian terms?' However, we know that most neo-Gramscian scholars like Robert W. Cox, Stephen Gill, and Andreas Bieler, focus on economic governance, global capitalism, and hegemony structures. They often treat human rights either as an element that legitimizes hegemonic orders or as a prolongation of the counter-hegemonic language. Thus, this book fills the gap in the literature by offering a neo-Gramscian interpretation of states' engagement with international human rights regimes, addressing the tension between sovereignty and human rights, not merely as a question of utility, but as a strategic move

51 Moravcsik, 'The Origins of Human Rights Regimes', 217.

52 Ana Carolina Garriga, 'Human Rights Regimes, Reputation, and Foreign Direct Investment', *International Studies Quarterly* 60, no. 1 (2016): 160–72, at 161; See also: Samuel P. Huntington and Joan M. Nelson, *No Easy Choice: Political Participation in Developing Countries* (Cambridge, MA: Harvard University Press, 1976).

53 Garriga, 'Human Rights Regimes, Reputation, and Foreign Direct Investment', 161.

within broader hegemonic structures. It expands the discussion beyond the liberal and realist paradigms by situating human rights commitments within the dynamics of global historical blocs, ideological leadership, and struggles for legitimacy.

From a neo-Gramscian perspective, the willingness of states to accept the sovereignty costs embedded in human rights regimes can be understood as part of broader hegemonic projects. Rather than acting purely out of material self-interest, states operate within historical blocs shaped by prevailing ideological, economic, and social orders. Human rights norms, while seemingly universal and emancipatory, can serve to reinforce a particular form of global order legitimizing dominant modes of governance and aligning domestic structures with international hegemonic interests. In this context, states may commit to international human rights treaties not merely as a matter of choice, but as a strategy to secure their position within a hegemonically constructed international system. Compliance with human rights conditionalities, especially for semi-peripheral or rising states like Turkey during its early EU candidacy, can be seen as a calculated move to gain access to the economic, political, and symbolic benefits of inclusion within the dominant order. Thus, even sovereignty concessions are framed within a wider struggle for legitimacy, integration, and influence within a hegemonic world structure shaped by liberal-capitalist norms.[54]

The application of a neo-Gramscian hegemony framework to Turkey's adherence to international human rights conventions reveals that its motivations were embedded within broader struggles over hegemony rather than purely rational calculations of utility. From this viewpoint, Turkey's commitment to these conventions can be interpreted as part of a strategy to align itself with the dominant norms of the liberal international order, thereby securing legitimacy both domestically and internationally. Rather than merely maximizing material self-interest, Turkey's engagement with human rights reforms under the Justice and Development Party reflected an effort to position itself within an emerging historical bloc, wherein adopting European norms could reinforce the party's internal authority and legitimacy as well as its external credibility. As a peripheral economy, Turkey found a boosting effect in integration with the EU. Human rights reforms, in this sense, served to bolster the AKP's hegemonic project, both by reshaping domestic consent, gearing up the Turkish economy, and by

54 Stephen R. Gill and David Law, 'Global Hegemony and the Structural Power of Capital', *International Studies Quarterly* 33, no. 4 (1989): 475–99.

accommodating the expectations of dominant transnational structures. However, as the AKP consolidated power and alternative sources of legitimacy emerged domestically, the incentives to maintain alignment with the liberal international human rights order diminished. In neo-Gramscian terms, the AKP's early reforms were an exercise in 'passive revolution' by adopting selected elements of the dominant global order to stabilize its own rule, while the later retreat from these commitments reflected a reassertion of a counter-hegemonic project aligned with new domestic and international power constellations.

The presence of the military in Turkey's civilian politics and institutions has been a consistent point of criticism by the European Union and a source of domestic discontent, particularly in light of the coup d'états in 1960, 1970, and 1980, which significantly regressed democratic progress each time. Historically, since the establishment of the Republic, the military positioned itself as the guardian of the Republic, secularism, and Kemalist values, posing subtle threats to civilian governance. The convergence of international and domestic interests under the AKP government facilitated the enactment of reforms aimed at purging military elements from civilian political structures, aligning with both EU criticisms and societal grievances. The neo-Gramscian hegemony lens demonstrates that the removal of military elements from Turkish political and institutional scenery allowed the AKP government to prepare a basis on which it finds the opportunity to accumulate the legitimacy and power to separate itself from the core (the EU) in order to build its contra-hegemony in the next phase.[55]

The second phase of human rights development in Turkey can be characterized as a plateau, where reforms continue, yet not incrementally. This stabilization phase is typical for candidate states, as evidenced by empirical research which shows that these states often implement a flurry of reforms to meet the Copenhagen criteria, only for their motivation to wane once accession negotiations commence. While this does not signify a reversal, the upward trend halts, giving way to a more tempered and stable continuation of reforms. The neo-Gramscian perspective suggests that this plateau phase reflects a moment of stabilization within a historic bloc, where initial reforms aligned Turkey with the hegemonic liberal international order, but deeper structural transformation was resisted. Early reforms were part of a 'passive revolution', which indicated selective adaptations to hegemonic norms aimed at preserving state autonomy and domestic power structures.

55 Stephen Gill, *Gramsci, Historical Materialism and International Relations* (Cambridge: Cambridge University Press, 1993), 30–32.

As the domestic configuration of power stabilized and Turkey secured partial recognition from dominant international actors, the impetus for further transformative change weakened. The plateau thus signals the limits of consent achieved through external pressures; without deeper internalization of the hegemonic project or continued material incentives, the process reached a point of relative equilibrium. In neo-Gramscian terms, Turkey's reforms served to manage contradictions between domestic power interests and external hegemonic expectations, but once the immediate legitimacy gains were secured, the historic bloc resisted further structural convergence, preferring a stabilized hybrid model rather than full alignment with liberal human rights norms.

The European Union wields dual influence mechanisms. On the one hand, there exists an implicit coercion where deviation from EU norms could jeopardize accession prospects or diminish benefits such as trade relations. Additionally, the EU's stance involves potential audience costs, adding a layer of pressure on states to conform to its standards and expectations. From a neo-Gramscian perspective, however, the EU's influence operates not solely through material incentives and disincentives but also through the diffusion of a broader hegemonic project. By embedding human rights norms within accession criteria and institutional frameworks, the EU seeks to reshape the domestic social order of candidate countries, fostering a new historic bloc aligned with liberal-capitalist values. This exercise of hegemony involves not just coercion, but the construction of consent among domestic elites and social forces, encouraging voluntary internalization of norms that ultimately stabilize the existing international order. Thus, the EU's human rights conditionality is as much a project of ideological leadership as it is of strategic bargaining.

In the third phase, human rights in Turkey experience a notable backslide, at times accelerating rapidly. From a neo-Gramscian perspective, the administrative, executive, and coercive apparatus of the state is dominated by the hegemony of the AKP government, as the leading class.[56] The deterioration in the human rights record reflects a broader crisis in the hegemonic project that had previously aligned Turkey's domestic order with European-led international norms. While institutionalism within regime theory suggests that international institutions facilitate cooperation by reducing transaction costs and reinforcing shared norms, neo-Gramscian analysis reveals that institutions serve deeper purposes: They are instruments through which dominant powers project

56 Cox, 'Gramsci, Hegemony and International Relations', 51.

and stabilize a particular historical bloc globally. Institutions like the Council of Europe and the European Union do not merely provide forums for dialogue; they embed the dominant liberal-capitalist values within domestic structures, aiming to cultivate passive consent among states like Turkey. However, as Hafner-Burton notes, the institutionalization of human rights can act as a 'double-edged sword'[57] – states may initially ratify instruments to secure legitimacy, only to later selectively disengage once external pressures weaken. In neo-Gramscian terms, Turkey's human rights regression indicates not just opportunistic deviation but a reconfiguration of the domestic power bloc away from the liberal order and towards a new alignment of forces favouring greater state autonomy and authoritarian governance. This shift reveals the fragile, contested nature of the hegemonic consensus that institutions attempt to sustain, especially when material conditions and domestic political interests diverge from the international project.

While liberal and constructivist scholars like Finnemore suggest that international law influences state behaviour through informational mechanisms and norm learning,[58] from a neo-Gramscian perspective, such processes can be understood as part of the broader project of hegemonic stabilization. According to Finnemore, international pressure facilitates a learning process that reduces violations.[59] Simmons further argues that states ratify human rights treaties in part due to 'social camouflage', aiming to align with regional norms and avoid audience costs. Koh describes this as the first stage of norm internalization, where transnational interactions bestow legitimacy upon emerging norms, gradually embedding them domestically.[60] However, a neo-Gramscian reading would reinterpret these developments not purely as voluntary learning or norm adoption, but as manifestations of hegemonic diffusion, mechanisms through which dominant powers universalize their preferred norms and embed them within national legal and political structures, thereby securing passive consent and stabilizing the

57 Emilie M. Hafner-Burton, Kiyoteru Tsutsui, and John W. Meyer, 'Human Rights in a Globalizing World: The Parad.ox of Empty Promises', *American Journal of Sociology* 110, no. 5 (2005): 1373–1411, at 1378.

58 Martha Finnemore, *National Interests in International Society* (Ithaca, NY: Cornell University Press, 1996), 141.

59 Beth A. Simmons, 'Mobilizing for Human Rights: International Law in Domestic Politics', in *Leading Works in International Law*, ed. Donna Lyons (Routledge, 2024), 88–90.

60 Harold Hongju Koh, 'Why Do Nations Obey International Law', *Yale Law Journal* 106 (1996): 2599–2660; Harold Hongju Koh, 'The 1998 Frankel Lecture: Bringing International Law Home', *Houston Law Review* 35 (1998): 623–81.

existing order. Rather than neutral processes of socialization, these dynamics reflect the asymmetric relations of power inherent in the construction and maintenance of international regimes.

Goodman and Jinks introduced the concept of acculturation,[61] whereby international law influences state behaviour by embedding norms as shared values through mechanisms such as mimicry, identification, and status maximization.[62] However, from a neo-Gramscian perspective, these microprocesses should not be viewed as neutral pathways to norm internalization but rather as mechanisms for consolidating hegemonic structures. Acculturation becomes a strategy through which dominant actors secure passive consent by embedding their preferred norms as common sense. In the Turkish case, while early human rights reforms may have reflected some degree of normative alignment, the EU's later behaviour, particularly during the third phase of backsliding, reveals the limits of value-driven approaches.

As human rights conditions in Turkey deteriorated, the EU failed to apply effective incentives or sanctions to reverse the trend. Instead, despite its professed normative identity, the EU leveraged Turkey's authoritarian turn to externalize its migration management through the 18 March 2016 EU–Turkey deal. This pragmatic shift highlights how hegemonic projects adapt to material exigencies, subordinating normative commitments to strategic interests when necessary. In line with international relations theories that suggest external pressure affects human rights performance, the waning of EU leverage facilitated democratic backsliding in Turkey.

Mainstream research, such as that of Simmons, Cole, and Moravcsik, has documented that democratizing states are more likely to ratify human rights treaties, largely because they seek to stabilize internal state–society relations.[63] Yet, from a neo-Gramscian perspective, this trend reflects not only voluntary democratization but also the embedding of a hegemonic world order wherein liberal norms serves to reproduce existing hierarchies. Turkey's reversal thus illustrates the fragility of norm compliance when external hegemonic support shifts and domestic elite coalitions realign.

The compliance literature offers suggestions about the link between human rights and democracy which explains why Turkey entered into

61 Goodman and Jinks, 'How to Influence States'.

62 Ibid., 626.

63 Beth A. Simmons, 'Should States Ratify? Process and Consequences of the Optional Protocol to the ICESCR', *Nordic Journal of Human Rights* 27, no. 1 (2009): 65–82; Wade M. Cole, 'Sovereignty Relinquished? Explaining Commitment to the International Human Rights Covenants, 1966–1999', *American Sociological Review* 70, no. 3 (2005): 472–95.

human rights commitments during its democratization period and then started to withdraw from them (as it did in 2021 from the Istanbul Convention) or deviate from them (such as from ECtHR rules) during the backsliding.

Simmons studied compliance in relation to human rights regimes. She argues that the majority of governments that adopt human rights do not do so in order to deviate from them. The non-democratic government that is less willing to comply often takes longer to ratify the agreement in order to avoid the obligations thereunder. This evidence suggests that participation in human rights regimes is not based on commitment.[64] Observation of the ratification of eighteen international human rights treaties shows that among 199 states, there are no states on earth that have ratified only one or fewer treaties, which means even non-democratic states are party members to at least one international human rights convention.[65] No state has ever placed reservations on human rights articles in the UN Charter. Considering formal rejections, we recall the eight abstentions to the adoption of the UDHR, which were made by members of the Soviet Bloc, Saudi Arabia, and South Africa. Hafner-Burton et al. questioned the 'strong inclination' of the rational of national governments that repress and violate human rights to join international human rights treaties. Their findings indicate that the adoption of international agreements which give increasing normative emphasis on human rights is how modern states seek international legitimation. On the other hand, global non-accountability leads to a vicious cycle, in which the given states only symbolically commit to the agreements they adopted.[66] Then again, Hafner-Burton found that democratizing states join human rights conventions with the will of complying. Neumayer says that those states are less likely to place treaty reservations.[67] This is how they communicate with the rest of the world, showing that they are not only paying lip service but taking action and bearing credible, legally binding costs on behalf of democratization.[68]

64 Simmons, 'Should States Ratify?'.

65 OHCHR, 'Status of Ratification Interactive Dashboard', accessed 10 March 2024, https://indicators.ohchr.org.

66 Hafner-Burton, Tsutsui, and Meyer, 'Human Rights in a Globalizing World: The Paradox of Empty Promises', 135–37.

67 Emilie M. Hafner-Burton, 'The Power Politics of Regime Complexity: Human Rights Trade Conditionality in Europe', *Perspectives on Politics* 7, no. 1 (2009): 33–37.

68 Emilie M. Hafner-Burton, Edward D. Mansfield, and Jon C.W. Pevehouse, 'Human Rights Institutions, Sovereignty Costs and Democratization', *British Journal of Political Science* 45, no. 1 (2015): 1–27.

The neo-Gramscian hegemony approach views compliance with international treaties not merely as a result of normative commitment, rational calculation, or transaction cost management, but as part of a broader strategy of hegemonic reproduction. States ratify and (selectively) comply with international legal commitments, including human rights obligations, as a means of integrating themselves into the dominant international order. Participation in international treaties helps confer legitimacy, access to material benefits, and a position within the structures of global governance shaped by hegemonic actors.

As mentioned above, Simmons' research demonstrates that many states do not adopt human rights treaties with a genuine commitment to full compliance.[69] Non-democratic governments, in particular, often delay ratification to postpone the costs of legal obligations, yet eventually join to avoid international isolation. Hafner-Burton and colleagues have shown that even highly repressive regimes ratify human rights treaties in order to gain international legitimacy, reinforcing their sovereignty while minimizing external scrutiny. Ratification becomes part of what Gramsci termed the 'passive revolution', the adaptation of dominant norms without substantive structural change.

The global human rights regime, characterized by almost universal participation (as seen in the ratification patterns of major treaties and the non-reservation of core UN Charter obligations), reflects this dual dynamic: widespread formal commitment combined with selective, strategic compliance.

Chayes and Chayes's managerial model, which emphasizes cooperation, dispute resolution, and problem-solving as drivers of compliance, captures important aspects of international law's role in facilitating stability.[70] However, it overlooks the deeper functions of international legal regimes as instruments of hegemonic governance. From a neo-Gramscian standpoint, the managerialist view naively assumes good faith and shared objectives, whereas actual compliance patterns reveal how states selectively align their behaviour with international obligations to preserve their position within the world system, balancing domestic elite interests, international legitimacy, and material integration.

In the case of international human rights regimes, democratizing states may initially comply more fully, as Neumayer and Moravcsik suggest,

69 Simmons, 'Should States Ratify?', 65.

70 Abram Chayes and Antonia Handler Chayes, 'On Compliance', *International Organization* 47, no. 2 (1993): 175–205.

seeking to gain credibility and to reinforce emerging elite coalitions. Yet, from a neo-Gramscian perspective, compliance is understood not as a fixed commitment but as a contingent and strategic behaviour shaped by the evolving balance of internal social forces and external hegemonic pressures. When these external pressures diminish, or when domestic power blocs consolidate authoritarian control, states may revert to symbolic compliance or even open non-compliance without jeopardizing their international standing. This dynamic is clearly evidenced in Turkey's trajectory.

Such a perspective sheds light on Turkey's sporadic non-compliance with the judgements of the European Court of Human Rights (ECtHR). The absence of robust enforcement mechanisms within the Council of Europe (COE) permits such violations to persist with relative impunity, illustrating a critical structural gap in the governance of international human rights. Rather than being anomalies, such instances of non-compliance can be understood as rational strategies within the broader hegemonic structure: by selectively adhering to human rights norms, states like Turkey navigate their dual imperatives of maintaining domestic authority while preserving the international legitimacy necessary for continued integration within the global order.

Infamously, international monitoring of human rights compliance remains either weak or altogether absent. Particularly in domains such as international asylum and migration governance, mechanisms for monitoring are notably deficient. While formal commitment to human rights treaties relieves states from the burden of genuine behavioural change, the absence or, as Hathaway terms it, the 'woefully inadequate'[71] nature of compliance monitoring enables states to pursue self-interest with minimal external restraint. From a neo-Gramscian standpoint, this phenomenon reflects the structural priorities of the international system: the symbolic adoption of human rights norms by states sustains the appearance of a rule-based international order while masking the uneven distribution of accountability and enforcement.

Although treaty-based monitoring bodies exist under many United Nations conventions, their impact is often limited by structural weaknesses and the dominance of hegemonic interests. Beyond international monitoring, domestic or sub-national monitoring mechanisms also warrant attention. Ideational approaches emphasize the internalization of international norms

71 Oona A. Hathaway, 'Do Human Rights Treaties Make a Difference?', *The Yale Law Journal* 111, no. 8 (2002): 1935–2042, at 2008.

at the domestic level, asserting that the highest levels of compliance are achieved when such norms are politically and socially institutionalized and incorporated into municipal law. Civil society organizations (CSOs) emerge as crucial actors within this domestic monitoring landscape. NGOs, established around specific social and political causes, act as watchdogs over governmental human rights practices. By exposing violations through digital platforms, traditional media, and transnational advocacy networks, these organizations not only stimulate domestic awareness but also activate international interest. Their efforts generate pressure from both within and beyond national borders, thus serving as a critical counterweight to state power.

Nevertheless, from a neo-Gramscian perspective, the efficacy of civil society itself is shaped by the broader relations of production and power: NGOs and advocacy networks operate within the structural constraints imposed by the prevailing hegemonic order. Their influence, particularly in sensitive fields such as asylum and migration, is often muted when their activities conflict with dominant political and economic interests.

This analysis reveals a profound gap in the enforcement and monitoring of human rights protections, especially concerning the rights of irregular migrants. Given the 'woefully inadequate' compliance monitoring mechanisms identified by Hathaway and others, combined with the strategic geopolitical imperatives of both Turkey and the European Union, there exists little incentive for rigorous oversight. Consequently, the rights of irregular migrants are frequently marginalized within policy frameworks, subsumed beneath broader political and security priorities. This neglect is compounded by both the lack of vigorous international scrutiny and the limited engagement or constrained effectiveness of civil society organizations in these specific domains. The resulting tacit acceptance of human rights violations within the asylum and migration regime underscores the critical need for enhanced mechanisms of international accountability and for a more assertive role of transnational advocacy networks in challenging and reshaping the prevailing hegemonic consensus.

As a significant component of international affairs, international legal perspective provides us with insights in relation to treaties. While traditional international legal scholarship predominantly focuses on the binding nature of treaty obligations post-ratification, a neo-Gramscian perspective compels us to reconsider treaties, including human rights instruments, as embedded within broader structures of hegemonic power. From this vantage point, treaties are not merely consensual legal acts but rather manifestations of a historically specific international order, sustained by the interplay between material capabilities, ideational domination, and institutional arrangements.

Due to the law of the instrument, legal scholars do not pay attention to the reasons that drive states towards treaty making. In legal scholarship the focus is mainly on the obligations created by any source of law, be it conventions or customs. The focus of the legal scholarship is rather on the process of and the aftermath of ratification, when the legal bindingness, and thus the obligations, start. In the international law literature, consent-oriented approaches are directly related to human rights regimes. Those theories hold that if a state does not enter into a treaty, then the treaty provisions do not bind the state. If a state enters a treaty this is because they intend to implement the provisions thereunder. When we consider such theories in relation to human rights, we discover a clash among the universality of human rights and international law. We have recorded a lot of evidence from the events of the twenty-first century. The great powers and their close allies, such as China, Russia, Israel, and Myanmar, engaged with various forms of international crimes. They are not parties to the Rome Statute of the International Criminal Court (ICC). Yet, neither the political circles nor the scholars of international law or the literature discuss their right to genocide, war crimes, crimes against humanity, and acts of aggression. While the international criminal law fell short in preventing such atrocities, the perpetrators are still responsible for their tortuous acts, referring to the peremptory norm, the *jus cogens* principle. In this sense, not ratifying a human rights treaty does not free a given state from content of the treaty, but some relevant mechanisms of monitoring, enforcement, etc. Another significant element of the consent-oriented theories departs from the *pacta sunt servanda* principle to argue that consent to join a treaty signals compliance readiness. This is mentioned in the Vienna Convention on the Law of Treaties (VCLT, 1969) that 'principles of consent, and of good faith and the *pacta sunt servanda*[72] are universally recognized' and as in article 26 'every treaty in force is binding upon the parties to it and must be performed by them in good faith'. However, there is abundant evidence to confute the consent-oriented approaches in situations where states have ratified a treaty but have then deviated from their obligations under it.

In the neo-Gramscian view, international law, including human rights regimes, functions as part of the 'superstructural' apparatus that reinforces prevailing hegemonies. Thus, the act of treaty ratification may reflect a

72 A Latin phrase meaning 'promises are kept'.

state's integration into a particular historical bloc, seeking legitimacy within a hegemonic framework that defines the contours of acceptable state behaviour.

In light of the discussions on consent-oriented theories within international law, Turkey's selective (non)implementation of the European Court of Human Rights (ECtHR) verdicts exemplifies a significant elements of this dynamic. While formal ratification of the European Convention on Human Rights (ECHR) signalled Turkey's alignment with the post–Cold War European liberal order, subsequent non-compliance reveals the fragility and contestability of that hegemonic structure. Turkey implemented its duties created by the ECHR and benefitted from verdicts such as *Opuz v. Turkey* (2009) that led Turkey taking the initiative in the formulation of the Istanbul Convention (the Convention on Preventing and Combating Violence against Women and Domestic Violence) of the Council of Europe and making ambitious efforts to elevate the relevant conditions in Turkey.[73] As internal social forces shifted and authoritarian consolidation progressed under the AKP government, the incentives to maintain symbolic alignment with European liberal norms waned, exposing the limits of ideological cohesion within the hegemonic project.

From a neo-Gramscian lens, the apparent gap between legal obligation and political practice is not merely a failure of enforcement but an expression of an underlying transformation in the balance of social forces. Compliance cannot be reduced to juridical consent; it is conditioned by the extent to which hegemonic norms resonate with, or are resisted by, domestic power configurations. In Turkey's case, the weakening appeal of European liberalism, compounded by the emergence of counter-hegemonic narratives emphasizing sovereignty, tradition, and national identity, facilitated the state's retreat from substantive compliance without necessitating overt withdrawal from the regime.

This approach also nuances the interpretation of the efficacy of human rights regimes. Rather than attributing compliance solely to enforcement mechanisms or rational self-interest, the neo-Gramscian perspective situates it within the broader contestation of hegemony at both the domestic and international levels. Hence, the selective adherence to human rights obligations is not anomalous but reflective of the continuous and contested process through which hegemonic orders are constructed, maintained, and challenged.

73 See Ergun Özbudun and Füsun Türkmen, 'Impact of the ECtHR Rulings on Turkey's Democratization: An Evaluation', *Human Rights Quarterly* 35 (2013): 985–1008.

## Comprehending the EU's Influence through a Neo-Gramscian Lens: Normative Power and Its Structural Limits

Understanding Turkey's interactions with the European human rights regime necessitates situating the external influence of the European Union (EU) within broader structures of power. Traditional regime theory often falls short in addressing the transformative impact of regimes on domestic structures. The European Union's influence, discussed extensively under the 'normative power Europe' (NPE) framework developed by Ian Manners, reveals both the potential and the limitations of a liberal international order striving for global norm diffusion.[74]

Manners posited that the EU's normative foundation is constructed upon five core norms: peace, liberty, democracy, the rule of law, and respect for human rights, enshrined in the *acquis communautaire* and *acquis politique.* These norms are propagated through mechanisms of contagion (unintentional transfer), transference (through trade or technical assistance), overt diffusion (direct influence), and the cultural filter (local adaptation or rejection). Tools for such propagation include EU delegations, the office of the Special Representative for Human Rights,[75] and trade agreements mandating adherence to International Labour Organization (ILO) conventions.[76] Human rights concerns are also institutionalized within the enlargement process, notably through the Treaty of Amsterdam[77] and the Copenhagen criteria,[78] which explicitly link accession to the fulfilment of democratic and human rights standards.

However, a neo-Gramscian perspective demands moving beyond the apparent altruism of these practices to reveal the underlying power relations shaping them. From this vantage point, the EU's promotion of norms functions not merely as a benign exercise in values diffusion, but

74 Ian Manners, 'Normative Power Europe: A Contradiction in Terms?', *JCMS: Journal of Common Market Studies* 40, no. 2 (2002): 235–58.

75 Strategic Communications, 'About Us: EU Special Representatives', *The Diplomatic Service of the European Union*, 15 November 2024, https://www.eeas.europa.eu/eeas/eu-special-representatives_en.

76 European Commission, 'Human Rights', accessed 16 November 2023, https://policy.trade.ec.europa.eu/development-and-sustainability/sustainable-development/human-rights_en.

77 The Treaty of Amsterdam (amending the Treaty on European Union, TEU) enshrines principles of liberty, democracy, respect for human rights, and fundamental freedoms and the rule of law as constitutional principles (new article 6, para. 1).

78 European Parliament, 'Democracy and Respect for Human Rights in the Enlargement Process of the European Union', accessed 16 November 2024, https://www.europarl.europa.eu/enlargement/briefings/20a2_en.htm.

as part of a broader strategy to consolidate a particular historical bloc, the liberal-democratic capitalist order, on a global scale. In this reading, the EU's normative power reflects the extension of a transnational consensus rooted in Western liberal values, sustaining material and ideational structures beneficial to dominant social forces.

The EU's transformative influence on Turkey prior to the start of accession negotiations can thus be interpreted as a process of passive revolution, whereby external pressures encouraged a reorganization of Turkey's domestic legal and political structures without fundamentally altering the existing power relations. Turkey's significant reforms in areas such as human rights, minority protections, and the abolition of the death penalty demonstrate how subaltern states may undergo structural adjustments in response to the incentives and conditionalities embedded within the hegemonic project.

Nonetheless, the neo-Gramscian approach highlights the fragility and contradictions within this hegemonic project. Once accession negotiations began, the EU's inconsistent application of its own principles manifested in shifting standards, the handling of minority protections, and the politicization of the Cyprus issue exposed the instrumental nature of the Union's normative claims. In Turkey, these inconsistencies fostered growing disillusionment with the EU, undermining the moral leadership necessary for sustained consent to the liberal-democratic order.

In particular, the absence of uniform criteria for minority rights protections[79] and the perceived hypocrisy surrounding the Cyprus dispute[80] illustrate that the EU's normative discourse was conditioned by material and geopolitical considerations. In Gramscian terms, the EU's failure to maintain an appearance of impartiality fractured the hegemonic consensus it sought to extend, allowing space for counter-hegemonic narratives within Turkey that framed the EU as a self-interested actor rather than a genuine community of values.

Thus, the Turkish case illuminates the limits of normative power when it is not consistently backed by a credible and transparent application of norms. The EU's partial and selective enforcement of human rights standards reveals that normative power operates within the constraints of broader material interests, power asymmetries, and the strategic imperatives of

79 Regarding the protection of minorities, which is one of the Copenhagen criteria, the European Union does not have well-structured measures and principles for determining the fulfilment of this obligation, nor have member states established their national minorities in order to protect them consistently within the Union.

80 The EU raising the Cyprus issue as a barrier before negotiations with Turkey, whilst not bringing up the very same topic before Greece, raises considerations of hypocrisy in Turkey.

dominant social groups. In neo-Gramscian terms, when the ideological apparatus of hegemony falters, when the mask of universality slips to reveal particularistic interests, the transformative potential of international regimes is fundamentally weakened.

In conclusion, while the EU possesses significant normative instruments and has achieved moments of influence, its inconsistent praxis during Turkey's accession process reflects the deep-seated contradictions of liberal hegemony. Without a commitment to a genuinely universal and consistent application of its own professed principles, the EU's normative project risks being exposed as a mechanism for reproducing existing power structures rather than genuinely transforming them. A neo-Gramscian lens thus not only contextualizes the EU's normative power within global configurations of domination and consent but also critically assesses its structural limits and vulnerabilities.

# 3. The Architecture of the European Human Rights Regime

**Abstract:** This chapter traces the development of the European human rights regime within the broader evolution of global human rights norms. It begins with the foundational influence of the Universal Declaration of Human Rights, highlighting how universal principles such as *jus cogens* and non-derogable rights shaped international expectations. The chapter then examines the institutional and normative architecture of the Council of Europe, focusing on the European Convention on Human Rights and the European Court of Human Rights. Finally, it explores the European Union's evolving role in human rights protection, particularly through its legal instruments and political conditionality mechanisms. By mapping this layered architecture, the chapter sets the groundwork for analysing how these regimes interact and affect Turkey's human rights trajectory.

**Keywords:** European human rights regime, Universal Declaration of Human Rights, Council of Europe, European Union, *jus cogens*, legal architecture

The rise of the modern (global) international human rights regime started with the adoption of the Universal Declaration of Human Rights (UDHR) on 10 December 1948 by the United Nations General Assembly (UNGA). Despite not being a legally binding document, it has been the most important influence as a political and legal departure point of all international human rights treaties, besides national legislation. The UDHR boldly laid the foundational norms and standards of human rights after 1945 by entitling all human beings equally, without exception, with inalienable rights. This is how the universality element of international human rights law was instigated. Universality should not be confused with international implementation. The UDHR is not the sole source of the universality. General principles of law, particularly *jus cogens* (thc compelling law), is another source which

Bayar, Tuğba. *The Rise and Relapse of European Human Rights in Turkey: The AKP Era, 2002–2024.* Amsterdam University Press/Central European University Press, 2025.
DOI 10.5117/9789048573813_CH03

is universally non-derogable. The principle of *jus cogens* holds that there are no legitimate or legal deviations from the ban of, for example, slavery, genocide, or war crimes.

## From Global Norms to European Protection

The Universal Declaration of Human Rights imposes specific obligations on states, which are inherently recognized as the principal protectors of human rights. These obligations require states to respect, protect, and fulfil human rights. Due to the intrinsic nature of human rights, their implementation predominantly occurs at the national level, underscoring the central role of sovereign states in the actualization of international human rights norms.

Those rights mentioned in the UDHR grew vertically and horizontally over the seven decades. Today, there is a vast number of regional and global human rights instruments for enhanced commitment. Human rights norms are also incorporated in customary law, such as the elements of human dignity, prohibition of arbitrary deprivation of life, equality, and solidarity.[1] Commitment to human rights is widely perceived as the key to peace, as also set forth by the UN Charter.

Subsequent to the UDHR, three UN documents were adopted. They are the International Covenant on Civil and Political Rights (ICCPR) and the International Covenant on Economic, Social and Cultural Rights (ICESCR). Contrary to the Universal Declaration, these are legally binding instruments. They categorize fundamental rights and provide us with more details of those rights, compared to the UDHR. Those conventions endorsed by the UN managed to reach the highest ratification rates and established the global (universal) regime for human rights together with numerous international organizations (IOs). As of 2024, 124 countries are states parties to the Rome Statute of the International Criminal Court (ICC). The rapid expansion of international human rights has been a pleasant surprise for the newly forming world order with the formulation of stacks of international treaties in a remarkable range. The UN regime was enlarging by adding up new human rights–related treaties, such as for the abolishment of slavery, for the protection of the child, etc. At the same time, regional human rights regimes started to mushroom around the globe, such as the European regime that springs from the European Convention on Human Rights (ECHR) endorsed

1 See William A. Schabas, *The Customary International Law of Human Rights* (Oxford: Oxford University Press, 2021).

by the Council of Europe (COE), the inter-American regime founded by the American Convention on Human Rights formulated by the Organization of American States (OAS), and African regimes based on the African Charter on Human and Peoples' Rights by the Organisation of African Unity. Keohane mentions that the complexity of international regimes means that they are intersecting to create linkages and hierarchies.[2] The regional human rights regimes are thus autonomous sub-levels of the global regime.[3] These regional legal regimes are designed to generate participation, monitor compliance of the member states, receive complaints, spot human rights violations, and hold the violator state accountable. Surely, national and international non-governmental organizations (NGOs) established to raise their human rights cause were also bourgeoning together with global and regional systems. For instance, as an international NGO, Amnesty International (1961) was awarded the Nobel Peace Prize for its defence of the value of human life.

Among regional organizations, the European regime is known to be the most effective and robust among all the regimes that bring democracies, material sources, and a well-established legal infrastructure together. It is composed of various organizations, institutions, and a collection of treaties, laws, and regulations. The inter-American and the European systems have similar organizations, a commission, and a court that allows individual applications and fosters friendly settlements between individuals and the violator state. However, the members of the European system are mostly well-established democracies. This is not the case for the inter-American system. The 2004 Arab Charter has the material sources to function but lacks a robust legal infrastructure. In contrast, the 1986 African Charter on Human and Peoples' Rights possesses a well-supported legal infrastructure. We do not observe a cross-cutting human rights system in Asia, due to various differences across the region in terms of geographical setting, the types of regimes and human rights approaches of the dominant states, and their economic relations. Despite the widening of international human rights regime(s), the number of rights-abusive governments has not decreased. At the same time, a number of governments have entered these agreements without having the urge to implement them. There had been serious international incidents, when human rights were employed to conceal unacceptable geopolitical goals. We have witnessed serious democratic

2 Robert O. Keohane, 'The Demand for International Regimes', *International Organization* 36 (1982): 325–55, at 334.

3 Jack Donnelly, 'International Human Rights: A Regime Analysis', *International Organization* 40, no. 3 (1986): 599–642, at 619–20.

backsliding in a lot of countries over the last decade and there have also been countries that have strayed away from their initial compliance.

The European regime was established in parallel to the universal system, as one regional regime, benefiting from the same sources. Known to be the most effective human rights regime on earth, the European human rights regime is based on a collection of international (regional) organizations, institutions, and treaties. As James Rosenau states, global governance emerges from the interaction between overlapping spheres of authority.[4] Likewise, the European human rights regime is a construction of disaggregate authorities spread among various actors, both supranational and intergovernmental. The success of this international human rights regime can be credited to the institutional structure, but I would rather praise the constructive political atmosphere. The war-weary states of Europe on the beginning of their democratization trajectory found a brilliant opportunity to demonstrate their consent to act under binding international obligations by facilitating the work of the European Convention on Human Rights (ECHR). Undeniably, geographical proximity, cultural (and almost political) homogeneity, and emerging multiple interdependence were active in the attainment of the goals of the convention. Additionally, Cold War polarization at the systemic level also contributed as European states closed ranks vis-à-vis the Soviets.

The three cores of this regime are the European Union, the Council of Europe, and the Organization for Security and Co-operation in Europe (OSCE). The Council of Europe is the oldest of these organizations, established to convey the values of the new world order.

Explaining the success of the European human rights system, the institutional design follows political lines. The simplicity of the text of the ECHR is an incontrovertible convenience for establishing a common denominator. For the same reason, its incorporation into national law has not been complicated. Its simplicity, therefore, is an important factor that prevented divergence and violations. By keeping the liability costs low, the regime achieved a high level of compliance. The introduction of the European Court of Human Rights was another addition to the regime, which added a significant element to its judicial structure. Each individual decision of the court was understood as an opportunity for improvement by the members and enabled the regime to progress in a gradual way. The slow evolution of the judicial institutions provided the regime with the

4 James N. Rosenau, 'Governing the Ungovernable: The Challenge of a Global Disaggregation of Authority', *Regulation & Governance* 1, no. 1 (2007): 88–97.

prospect of elaboration, which resulted in steadfast implementation. The organizational structure of the court facilitated this.

The newly emerging global order of the post–World War II era was built upon the lessons learnt from the horrors of the previous wars. The cure to the isolationism that gave rise to a formidable international competition was 'cooperation' among nations. On the one hand, the world was divided into Western and Eastern Blocs, led by the United States and the Soviet Union. On the other hand, mushrooming international (global and regional) organizations started to bring states together to address various issue areas. In this global context, Winston Churchill, one of the founding fathers of the ideal of a united Europe, gave a speech at the University of Zurich in 1946 to propose his vision:

> [I]f Europe were once united in the sharing of its common inheritance there would be no limit to the happiness, prosperity and glory which its 300 million or 400 million people would enjoy. [...] We must build a kind of United States of Europe.[5]

In this famous speech, he underscored the necessity for the recreation of the Franco–German partnership to pioneer further integration. The united Europe idea of Churchill was not depicted as a rival to the United Nations, but as a booster and supplement to it.

Two years later, the Congress of Europe in the Hague (also known as the Hague Conference) was held between 7 and 10 May 1948.[6] The honorary chair of the Congress was Winston Churchill. Under his auspices, seventeen European states gathered alongside observers from the United States and Eastern Europe. The conference aimed to establish multiple ties among European nations under the coordination of their parliaments. Three committees were formed for closer elaboration of the integration elements: the Economic and Social Committee, the Political and Legal Committee, and the Cultural Committee. While the Economic and Social Committee focused on themes around removing the barriers to inter-European trade, the Political and Legal Committee made efforts towards the creation of a common plenary body, an assembly, to be elected by universal suffrage. Chaired by the former French prime minister, Paul Ramadier, the Cultural

5 Winston Churchill, 'Winston Churchill, Speech Delivered at the University of Zurich, 19 September 1946', https://rm.coe.int/16806981f3.

6 Seventeen countries were represented, and observers from Eastern Europe and the US also attended.

Committee was in charge of formulating binding human rights values that would lead states to be responsible for their human rights violations vis-à-vis the subjects under their jurisdiction. The political resolution of the Congress proposed (i) the establishment of the European Assembly, (ii) the drafting of the Charter of Human Rights that established 'standards to which a state must conform if it is to deserve the name of a democracy',[7] (iii) the establishment of a Supreme Court 'with adequate sanctions for the implementation of this Charter',[8] and (iv) world unity. The necessity of adopting the Charter of Human Rights was repeated in the Cultural Resolution, which also called for establishment of the European Youth Institute and the European Cultural Centre.[9]

As a result of the efforts of the Cultural Committee, the foundation of the Council of Europe was adopted on 5 May 1949 by the Treaty of London (also known as the Statute of the Council of Europe). The Council of Europe came to being as the very first parliamentary assembly. In this sense, we can make two inferences: (i) although this is rarely mentioned in European studies, the integration was predominantly led by parliamentarians, and (ii) the human rights ideal was not a spin-off element to integration, it was a central cause from the beginning.

## The Council of Europe

The Council was founded by ten states: Belgium, Denmark, France, Ireland, Italy, Luxembourg, the Netherlands, Norway, Sweden, and the United Kingdom. It has gone through two enlargement waves. The first wave included the addition of Cyprus in 1962, Malta in 1967, and Switzerland and Greece in 1974. (Greece had already signed in 1950 but had withdrawn its signature in 1969.) The Iberian accession took place when Portugal joined in 1976 and Spain in 1977. The second wave of enlargement hit following the collapse of the Soviet Bloc when Eastern European states and Russia joined the Council. The Russian Federation withdrew its membership in 2022 following the opinion adopted by the Parliamentary Assembly of the Council of Europe

7 Congress of Europe, 'Political Resolution of the Hague Congress (7–10 May 1948)', 1948, https://www.cvce.eu/obj/political_resolution_of_the_hague_congress_7_10_may_1948-en-15869906-97dd-4c54-ad85-a19f2115728b.html.

8 Ibid.

9 Congress of Europe, 'Cultural Resolution of the Hague Congress (7–10 May 1948)', 1948, https://www.cvce.eu/en/recherche/unit-content/-/unit/04bfa990-86bc-402f-a633-11f39c9247c4/4ab19baa-6d0e-4de8-9d9c-6391612bf22a/Resources.

(PACE) due to Russia's invasion of Ukraine. Currently, the COE has forty-six member states and almost 800 million citizens. Additionally, there are six states with observer status: Canada, the Holy See (Vatican), Israel (observer to the Parliamentary Assembly), Japan, Mexico, and the United States. In this sense, although the COE was founded as a regional organization, its influence reaches beyond the borders of Europe. In 2024, the PACE recommended inviting Kosovo to become a member of the COE.[10] This opinion resolution was published in line with UN Security Council Resolution no. 1244 that defines the status of Kosovo as a territory under the protectorate of the UN and also as a territory within Serbia.

The COE was established soon after the most prominent proclamation of the century, the Universal Declaration of Human Rights (UDHR) by the UN General Assembly (UNGA) on 10 December 1948. Its first initiative was to formulate a human rights convention as inspired by the UDHR. It was the inspiration for the preparation of the European Convention on Human Rights (formerly known as the Convention for the Protection of Human Rights and Fundamental Freedoms) that was opened for signature on 4 November 1950 in Rome. Turkey signed it in the same year and ratified on 10 March 1954.

Although the EU and the Council of Europe (COE) are two independent international actors, a closer look at the establishment of the COE reveals the shared foundational elements of the two organizations. The very first human rights initiative of the Europe, the ECHR, functioned to construct the European community as a corpus, where human rights was an integral and natural element of it. Furthermore, the ECHR is mentioned in the Treaty on European Union (TEU), where this referral represents a bond between the two entities, the COE and the EU. The EU is one of the top contributors to the COE's joint programmes. The ECHR, article 6, paras. 2 and 3, states that the Union shall accede to it, and it is a document reflecting the common constitutional tradition of all Union members and thus constituting the general principles of EU law. The convention reiterates the phrase 'prescribed by law', which is a referral to both EU law and the municipal law of the member states.[11] The member states incorporated the ECHR 'in the rank of a statute' (as in Germany) and it is assumed to be a source to support the interpretation of fundamental rights in line with the national constitution. In some other

10 Parliamentary Assembly of the Council of Europe, 'Opinion 302: Application by Kosovo for Membership of the Council of Europe', 15 April 2024, https://pace.coe.int/en/files/33496.

11 Verica Trstenjak, 'Limitations of Fundamental Rights in EU Law: Are Human Rights Absolute?', *European Review* 32, no. 2 (2024): 135–49, https://doi.org/10.1017/S1062798723000509.

member states the convention is incorporated in the 'constitutional rank' (as in Austria and Spain) as an international treaty that is superior to regular legislation. The courts, including the Constitutional Court, cite the ECHR as well as ECtHR jurisprudence 'regularly and extensively'.[12]

The Council of Europe declares its main mission to be to promote three norms, democracy, human rights, and the rule of law, across Europe and beyond. It aims to promote basic elements of human rights, such as freedom of thought (article 9), freedom of expression (article 10), freedom of assembly and association (article 11), and the right to an effective remedy (article 13) as indisputable supranational values. To this end the COE devises international agreements for further promotion and encouragement of human rights practices – for example, it endorsed the Istanbul Convention in 2011, the Convention against Trafficking in Human Organs in 2015, and the Convention on an Integrated Safety, Security, and Service Approach at Football Matches and Other Sports Events in 2016.

The COE's duties are shared among seven main entities: the Chairmanship, the Committee of Ministers, the Parliamentary Assembly, the Congress of Local and Regional Authorities, the European Court of Human Rights, the Commissioner for Human Rights, and the Conference of International Non-governmental Organizations (INGOs). Additionally, monitoring bodies contribute to the dissemination of human rights. The duties of these organs are well defined and they play a central role in the achievements of the COE. Since the human rights issue area does not belong to the high politics cluster, states are less willing to cooperate under human rights regimes. However, the COE was established as a bulwark against armed conflicts and atrocities by promoting the three COE norms. It has succeeded in expanding its influence over a broad geography with a regime praised as a legitimate and effective international framework to promote and monitor fulfilment of human rights standards as responsibilities at the domestic level.

The three norms were present at the time of European integration and the creation of its liberal and rights-respecting state mechanisms. One of the greatest achievements of the COE is the abolition of the death penalty within its sphere of influence, which is a vertical expansion of the right to life. Its contributions to the expansion of freedom of expression and gender equality in Europe are also undeniable. The COE monitors its member states for compliance and provides them with advice for improvement. The Council hosts fourteen specialist monitoring bodies – including the European Committee of Social Rights, the European Committee for the Prevention

12 Krisch, 'The Open Architecture of European Human Rights Law', 186–87.

of Torture and Inhuman or Degrading Treatment or Punishment (CPT), the Council of Europe Convention on Preventing and Combating Violence against Women and Domestic Violence (and its monitoring organ, the Group of Experts on Action against Violence against Women and Domestic Violence, GREVIO) – besides committees on human trafficking, racism and intolerance, protection of children against sexual exploitation and sexual abuse, national minorities, freedom of information, data protection, cybercrimes, corruption, recovery of criminal assets, money laundering, and fake medical products. In the monitoring process, the Council measures the compliance of the state parties to the aforementioned international treaties and thereunder established specialist monitoring bodies. The experts in these monitoring bodies go to member states to collect data via site visits, observations, and reports. In addition to the specialist monitoring bodies, there are currently ten specialist advisory bodies of the COE. They also assess the commitment of the member states to the COE standards and make recommendations for improvement.

The specialist advisory bodies have been formed to deal with constitutional matters, justice, judges, prosecutors, drug policies, doping and manipulation in sport, fairer and safer sport, history teaching, cultural support, the audio-visual market, and legal information. The institutional structure of the Council contributed to the development of fundamental rights in member states in different ways. The legal instruments formulated by the Council are central in this development. Turkey has also benefited directly from the European Convention, besides the European Social Charter, the European Charter of Local Self-government, the Istanbul Convention, the Lanzarote Convention, and many others. The European Convention is cited by the election manifestos of both Erdoğan's party, the AKP, and the main opposition party, CHP (Republican Peoples Party), to declare their approach to fundamental rights and freedoms.

As a sub-organ of the COE, the European Court of Human Rights (ECtHR) was founded in 1959 to interpret the ECHR. It was established as a permanent international court where individuals are allowed to lodge complaints against their own state, based on violations of the ECHR. The court offers regional jurisprudence on member states' implementation of human rights. With its organizational structure and diligent processes, the ECtHR functions as the heart of the European human rights regime, where standards and the normative meaning of the rights are defined for implementation. The normative expansion of the right to life by the abolition of the death penalty is a prominent example. Creation and consolidation of the rule of law culture is another one.

Relations with the COE gained a new dimension later, in 1987, when Turkey adopted the right to individual application (in article 34, formerly article 25 of the Convention) that allows 'any person, non-governmental organization, or group of individuals' to lodge a complaint about a violation of their human rights against their own state. (Interstate applications are also allowed according to article 33, which was formerly article 24.) The acknowledgement of the individual application right was followed by Turkey's recognition of the ECtHR's jurisdiction in 1989. Since then, the court has become a 'normative power centre' with a high density of individual applications from Turkey.[13] The court procedures are designed under the ECHR and, partially, by the rules of the court.

Turkey's relations with the court have become a significant indicator of its trajectory away from democratization. For instance, the court ordered the Turkish state to pay compensation for its failure to protect woman from gender-based violence in *Opuz v. Turkey*.[14] This decision motivated Turkey (during its Europeanization/democratization years) to play a leading role in the formulation and adoption of the Istanbul Convention. On the other hand, Turkey is currently on a democratic backsliding track[15] – for example, it failed to implement the ECtHR decisions ordering the release of Osman Kavala and Selahattin Demirtaş.

It is, however, possible to approach the relations between the court and the AKP government from another perspective. The distrust of the AKP elites towards the ECtHR was established in the 1990s, when it brought a suit against Turkey for the reinstatement of rights and freedoms.

The AKP elites' experience with the ECtHR when they faced rights derogations caused distrust. In the cases of *Leyla Şahin v. Turkey* and *Kurtulmuş v. Turkey*, the applicants made complaints against the Turkish state that they were, respectively, deprived of a studentship at the medical school and of a professor position at the university, after a disciplinary procedure, for wearing a headscarf. In the case of Leyla Şahin, the chamber unanimously held that a headscarf ban was not a violation of her right to education and

13 Selçuk Kahraman and Önder Kutlu, 'International Organisations on National Politics: Council of Europe Effects on Political Party in Turkiye', *Otoritas: Jurnal Ilmu Pemerintahan* 14, no. 2 (2024): 429–49, at 433.

14 ECtHR, *Opuz v. Turkey*, no. 33401/02, 9 June 2009.

15 Berk Esen and Sebnem Gumuscu, 'Why Did Turkish Democracy Collapse? A Political Economy Account of AKP's Authoritarianism', *Party Politics* 27, no. 6 (2021): 1075–91; Meltem Muftuler-Bac, 'Backsliding in Judicial Reforms: Domestic Political Costs as Limits to EU's Political Conditionality in Turkey', *Journal of Contemporary European Studies* 27, no. 1 (2019): 61–76.

her right to religious expression.[16] The court ruled in favour of Turkey, relying on article 9, para. 2, according to which freedom of thought, conscience, and religion are subject to limitations as prescribed by law.

The judgements indicated that the state is entitled to implement limitations to the extent necessary for the preservation of the secular features of the state, for protecting the rights and freedoms of others, public order and public safety as well as for providing neutrality and impartiality. The court's interpretation of the article underlines that not all religiously motivated acts are thereunder protected.

In *Kurtulmuş*,[17] the court declared the inadmissibility of the application that the dress code was applied to all members of society for the protection of secularism and of the neutrality of the civil service, and particularly of education provided by the state. The court noted that the measures were not based on the applicant's religion. The court decisions, in both of the cases, approving the prohibition rather than focusing on individual rights and freedoms, provoked reactions from religious conservatives. The decisions led people in these circles to criticize the court for its approach towards religious symbols and items of clothing and the presupposition that they prevented well-functioning, pluralist democracies. The conservative faction held that pluralism was only possible without discrimination against religious people and this kind of a societal system could not be spoiled by the use of the headscarf.[18] This proposition contradicted the court's understanding of pluralist societies, which embraced a variety of identities, ideologies, beliefs, and opinions under the denominator of freedoms such as the freedom of expression. In this context, the court's decisions established a milestone in the perception of the conservatives – that is, strategic modernists acting as a branch of political Islam[19] that was later embodied in the AKP[20] – of European values relating to democracy,

16 Leyla Şahin claimed that her rights under articles 8, 9, 10, and 14 of the European Convention on Human Rights and article 2 of Protocol no. 1 of the ECHR are violated by the headscarf ban and the subsequent suspension of her studentship at Istanbul University.

17 Sevgi Kurtulmuş applied to the European Court of Human Rights for the reinstatement of her rights guaranteed by articles 8, 9, and 10 of the European Convention on Human Rights and article 1 of Protocol no. 1 of the ECHR.

18 Mert Hüseyin Akgün, 'Başörtüsü Özgürlüğü ve Anayasal Güvence Arayışı', SETA, January 2023, 26–29, https://www.setav.org/assets/uploads/2023/01/R214.pdf.

19 Daniel Brumberg, 'Rhetoric and Strategy: Islamic Movements and Democracy in the Middle East', in *The Islamism Debate*, ed. Martin S. Kramer (Syracuse, NY: Syracuse University Press, 1997), 11–33.

20 Senem Aydın Düzgit and Ruşen Çakır, 'Turkey: A Sustainable Case of De-radicalisation?', in *Islamist Radicalisation: The Challenge for Euro-Mediterranean Relations*, ed. edited by Michael

human rights, and secularism.[21] The decisions led to scepticism about the COE's understanding of tolerance and pluralism, because the court failed to provide concrete examples of individual violations of the neutrality principle.

The COE member states internalized the human rights standards, particularly as a result of the efforts by the European Court of Human Rights and the Committee of Ministers because the ECtHR holds the states responsible for their violations and the Committee of Ministers examine the implementation of the orders of the court by the convicted state.

The Committee of Ministers is entitled to determine the loopholes in the human rights system and to formulate international agreements to address these gaps. The Committee of Ministers serves as the principal decision-making body of the Council of Europe, with its Secretariat ensuring the effective operationalization of the mandate. Tasked with organizing and facilitating high-level meetings, including those concerning the supervision of the execution of judgements from the European Court of Human Rights as per article 46 of the European Convention, the Secretariat is instrumental in preparing and managing interactions among heads of state, government ministers, and their deputies. It supports the presidency in orchestrating meetings and enhancing communication flows within the Council, while also aiding rapporteurs, working groups, and thematic coordinators in fulfilling their responsibilities. Additionally, the Secretariat enhances liaisons among permanent representations and various Council of Europe bodies and fosters external relations with other international institutions. It plays a key role in preparing documentation, maintaining confidentiality and transparency, and coordinating follow-up actions on decisions. The Secretariat also orchestrates dialogue with pivotal entities such as the Parliamentary Assembly and the European Court of Human Rights, ensuring the committee's decisions are well-communicated and effectively implemented. Furthermore, it manages the Committee of Ministers' website and engages with media and public relations to amplify the visibility and impact of the committee's work, reflecting its central role in advancing the Council of Europe's mission.

Emerson, Kristina Kausch, and Richard Youngs (Brussels: Centre for European Policy Studies, 2009), 87–108.

21 Ibid.

## The European Union's Emerging Human Rights Role

Although the European Union was not established as a human rights organization, its evolving role has significantly shaped the broader European human rights architecture. Initially driven by economic integration, the EU increasingly incorporated human rights considerations into its external and internal policies. Through the use of conditionality in accession processes, trade agreements embedding human rights clauses, and the establishment of mechanisms such as EU delegations and the Special Representative for Human Rights, the Union has extended its normative influence across Europe and beyond. As a result, the EU today stands as a critical actor in promoting and protecting human rights, complementing the work of specialized institutions like the Council of Europe and the OSCE.

In conclusion, the architecture of the European human rights regime illustrates a robust and multifaceted framework for the promotion and protection of fundamental rights across the continent. Rooted in the principles established by the Universal Declaration of Human Rights and reinforced through a range of regional instruments and institutions, this regime stands as a testament to Europe's enduring commitment to human dignity and justice. The European Court of Human Rights, alongside the Council of Europe, plays a pivotal role by offering individuals a judicial avenue to challenge state actions, thereby enhancing state accountability and adherence to human rights standards. Complemented by the contributions of the European Union and the OSCE, the intricate network of treaties, monitoring bodies, and institutional collaborations fosters both compliance and a culture of rights and democratic governance that transcends national boundaries. The effectiveness of this regime is not solely the result of its legal mechanisms, but also reflects a broader European identity that places human rights at its core. Thus, the European human rights architecture remains a cornerstone in the global pursuit of a just and equitable international order.

# 4. Turkey's Human Rights Trajectory until 2002

**Abstract:** This chapter traces the evolution of human rights in Turkey from the foundation of the Republic through to the AKP's rise in 2002, identifying key ruptures and continuities across four political periods. Drawing on a neo-Gramscian framework, it examines how human rights were shaped by domestic hegemonic struggles and external pressures, particularly from European actors. The chapter explores the authoritarian foundations of the early Republic, the impact of repeated military interventions, and the gradual liberalization and Europeanization processes that gained traction in the late 1990s. It argues that by 2002, Turkey had entered a moment of conditional opening, with human rights increasingly tied to EU accession dynamics. This historical grounding sets the stage for understanding both the promises and contradictions of the AKP's human rights agenda in the following years.

**Keywords:** Turkey, human rights, military coups, EU conditionality, neo-Gramscian theory, democratization

Understanding Turkey's human rights trajectory under the Justice and Development Party (AKP) requires a careful examination of the longer historical patterns that preceded its rise to power. This chapter explores the evolution of human rights in Turkey from the establishment of the Republic in the 1920s to the end of 2002, highlighting the continuities and ruptures that have shaped the country's political and legal landscape. Drawing on a neo-Gramscian perspective, the analysis frames human rights not merely as legal commitments but as part of broader hegemonic struggles between state authority, civil society, and international actors.

From the early republican era's emphasis on state sovereignty and modernization to the turbulent periods of military interventions and restricted

Bayar, Tuğba. *The Rise and Relapse of European Human Rights in Turkey: The AKP Era, 2002–2024*. Amsterdam University Press/Central European University Press, 2025.
DOI 10.5117/9789048573813_CH04

political freedoms, Turkey's human rights record reveals a complex interplay of internal power dynamics and external influences. The chapter traces the slow emergence of a human rights discourse, the influence of European institutions, and the conditional openings towards democratization in the late 1990s, setting the stage for the transformative, but ultimately uneven, reforms of the AKP era. By situating the post-2002 developments within this longer historical trajectory, the study provides a deeper understanding of the structural conditions that have both enabled and constrained human rights progress in Turkey.

## 1920–46: Early Republic

Since the introduction of high ideals of the early emerging republic in the 1920s, Turkey has been recording unsteady improvements in the consolidation of human rights. After the foundation of the Turkish Grand National Assembly, Atatürk declared that 'sovereignty belongs to the nation unreservedly and unconditionally'. The newly emerging republic integrated the nation into the governance by freeing them from the authoritarian rule of the sultan and the caliph. In a sense, the folk was made the new master of the state. The subjects of the empire were elevated to the status of citizens by gaining several rights and liberties. Additionally, courageous reforms were recorded to modernize every aspect of life. Ironically, the progressive reforms were undertaken under the single-party rule of the Republican People's Party (Cumhuriyet Halk Partisi, CHP). After the instigation of the multiparty era, progress was sporadically interrupted by backslides by the hands of military invasions and domestic political priorities.

## 1946–80: Three Military Coups

The emergence of the post-war world order coincides with Turkey's transition to a competitive electoral system in 1946. While improving its democratic experience, Turkey was eager to engage with international advancements. Thus, it became one of the founding members of the UN system as it attended the 1945 San Francisco Conference (the United Nations Conference on International Organizations) and signed the UN Charter. Turkey also participated in the drafting of the Universal Declaration of Human Rights (UDHR) in 1946, which commenced under the newly established Commission on Human Rights. Turkey adopted the UDHR as it was published in the official gazette on 27 May 1949.[1]

Owing to the Republic's traditional Western orientation, Turkey hurried to be one of the earliest members of the Council of Europe by adopting the Treaty of London (the Statute of the Council of Europe) in 1950, one year after its establishment, and ratified it in 1954. Despite the early leap, Turkey hesitated to remain engaged with the globally enduring human rights progression by not signing the instruments adopted by the United Nations General Assembly, such as the International Covenant on Civil and Political Rights (ICCPR, 1966), and the International Covenant on Economic, Social and Cultural Rights (ICESCR, 1966). Human rights entered the Turkish political agenda after the 1980s and started to influence Turkish laws and development by the 2000s due to the prospective EU candidacy negotiations.

From 1946 until 1980, the era was marked by political upheavals ceased by military coup d'états. The four constitutions of 1921, 1924, 1961, and 1982 (with numerous amendments) hint at the development of human rights in Turkey. Turkey's human rights trajectory did not follow a linear track. It is rather full of paradoxes. For example, the single-party governance of the 1920s is an authoritarian rule by nature. The party ban on the Progressive Republican Party (Terakkiperver Cumhuriyet Fırkası, TCP) was a severe counterattack on democracy since one of the indispensable foundations of democracy is the existence of multiple political parties across the political spectrum.

On the other hand, the single-party government enacted numerous liberalization reforms. The transition to the competitive electoral system in 1945 was supposed to enhance the democratic experience in Turkey until it paved the way for another authoritarian rule by the Democrat Party (Demokrat Parti, DP) led by Adnan Menderes. The DP employed a religio-populist discourse as a challenge against the reforms. The economic failure of the DP government was concealed under the religious, nationalistic gestures and favours that generated hate against the other in society. The other was portrayed as the non-Turkish and non-Muslim. When the *Istanbul Ekspres* newspaper published false stories about the bombing of Atatürk's house in Thessaloniki, masses flooded the streets of Istanbul looting businesses, residences, schools, monuments, and holy

1 T.C. Resmi Gazete, 'İnsan Hakları Evrensel Beyannamesi', 7217 § (1949), https://www.resmigazete.gov.tr/arsiv/7217.pdf.

shrines of mainly Greek but also Armenian and Jewish minorities.[2] The infamous 6–7 September 1955 riots marked a dramatic backlash in human rights development in Turkey. As a result of the fearful atmosphere created intensely in Istanbul, as well as in other parts of Anatolia, minorities under Turkish citizenship, particularly thousands of Greeks, left Turkey for Greece and other countries.

The DP term ended with a military intervention on 27 May 1960. Menderes and two prominent ministers, Fatin Rüştü Zorlu, the minister of foreign affairs, and Hasan Polatkan, the finance minister, were tried on various charges and executed by hanging on 17 September 1961. The 1960 coup d'état signifies another twist in Turkey's human rights progression. The military coup of May 1960 was a democratic shortcoming, indicating the tensions between the democratically elected representatives and the military elites that label themselves as the protectors of the Republic and Kemalist values.

The 1961 constitution was prepared at the behest of the military junta. Opposite to what is expected from repressive juntas, the 1961 constitution was not devised for an authoritarian state. The human rights approach of this constitution was quite libertarian compared to the 1924 constitution, as it held that rights and liberties cannot be left up to the appreciation of governments. The 1924 constitution acknowledged the natural law that 'every Turk is born free and lives freely' (article 68) and it listed fundamental rights (articles 70 to 83) without any details. The human rights dimension of the state is underlined in the constitution of 1961. Article 2 of the 1961 constitution says that 'the Turkish Republic is a nationalistic, democratic, secular and social state governed by the rule of law, based on human rights and the fundamental tenets outlined in the preamble'. This article demonstrated that the state prioritizes human rights by putting individuals at the centre and deploying the state to protect and promote human rights. In other words, human rights constituted the basis of the state.

In this sense, human rights were formally institutionalized by the 1961 constitution that characterizes Turkey as a social state (article 2) with an emphasis on social justice (articles 10 and 11), social rights (section 3), and social security (section 6). The 1961 constitution maintains that rights and liberties can only be limited by law (article 11). This principle is repeated under several other articles, such as freedom of travel and residence (article 18), freedom

2 Helsinki Watch Report, 'Denying Human Rights and Ethnic Identity: The Greeks of Turkey' (Human Rights Watch, March 2022), https://www.hrw.org/sites/default/files/reports/TURKEY923.PDF.

of the press (article 22), the right and freedom to congregate (article 28), the right to form associations (article 29), and the right to property (article 36). Additionally, the 1961 constitution contained a separate section covering social and economic rights. As a reaction to the authoritarianism observed during the period of DP rule, the 1961 constitution aimed to create an effective system of checks and balances.

Additionally, it introduced new institutions, such as the Administration of Turkish Radio and Television (article 121) to ensure impartiality of broadcasts and news; the Court of Accounts (article 127), responsible for examining and auditing of public enterprises; the State Planning Organization (article 129) to carry out development-related matters; the Supreme Council of Judges (article 143) for the monitoring and supervision of judges and their adherence to the rule of law; and the Constitutional Court (article 145), responsible for reviewing the constitutionality of laws. It also addressed professional organizations (article 122) as an enhancement of the right to associate and organize. Contrary to the establishment of the institutions mentioned above that aimed to contribute to the effective functioning of democracy, the 1961 constitution also founded a democratically controversial institution: the National Security Council (Milli Güvenlik Kurulu, MGK) (article 111). The Council foresaw the participation of the armed forces in politics. It is led by the president and it consists of cabinet members, including the chief of the general staff (as the principal military officer) and representatives of the armed forces. According to the constitution, the function of the Council was to advise on issues related to national security. The establishment of the MGK marked the institutionalization of military tutelage over Turkish democracy. The most undemocratic feature of the MGK was the lack of civilian control of the Ministry of Defence over the army.[3] Moreover, the military was autonomous in many ways. Judicial autonomy was provided in the 1961 constitution (article 138) by the establishment of military courts such as the High Military Administrative Court of Appeals (Askerî Yüksek İdare Mahkemesi) (article 140) and the Military Court of Cassation (Askerî Yargıtay) (article 141) to try individuals for military offenses, as well as offenses committed against military personnel. The fiscal autonomy of the army was also maintained as its budget was exempted from parliamentary supervision.[4]

3 Aylin Güney and Petek Karatekelioğlu, 'Turkey's EU Candidacy and Civil–Military Relations: Challenges and Prospects', *Armed Forces & Society* 31, no. 3 (2005): 439–62.

4 Ibid., 528.

In a nutshell, the 1960 coup took its toll on the democratic development of Turkey and left a lasting dent in democracy by introducing military tutelage over civilian democracy. Contrariwise, the 1961 constitution was of a liberal character to acknowledge universal fundamental rights and to limit the state's retrenchment for the rights and liberties. In Turkey's democratic trajectory, the liberal atmosphere created by the 1961 constitution is seen as the cause of the political polarization and anarchy that paved the way for the 1980 military takeover. The unprecedented urbanization that caused dramatic socio-economic change, particularly in the cities, accompanied the factors mentioned above, led to an escalation in violence. The civic activism enabled by the constitution was also held to be behind the rise in student and labour groups.

Conversely, the governments of this era, mainly run by the Justice Party (Adalet Partisi, AP), regarded the libertarian constitution as excessive for Turkey, subtly blaming it for the social chaos. Süleyman Demirel's AP focused its energy pragmatically on the economy and industrialization while avoiding the disapproval of the army, which was keeping a close watch over political activity. The fundamental transformation of the Turkish economy and society started to create new social strata, resulting in ideological tensions. The legendary 1968 youth protests and the polarized socio-political unrest that followed led to the military takeover of 12 March 1971 to oust the elected government. The pause in tensions ended immediately after the return to civilian politics in 1973. The polarization and rivalries among ideological groups resulted in gunfights in the cities. The increasing violence was concluded by the military coup that took place on 12 September 1980.

Blaming the anarchy on the former constitution, the junta of 1980 aimed to depoliticize society and limit the abundant liberties to prevent further turmoil.[5] Thus, as already put forward by Ergun Özbudun, a restrictive constitution was prepared in 1982 with a strict statist approach.[6] The constitutional shift regarding human rights from the 1961 to the 1982 constitutions is visible in the wording of article 2 of both constitutions, which defines the characteristics of the Republic. According to the 1961 constitution, the Turkish Republic is 'based on' human rights, whereas according to the 1982 constitution, the Republic is 'respecting' human rights. The expression signifies the shift of focus from people to state. The

5 Anka Hukuk, 'Kenan Evren'in 1980 Anayasası'nı Tanıtma Konuşmaları', 5 September 2023, http://www.ankahukuk.com/kenan-evrenin-1980-anayasasini-tanitma-konusmalari/.

6 Ergun Özbudun, *The Constitutional System of Turkey: 1876 to the Present* (New York: Palgrave Macmillan, 2011).

former one indicated that human rights comprise the existential reason for the state. Nonetheless, the latter means that human rights is not the founding value anymore. The human rights bearing of the 1982 constitution is presented under article 12, which declares, 'everyone possesses inherent fundamental rights and freedoms which are inviolable and inalienable. The fundamental rights and freedoms also include the duties and responsibilities of the individual towards society, his family, and other individuals'.[7] In this sense, human rights are conditional on the responsibilities of the individual vis-à-vis the entire society. The attack on human rights after the 1980 military takeover generated disapproval and criticism as a result of the detention of 650,000 people, the execution of 50, the widespread use of torture, and 299 lives lost due to torture and prison conditions.[8] Yet, the Cold War situation prohibited the Western World from concentrating on human rights regression in Turkey. The transfer of power in 1983 over the civilian rule of a single-party government led by Turgut Özal of the Motherland Party (Anavatan Partisi, ANAP) continued with an intense focus on the liberalization of the economy, replacing import substitution with an export-centric model.

Interparliamentary relations between the European Community (EC) and Turkey were formally suspended after the military coup of 12 September 1980 until the aftermath of the elections held on 29 November 1987. Following the dissolution of the USSR, the Turkish government started accelerating its efforts to increase Turkey's suitability for EU candidacy. The early efforts concerned economic improvement. Due to Turkey's role in containing the USSR, and also as a NATO power, the Western world turned a blind eye to human rights violations in Turkey to a great extent. The fall of the Soviets thus created an impetus to correct the human rights conditions in Turkey.

## 1980–99: Liberalization and European Integration

When the ANAP came to power and Özal became prime minister in 1983, Turkey's relations with its Western partners were almost frozen as a result of the 1980 coup d'état. Bilateral relations were poor and Turkey was

7 Republic of Turkey, 'The Constitution of the Turkish Republic (November 7, 1982)', https://www.anayasa.gen.tr/1982Constitution-EYasar.htm.

8 Erdoğan Çağatay Zontur, 'Turkish President Remembers 1980 Military Coup Victims', *Anadolu Agency*, 12 September 2019, https://www.aa.com.tr/en/turkey/turkish-president-remembers-1980-military-coup-victims/1580335.

inadequately represented in the Council of Europe (COE). Five European countries lodged a complaint against Turkey at the European Court of Human Rights (ECtHR).[9] Turkish government started to make new efforts to show it wanted to resume following the Westernization ideal of the Republic and was open to the neoliberal global order. One of the earliest human rights initiatives of the Özal government was to sign and ratify the Convention on the Elimination of All Forms of Discrimination against Women (CEDAW) in 1985. The convention went into effect in 1986. CEDAW was signed with reservations on article 9, para. 1; article 15, paras. 2 and 4; article 16, para. 1, subparas. (c), (d), (f), and (g); and article 29, paras. 1 and 2.[10] The primary obligation of CEDAW member states is to eradicate gender inequalities.

Interestingly, the cabinet ratifying this agreement did not consist of any women.[11] The adoption of CEDAW was noteworthy for the government, owing to the liberalization policies it was pursuing. In terms of correcting its relations with the Western countries, it is noteworthy that in 1986 the government of Turkey held the chairmanship of the Ministerial Council Meeting of the Organisation for Economic Co-operation and Development (OECD).[12]

The European Parliament (EP) harshly criticized the human rights violations with eleven resolutions as a result of the military takeover. It set six conditions for restoring EC–Turkey relations: (i) abolition of the death penalty, (ii) prohibition of torture, (iii) right to fair trial, (iv) ending of collective trials, (v) recognition of the right of individual application to the European Court of Human Rights, and (vi) removal of restrictions

9 France, Norway, Denmark, Sweden, and the Netherlands versus Turkey. These states submitted an application against Turkey related to outcomes of the coup d'état that the Turkish parliament was dissolved and its powers were transferred to the National Security Council. The laws and decrees abrogated by the Council caused derogation of constitutional rights and violations such as torture, inhuman or degrading treatment in a widespread and systematic practice; and also caused restrictions on political parties, trade unions, and the press; and, lastly, the detention and criminal proceedings under martial law.

10 UN, 'Convention on the Elimination of All Forms of Discrimination against Women (Status on 11.11.2023)', accessed 11 November 2023, https://treaties.un.org/pages/ViewDetails.aspx?src=TREATY&mtdsg_no=IV-8&chapter=4&clang=_en#EndDec. On 20 September 1999, Turkey decided to withdraw its reservations with regard to article 15, paras. 2 and 4, and article 16, para. 1 (c), (d), (f) and (g). Following the 2001 and 2004 amendments to the Turkish Civil Code, Turkey decided to withdraw its reservation with regard to article 9, para. 1, on 29 January 2008.

11 TBMM, 'I. Özal Hükümeti Bakanlar Kurulu 13.12.1983–21.12.1987', accessed 11 November 2023, https://www5.tbmm.gov.tr/hukumetler/old_files/HB45.htm.

12 Turkey assumed the chairmanship for the second time after twenty-six years in 2012.

on freedom of political activity, trade union rights, and expression.[13] Özal wanted to satisfy these expectations as soon as possible. To this end, he announced in 1986 the aim to introduce individual complaint rights,[14] and Turkey recognized the right of Turkish citizens to file individual complaint petitions against the Turkish state in 1987 by removing the conditions it placed on article 25 of the ECHR.

The Convention against Torture and Other Cruel, Inhuman or Degrading Treatment or Punishment (CAT) was adopted in the UN General Assembly (UNGA) on 10 December 1984 and entered into force on 26 June 1987.[15] Turkey signed the CAT on 25 January 1988 and entered it into force as of 1 September 1988. Turkey acknowledged the interstate and individual right to complaint. These procedures became operative in Turkey as a part of the liberalization movement carried out by Prime Minister Özal. Turkey has attracted international criticism as a result of the widespread torture of detainees, prison conditions, and death penalties. To leave the faults of the state in the past, to wipe the slate clean, to create legal adherence to prevent further abuse incidents in Turkey, Özal's initiative for the ratification of the CAT and becoming a party to the Council of Europe's Convention against Torture were significant steps. Turkey submitted two remarkable notifications and one reservation at the convention. The first notification concerns Turkey's recognition of the authority of the European Committee for the Prevention of Torture and Inhuman or Degrading Treatment or Punishment (CPT) to admit and examine the complaints regarding Turkey's non-compliance with its obligations under the convention. The second notification concerns Turkey's recognition of the authority of the committee to admit and examine individual complaints. The reservation Turkey placed is in article 30, para. 2, of the convention. In this regard, Turkey rejects the arbitration procedure owing to disputes under this convention.[16] In line with its EU membership aspirations, Turkey accepted article 25 of the ECHR in 1987, which endows individuals the right to lodge

13 European Parliament, 'Report Drawn on Behalf of the Political Affairs Committee on the Human Rights Situation in Turkey', Working Documents, A Series, 9 October 1985, 8, art. 2(a, b, c, d, e, f), http://aei.pitt.edu/49213/.

14 TBMM, *Başbakan Turgut Özal'ın Konuşma, Mesaj, Beyanat ve Mülakatları: 13.12.1986–12.12.1987* (Nisan 1987), 13, https://acikerisim.tbmm.gov.tr/items/893ad1e3-bd59-4f45-a407-1dad9903f9a2/full.

15 UNGA, 'Convention against Torture and Other Cruel, Inhuman or Degrading Treatment or Punishment', 39/46 § (1984), https://www.ohchr.org/en/instruments-mechanisms/instruments/convention-against-torture-and-other-cruel-inhuman-or-degrading.

16 According to article 30 of the convention, reservation can always be taken back following a notification submitted to the UN General Secretariat.

complaint applications against the state. Finally, due to its recent efforts to restore its democracy, Turkey submitted its formal application to the European Economic Community (EEC) on 14 April 1987. Simultaneously, Turkey submitted membership request letters to the European Coal and Steel Community (ECSC) and the European Atomic Energy Community (EAEC or Euratom).[17] When the government applied, the German chancellor, Helmut Kohl, told Turkish prime minister Özal that neither Turkey nor the European Community was ready for Turkey's membership in the Community.[18] Despite being ambitious and eager, Özal was also aware of the impediments. In a speech, he said that the negotiations of the former applicants lasted for nine years, and it is obvious that Turkey's will be even tougher.[19] Spain and Portugal were the two candidates that acceded to the Community in 1986. This accession is also known as the Iberian Enlargement or the Third Enlargement.[20] Their accession was more of a deepening than an enlargement process, which is what the accession of Turkey would have meant. In addition to developmental problems and difficulties related to institution building, Özal underlined the identity-related barriers. He stated that the Community is composed of Christian majorities, whereas Turkey is a Muslim majority country.[21] The international relations literature is filled with works that hold that Turkish identity is a key element in the issue of accession to the EU.[22]

17 The applications were based on article 237 of the Rome Treaty, article 98 of the European Coal and Steel Community, and article 205 of Euratom.

18 Amanda Paul, 'Turkey–EU Relations: Forever Engaged, Never to Be Married?', Heinrich Böll Stiftung, 8 July 2015, https://eu.boell.org/en/2015/07/08/turkey-eu-relations-forever-engaged-never-be-married.

19 TBMM, 'Başbakan Sayın Turgut Özal'ın Anavatan Partisi TBMM Grubunda Yaptığı Konuşma', in *Başbakan Turgut Özal'ın Konuşma, Mesaj, Beyanat ve Mülakatları: 13.12.1986–12.12.1987* (Nisan 1987), 259, https://acikerisim.tbmm.gov.tr/items/893ad1e3-bd59-4f45-a407-1dad9903f9a2/full.

20 The enlargement process occurred under six periods: the First Enlargement contained the accession of Britain, Ireland, and Denmark in 1973. The Second Enlargement was the accession of Greece in 1981. The Third Enlargement was the so-called Iberian Enlargement. The Fourth Enlargement was the accession of Austria, Finland, and Sweden in 1995. The Fifth Enlargement had two parts: the accession of Hungary, Poland, the Czech Republic, Slovakia, Slovenia, Latvia, Lithuania, Estonia, Malta, and the Greek Cypriot Administration of Southern Cyprus in 2004 and, in 2007, the accession of Romania and Bulgaria. The Sixth Enlargement happened in 2013 with the accession of Croatia.

21 TBMM, 'Başbakan Sayın Turgut Özal'ın Anavatan Partisi TBMM Grubunda Yaptığı Konuşma', 260.

22 See Meltem Müftüler-Baç, 'The Never-ending Story: Turkey and the European Union', *Middle Eastern Studies* 34, no. 4 (1998): 240–58.

The EU declared Turkey's eligibility in 1989. However, on 18 December 1989, the Commission published a report on its examination of Turkey's political and economic situation, noting that Turkey's level of development suggested that it would not be able to address the adjustment problems it would face if it were to accede in the medium term. Two points are highlighted: (i) Turkey, with its large geographical area, would eventually have the largest population in the Community, and (ii) its general level of development is lower than the European average.[23] The Commission also noted that 'although there have been developments in recent years in the human rights situation and respect for the identity of minorities, these have not yet reached the level required in a democracy'.[24] In this report, the Commission clearly stated the discomfort of the Community about Turkey's accession. The conclusion of the report deliberately leaves out discussion of accession or enlargement. Instead, it focuses on intensifying political links as foreseen under the Association Agreement by the completion of the Customs Union (CU), by the resumption of financial cooperation, by the promotion of industrial and technological cooperation, and by strengthening political and cultural ties.[25]

To fill the human rights–related gaps, Turkey recognized in 1990 the compulsory jurisdiction of the European Court of Human Rights (ECtHR).[26] Turkey's most ambitious EU adjustments and the greatest improvements in human rights were achieved afterwards.[27]

Turkey signed the Association Agreement, also known as the Ankara Agreement, with the European Economic Community (EEC) on 12 September 1963 'to promote a continuous and balanced strengthening of trade and economic relations between the Parties'.[28] The Ankara Agreement comprised three stages to be covered in twenty-two years, until 1995: a

23 Commission of the European Communities, 'Commission Opinion on Turkey's Request for Accession to the Community', 20 December 1989, 4, http://aei.pitt.edu/4475/1/4475.pdf.

24 Ibid., 7.

25 Ibid., 5–7.

26 Ministry of Foreign Affairs of the Turkish Republic, 'Human Rights', 2023, https://www.mfa.gov.tr/İnsan-hakları.en.mfa.

27 Frank Schimmelfennig, Stefan Engert, and Heiko Knobel, 'Costs, Commitment and Compliance: The Impact of EU Democratic Conditionality on Latvia, Slovakia and Turkey', *JCMS: Journal of Common Market Studies* 41, no. 3 (2003): 495–518; Meltem Müftüler Baç, 'Turkey's Political Reforms and the Impact of the European Union', *South European Society and Politics* 10, no. 1 (2005): 17–31.

28 European Parliament, 'EU–Turkey Association Agreement (the "Ankara Agreement")', accessed 15 October 2023, https://www.europarl.europa.eu/delegations/en/d-tr/documents/eu-texts.

preparatory stage, a transitional stage, and the final stage.[29] The transitional and final phases were to achieve the EC–Turkey Customs Union. The process was suspended first in 1973 by the Süleyman Demirel government owing to the conditions created by the coup d'état of 1971 and by the 1973 OPEC oil crisis. Then, for a second time, it was unilaterally suspended in 1978 by Prime Minister Bülent Ecevit as a result of the deterioration in the Turkish economy. An increase in imports – unaccompanied by an increase in the volume of exports – was deepening the trade deficit. Political turmoil, growing external debt, climbing inflation, and shortages of essential consumption goods established the basis of the suspension decision.[30] The European Parliament's suspension decision came in 1982 as a reaction to the 1980 coup d'état. As the European Commission (EC) announced Turkey's eligibility (instead of candidacy), it recommended operationalization of the Ankara Agreement (instead of opening accession negotiations).[31] Turkey and the EU reached the Customs Union Agreement in 1995, as foreseen in the Ankara Agreement.[32] Both Turkish society and the government perceived the conclusion of the CU as a pivotal step towards full membership in the Union, despite the fact that the CU's impact was still contested and that it had as many negative as positive effects on Turkey's trade.[33] The impacts of the CU were assessed on production and on trade (in terms of competition capacities, contribution to technological development, and on foreign direct investment). In order to harmonize with the CU, Turkey passed legislation on intellectual property rights, patent rights, copyright law, and laws in line with the EU's trademarks regulations.

As a result of the steady economic growth achieved by the efforts of the Özal government, the Walter Report of the European Parliament (EP) considered on 15 September 1988 the resumption of the Agreement.[34] The

29 European Parliament, 'Report of the Committee on Foreign Affairs and Security on EC–Turkey Relations', 22 May 1992, 4, http://aei.pitt.edu/48471/1/A9400.pdf.

30 Baskın Oran, 'Dönemin Bilançosu', in *Türk Dış Politikası: Kurtuluş Savaşı'ndan Bugüne Olgular, Belgeler, Yorumlar*, ed. Baskın Oran (İstanbul: İletişim Yayınları, 2011), 655–81.

31 Official Journal of the European Communities, 'Decision on the EC–Turkey Association Council', L 35/1 96/142/EC § (1995).

32 Commission of the European Communities, 'Commission Opinion on Turkey's Request for Accession to the Community'.

33 The Customs Union is an integration process that establishes mutual tax exemptions among the union members and adopts common customs tariffs vis-à-vis third countries.

34 European Parliament, 'Report of the Committee on Foreign Affairs and Security on EC–Turkey Relations', 7.

EP stated that 'the Agreement could only be considered when democracy in Turkey was fully restored and human rights were respected'.[35]

With the dissolution of the Soviet Union, Turkey lost its significance as a buffer zone against the West. The changing conditions forced Turkey to question its role within the Western world. The long years of security partnership had come to an end. Turkey was supposed to adjust to its European partners' political and economic standards. It is evident that Turkey had to put more emphasis on values such as human rights, the rule of law, and pluralistic democracy. Thus, Turkey started internationalizing its human rights by the late 1980s and early 1990s due to the changing domestic and systemic conditions. The decade of the 1990s is when Turkey, on the one hand, tried to improve its human rights standards to bring them in line with the EU ideals, and, on the other hand, it faced serious impediments to achieving this aim, such as counterterror, rising radicalism, the postmodern coup, and the challenging economy.

In this context, a human rights inquiry commission was established under the auspices of the Turkish Grand National Assembly in 1990 aimed at the institutionalization of human rights domestically.[36] In the 1991 elections, Süleyman Demirel introduced an emancipatory discourse to Turkish politics, hoping to associate his nationalist-conservative identity with modernism and innovations. He included human rights elements in his campaign, promising the establishment of a ministry of human rights and transparent police stations,[37] besides making references to UDHR as 'the common values of humankind'.[38] In 1991, a state ministry in charge of human rights was introduced to follow and coordinate human rights issues. The Kurdish question arose in Turkish politics in the 1990s. The terror problem rising from the 1980s onwards curbed human rights efforts largely. Besides terror itself being a grave violation of human rights by targeting civilians, there were also extensive allegations that terror was being handled via arbitrary arrests, the use of nightsticks, brutal beatings, and torture in police detention, besides forced disappearances.[39] The politicization of Kurdish ethno-nationalism and the sharp rise of the secessionist PKK's attacks on civilians has since been the basis of the Kurdish problem in Turkey. This term coincides with

35 Ibid., 13.

36 '3686 Sayılı İnsan Haklarını İnceleme Komisyonu Kanunu', 20719 3686 § Tertip 5, Sayı 20719 (1990), https://www.mevzuat.gov.tr/mevzuat?MevzuatNo=3686&MevzuatTur=1&MevzuatTertip=5.

37 Vahap Coşkun, 'Demirel (II): "Ben Devlet Fikrinin Adamıyım"', *Perspektif*, 18 August 2023, https://www.perspektif.online/demirel-ii-ben-devlet-fikrinin-adamiyim/.

38 Tanıl Bora, *Demirel* (İletişim Yayınları, 2023), 394.

39 Ibid., 394–95.

when the Organization for Security and Cooperation in Europe (OSCE) concluded its outline on human rights standards in 1990, with a particular emphasis on minority rights and non-discrimination.[40] Then, in 1992, the Treaty on European Union (TEU), which is also known as the Maastricht Treaty, was adopted to oblige the Union to respect the national identities of its members. The following year, in 1993, the European Council (EC) in Copenhagen defined the accession criteria to the Union.[41] The 'Copenhagen criteria' count democracy and human rights, particularly the 'respect for and protection of minorities', as a part of the political criteria that Turkey had to encounter recursively. The TEU was amended in March 1996 by the subsequent Treaty of Amsterdam that refers to the Convention for the Protection of Human Rights and Fundamental Freedoms (also known as the European Convention on Human Rights, ECHR). As article 7 of the Amsterdam Treaty encourages the EU to respect fundamental rights as guaranteed by the ECHR, the latter openly prohibits discrimination by association with a national minority.[42]

As a result of the developments in Europe regarding minority rights, the Union, the COE,[43] and the OSCE[44] demanded that Turkey adopt a minority-centred approach to human rights. They called on the Turkish government to recognize Kurdish identity constitutionally as a national racial or ethnic minority.[45] The Kurdish language was not banned in the context of cultural activities, but it was not allowed in radio/television broadcasting or political communication and education.[46] Contrary to common belief, Kurds were

40 OSCE, 'Document of the Copenhagen Meeting of the Conference on the Human Dimension of the CSCE', 29 June 1990, arts. 31–40, https://www.osce.org/odihr/elections/14304.

41 European Commission, 'Accession Criteria', accessed 29 December 2023, https://neighbourhood-enlargement.ec.europa.eu/enlargement-policy/glossary/accession-criteria_en.

42 Council of Europe, 'European Convention on Human Rights' (1950), art. 4, https://www.echr.coe.int/documents/d/echr/convention_ENG.

43 COE Parliamentary Assembly, 'Humanitarian Situation of the Kurdish Refugees and Displaced Persons in South-East Turkey and North Iraq', Assembly debate on 25 June 1998 (22nd Sitting), 25 June 1998, https://assembly.coe.int/nw/xml/XRef/Xref-XML2HTML-en.asp?fileid=16638&lang=en, article 13.4.

44 OSCE, 'Istanbul Document 1999', 1999, 5–7, https://www.osce.org/files/f/documents/6/5/39569.pdf.

45 European Commission, 'Turkey 1998 Regular Report', 27 November 1998, 19, https://neighbourhood-enlargement.ec.europa.eu/turkey-regular-report-1998_en; European Commission, 'Turkey 1999 Regular Report', 13 October 1999), 14, https://op.europa.eu/en/publication-detail/-/publication/bbe56597-782f-42d2-b16e-90ed9dbd28c9.

46 Tarlach McGonagle, Bethany Davis Noll, and Monroe Price, eds., *Minority-Language Related Broadcasting and Legislation in the OSCE* (Vienna: OSCE, 2003), 450–58; European Commission, 'Turkey 1999 Regular Report', 10–14.

not banned from political participation or economic life. The EU underlined the significance of objective and independent coverage of the issue.[47] For the Turkish government, the Kurdish question was a security issue, one that directly threatened Turkey's territorial integrity and sovereignty.

On the other hand, the European perception of the problem was centred around Kurdish culture, identity, and language.[48] The settlement of the Kurdish question became the proving ground of Turkey's level of democratic attainment for the European partners, which had a direct impact on Turkey's membership bid. The human rights–related demands of the European institutions, such the Assembly of the Western European Union (WEU) calling for the endowment of autonomy rights,[49] increased Turkish officials' suspicion of political foul play against the country's territorial integrity and led them to question the credibility of the European human rights policy.[50] The European disregard for the militarized separatist activities of the terrorist organization PKK (Partiya Karkerên Kurdistanê/Kurdistan Workers' Party) distanced Turkish officials from the human rights calls of Europe. The terrorist activities of the PKK included killing civilians, random shootings and beatings, and the kidnapping and severe abuse of young people as a part of terrorist recruitment. The result was deteriorating living conditions, the destruction of property, the evacuation of villages, and the eviction of villagers.[51]

Human rights authorities widely criticized the counterterrorism fight in Turkey in which torture and ill-treatment was routinely used.[52] Additionally, extrajudicial executions and forced disappearances had been a serious concern throughout the 1990s. European institutions criticized the state's imposition of a state of emergency in south-eastern Turkey and the militarized mishandling of the situation.[53]

47 European Commission, 'Turkey 1998 Regular Report', 16.

48 Ibid., 19–20.

49 Assembly of the Western European Union, 'Proceedings: Fortieth Ordinary Session Third Part', June 1995, 107, http://aei.pitt.edu/66919/1/WEU148.pdf.

50 Fusun Türkmen, 'Turkey's Participation in Global and Regional Human Rights Regimes', in *Human Rights in Turkey*, ed. Zehra F. Kabasakal Arat (Philadelphia: University of Pennsylvania Press, 2007), 249–61, at 256.

51 See MERIP, 'Document: Forced Evictions and Destruction in Villages in Turkish Kurdistan', *Middle East Report* 199 (Summer 1996), https://merip.org/1999/06/forced-evictions-and-destruction-in-villages-in-turkish-kurdistan/; Amnesty International, 'Turkey: No Security without Human Rights', 30 September 1996, EUR/44/84/96, https://www.amnesty.org/en/documents/eur44/084/1996/en/, sec. 3.

52 Amnesty International, 'Turkey', sec. 2.

53 European Commission, 'Turkey 1998 Regular Report', 9.

As a reaction to the democratization calls of the EU, the government of Prime Minister Tansu Çiller prepared an amendment proposal – a democratization package – in 1995. The primary aim of the amendments was to increase democratic participation, endow public servants with the right to form and become a member of syndicates, and allow the right to bargain collectively and to strike. The following amendments were undertaken: the ban on the political activities of associations was removed (article 33, para. 4); the right to association for civil servants was granted (article 33, para. 7); by the removal of the former article 52 the political ban on syndicates was removed; syndicate rights of public servants were acknowledged (article 53, para. 3); the voting rights of Turkish citizens living abroad were secured by constitutional guarantee (article 67, para. 2); the voting age was reduced to eighteen from twenty (article 67, para. 3); voting rights were provided to prisoners (article 67, para. 5); the minimum age of political party membership was reduced to eighteen from twenty-one (article 68); the provision that prohibited political parties from opening auxiliary branches, such as women's and youth branches, was abolished (article 68, para. 6); he provision allowing for a ban on political parties' statutes and programmes was expanded to also cover their political activities (article 68, para. 4); the ban on political party membership by academics and higher education students was removed (article 68, para. 6); besides other amendments. The contested Anti-Terror Law was amended for its article 8 that allowed journalists and academics to be convicted of the crime of spreading terrorist propaganda.

Although these constitutional amendments obviously improved the democratic standing of the Turkish Republic, they did not directly contribute to minority rights. The failure to progress human rights conditions led to objections to Turkey's membership. The British foreign secretary Robin Cook condemned the violations in Turkey and criticized 'those regimes who grotesquely violate human rights and repeatedly fail to respond to demands for an improvement in standards'.[54] It is obvious that there was a colossal disparity between the approaches of the Turkish government and the European governments. While Turkish officials continued to focus on 'separatist terrorism', the European partners saw the matter as a demand for 'regional autonomy'.[55] The Parliamentary Assembly of the Council of Europe decided in 1996 that the human rights situation in

54 UK Parliament, Lords Chamber, 'Turkey: Human Rights', 18 July 1997, https://api.parliament.uk/historic-hansard/lords/1997/jul/18/turkey-human-rights.

55 Ibid.

Turkey should remain under the monitoring procedures of the COE. Most cases of violations of civil and political rights were connected in one way or another to the responses of the government and military to issues in the south-east of the country. The EU's reaction to Turkey's counterterror activities was clearly stated in the European Commission's 1998 progress report on the nation: 'In combating terrorism in the south east, Turkey needs to exercise restraint, to make greater efforts to uphold the rule of law and human rights and to find a civil and not a military solution.'[56] Moreover, the 1998 report states that, despite repeated official declarations by the government to end such practices, instances of ongoing torture, forced disappearances, and extrajudicial killings are regularly recorded. In many cases, individuals detained in police stations and without access to outside contact were subjected to torture during this time. The cases are so well-documented that there is no doubt regarding the responsibility of the police authorities. These incidents raised questions about the effective oversight and supervision of the security forces. Appropriate disciplinary standards for these officers was lacking. Prosecutions for crimes committed by state officials, including police and gendarmerie, were usually subject to the approval of administrative authorities and, when compared to European standards, resulted in relatively lenient sentences. Thus, systematic judicial prosecution of crimes committed by law enforcement officers was not ensured. The 1998 report also confirmed that the conditions in Turkish prisons did not comply with the standards set by the Council of Europe or the minimum standards of the United Nations. Most prisons were overcrowded and did not provide adequate healthcare services. Prison staff were often military personnel, which led to several riots in prisons in 1996.

Besides the PKK, other radical movements started to surface on Turkish soil, predominantly in south-eastern Anatolia. Those groups were, namely: the Islamic Movement Organization (İslami Hareket Örgütü, İHÖ); the Jarusalem Warriors (Kudüs Savaşçıları); the Islamic Raiders of the Great East–Front (İslamî Büyük Doğu Akıncılar Cephesi, İBDA-C); the Revolutionary People's Liberation Party/Front (Devrimci Halk Kurtuluş Partisi-Cephesi, DHKP/C); the Turkish Workers and Peasants Liberation Army (Türkiye İşçi Köylü Kurtuluş Ordusu, TİKKO); and the Union of Islamic Communities and Congregations (İslamî Cemiyetler ve Cemaatler Birliği, İCCB); besides other indigenous groups.[57] They were engaged in violent terrorist

56 European Commission, 'Turkey 1998 Regular Report', 9.

57 Ibid., 9.

activities such as mass killings, kidnappings, and torture. Among them, the most prominent one was Turkish Hezbollah (The Party of God), led by Hüseyin Velioğlu.[58] Although this organization was established to replace the secular Turkish state with an Islamic one, Hezbollah was predominantly occupied with challenging the PKK for effective leadership.[59] Therefore, it has been argued that the state tolerated the activities of Hezbollah due to its anti-PKK stance.[60] The rise of fundamentalism in Turkey was taken by various national and international non-governmental organizations, such as Amnesty International, as proof of climbing human rights violations in Turkey. It was also argued that they serve to provide an excuse for measures undermining human rights.[61]

Islamism was on the rise in the government, too. It was presented as an antithesis to Kemalism and the founding values of the Turkish Republic. The flag bearer of this ideology was Necmettin Erbakan, the leader of the pro-Islamist Welfare Party (Refah Partisi, RP), and his coalition partner, Tansu Çiller, of the True Path Party (Doğru Yol Partisi, DYP), who formed the fifty-fourth government of Turkey (1996–97). While RP ran the administration with a pragmatic hand, its party members voiced their unhappiness about the system at national celebrations and on national mourning days, such as the annual Commemoration of Atatürk, Youth and Sports Day. Erbakan's invitation to cult leaders to a fast-breaking dinner at the end of Ramadan in 1997 was interpreted as a direct challenge to the secular Republic.[62] Still assuming itself to be the true protector of the Republic, commanders of the Turkish armed forces held an extraordinary session to discuss the new communication modus of the government, and, as a result, they warned the administration to curb its anti-secular activities. Unlike the former military coups, the army called on civil society to assume its patriotic duty this time.

On 28 February 1997, the army carried out the bloodless 'postmodern coup' – so-called due to the fact that it occurred without dissolving parliament or suspending the constitution – by publishing a memorandum

58 Born as Hüseyin Durmaz.

59 Gareth Jenkins, *Political Islam in Turkey: Running West, Heading East?* (New York: Palgrave Macmillan, 2008), 190.

60 Zehra F. Kabasakal Arat, 'Collisions and Crossroads: Introducing Human Rights in Turkey', in *Human Rights in Turkey*, ed. Zehra F. Kabasakal Arat (Philadelphia: University of Pennsylvania Press, 2007), 1–16, at 8, https://doi.org/10.9783/9780812201147.

61 Ibid., 3.

62 Milliyet, 'Tartışılan Iftar Yemeği', 11 January 1997, https://www.milliyet.com.tr/siyaset/tartisilan-iftar-yemegi-5389678.

designed to contain the spread of the separatist Islamist ideology. This separatism was ascribed to the PKK before the coup and then to political Islam after it. The memorandum pushed the Welfare Party to withdraw from the government owing to its Islamist, anti-secular activities. The coup resulted in the oppression of religious groups in Turkish society. Their education and employment rights, particularly those of veiled women, were denied. The state established different rules for groups of citizens according to their faith. Ideals such as freedom of thought/religion/conscience/expression, respect for private and family life, and equality of opportunity perished. Certain sections of society enjoyed these rights and freedoms and had access to public services and opportunities, while others did not. The official reaction of the Union was stated in the 1998 Turkey Progress Report, one year after the coup, expressing concerns over the 'ambiguities in the Turkish legal system with regard to civilian political control of the military'.[63]

The conclusion of the Customs Union on 6 March 1995, which the Association Agreement envisioned, was another step in Turkey's convergence towards Europe, particularly in monetary terms. It was taken as proof of Turkey's ability to engage within the competitive free trade atmosphere. Özal's efforts to boost international trade ties and the economy had been noteworthy in this process. Turkey became the first applicant to settle a customs union. As a result, the hopes of joining the EU were boosted.

However, while eleven other states' candidacy was accepted, Turkey's candidacy was rejected at the 1997 Luxembourg Summit on the ground that it still did not satisfy the Copenhagen criteria. Besides calling for improved relations with Greece, for making progress towards a resolution of the Cyprus issue, and for the fulfilment of economic and political criteria, the summit reminded Turkey of 'the alignment of human rights standards and practices on those in force in the European Union; [and] respect for and protection of minorities'.[64] The immediate reaction of Turkey was to challenge the instigation of membership negotiations with the Greek Cypriot state, claiming that it was a violation of the 1959 London and Zürich

63 European Commission, 'Turkey 1998 Regular Report', 10.

64 European Parliament, 'Luxembourg European Council 12 and 13 December 1997 Presidency Conclusions', accessed 4 March 2024, https://www.europarl.europa.eu/summits/lux1_en.htm#:~:text=The%20European%20Council%20meeting%20in,the%20divisions%20of%20the%20past.

Agreements and the 1960 Guarantee Treaty. According to the treaty, the Republic of Cyprus

> undertakes not to participate, in whole or in part, in any political or economic union with any State whatsoever. It accordingly declares prohibited any activity likely to promote, directly or indirectly, either union with any other State or partition of the Island.[65]

Turkey's response was to remind international society of the legal regulation.[66] When Turkey suspended its dialogue with the Union,[67] German foreign minister Klaus Kingel said that Turkey's membership depended on its level of human rights, its relations with Greece, and the Kurdish question.[68] The main agenda of the Cardiff Summit on 15–16 June 1997 and then the Vienna Summit of the European Council on 11–12 December 1998 was enlargement, and the outcome of this meeting for Turkey was a repeat of the Luxembourg Summit. Obviously, while the impediments before other candidacies were of an economic nature, Turkey's impediments were predominantly political. During the Cardiff Summit, based on the Association Agreement, the Council asked for the preparation of a progress report on Turkey by the Commission, despite the fact that Turkey was not a candidate yet.[69]

One significant human rights incident took place on 23 September 1998, when the Supreme Court of Appeals confirmed the verdict issued by the State Security Court (Devlet Güvenlik Mahkemesi, DGM) against Recep Tayyip Erdoğan, then the mayor of Istanbul and a member of the Virtue Party (Fazilet Partisi, FP). Erdoğan was sentenced to ten months in prison, disqualified from his mayoral duties, and banned from participating in future elections. He was convicted for inciting hatred by reading a poem. The EU stated concerns regarding democratic pluralism and freedom of

65 'Treaty of Guarantee: UK, Greece and Turkey and Cyprus', Pub. L. no. Nicosia (1960), https://peacemaker.un.org/sites/peacemaker.un.org/files/CY%20GR%20TR_600816_Treaty%20of%20Guarantee.pdf, article 2.

66 T.C. Dışişleri Bakanlığı, 'Türkiye Cumhuriyeti Dışişleri Bakanlığının AB Lüksemburg Kararı İle İlgili Açıklaması', 14 December 1997, https://www.mfa.gov.tr/turkiye-cumhuriyeti-_disisleri-bakanliginin_-ab-luksemburg-karari-ile-ilgili-aciklamasi_-14-aralik-1997.tr.mfa.

67 Reuters, 'EU, Turkey Seek to Tone down Membership', 18 December 1997, http://www.infoseek.com/Content?arn=a0972LBY655reulb-19971218&col=NW.

68 Daily Telegraph, 'Snubbed Turks Set to Withdraw EU Application', 18 December 1997, http://www.telegraph.co.uk/et?ac=000142848523311&pg=/et/97/12/18/wtur18.html.

69 European Parliament, 'Cardiff European Council Presidency Conclusions', 15 June 1998, https://www.europarl.europa.eu/summits/car1_en.htm, art. 64.

expression in Turkey for the prosecution of democratically elected politicians for expressing their views non-violently.[70]

Turkey's Constitutional Court has adjudicated on the dissolution of forty political parties, ordering the closure of nineteen, since 1982.[71] The majority of these dissolutions occurred during the 1990s, with verdicts predominantly based on three grounds: violations of secular principles, separatism, and formal procedural issues. Numerous Kurdish parties were disbanded due to allegations of separatism. For instance, in 1993, the People's Labour Party (Halkların Emek Partisi, HEP) was banned by a vote of ten to one, and the Freedom and Democracy Party (Özgürlük ve Demokrasi Partisi, ÖZDEP) and the Socialist Party of Turkey (Türkiye Sosyalist Partisi, TSP) were banned unanimously. This pattern continued with the Democracy Party (Demokrasi Partisi, DEP) in 1994, the Socialist Unity Party (Sosyalist Birlik Partisi, SBP) in 1995, the Party for Democratic Change (Demokratik Değişim Partisi, DDP) in 1996, the Labour Party (Emek Partisi, EMEP) in 1997, the Democratic Mass Party (Demokratik Kitle Partisi, DKP) in 1999, the People's Democracy Party (Halkın Demokrasi Partisi, HADEP) in 2003, and the Democratic Society Party (Demokratik Toplum Partisi, DTP) in 2009. They were all banned unanimously, except the Democratic Mass Party and the Party for Democratic Change. Additionally, other parties faced dissolution for engaging in activities that contravened the state's secular principles. Notably, the Welfare Party (Refah Partisi, RP) was banned in 1998 by a vote of nine to two, and the Virtue Party (Fazilet Partisi, FP) followed in 2001 with an eight to three vote. However, in 2008, the Justice and Development Party (Adalet ve Kalkınma Partisi, AKP), led by Erdoğan, narrowly escaped a similar fate, with the Constitutional Court split five to six against the ban.

The parliament enacted amendments to the Political Parties Law in August 1999 to enhance the protections against the closure of political parties and the barring of their members from future political participation. By the amendment, the provision that allowed for the dissolution of political parties if the Republic's chief public prosecutor found deficiencies or non-compliances during the formation stage of the parties, and these were not rectified despite notification, was repealed (article 9). Consequently, the function of the prosecutor in the establishment phase of political parties was eliminated. Later in 2004, the Law on Political Parties was amended.

70 European Commission, 'Turkey 1998 Regular Report'.

71 Osman Can, 'The Motion before Turkey's Constitutional Court to Ban the Pro-Kurdish HDP', *Stiftung Wissenschaft Und Politik*, 17 June 2021, https://www.swp-berlin.org/en/publication/the-motion-before-turkeys-constitutional-court-to-ban-the-pro-kurdish-hdp.

The amendment limited the possibility of party dissolution. The effort was praised by the commission as an advancement of political rights in Turkey.[72]

## 1999–2002: Turkey's Candidate Status

The Helsinki Summit of the European Council on 11–12 December 1999 unexpectedly declared that the Council was content with Turkey's reforms and developments and thus formalized Turkey's candidacy.[73] Earlier in the same year the PKK leader had been apprehended, on 15 February 1999 in Kenya, and had been transferred to Turkey, where he was sentenced to death on 29 June 1999. When the decision was under appeal, it was becoming clear that the execution of the sentence would put Turkey's candidacy under question. As a result of the Helsinki Summit, the Council offered Turkey an accession partnership for an augmented political dialogue directed at the full incorporation of the Copenhagen criteria and financial assistance, to help Turkey prepare to join the EU, as a pre-accession strategy. In 2000, as foreseen in the pre-accession strategy, the Commission prepared the accession partnership documentation for Turkey, which welcomed it by stating its commitment to the Helsinki Conclusions, and by promising to make further efforts, which it did in its 'Priorities in the Democratization Process' declaration.[74] Within this frame, the three-party coalition (of the DSP, MHP, and ANAP) initiated its first reforms to harmonize with the expectations of the EU. In March 2001 the government proclaimed the National Programme for the Adoption of the Acquis (NPAA).[75] In October 2001, a constitutional amendment was formulated to strengthen fundamental rights and liberties in Turkey and to limit the death penalty to warfare conditions.

The amendment introduced liberal principles in the field of fundamental rights and freedoms, reducing restrictions on these rights and freedoms. The reasons for these amendments included ensuring freedom of thought,

72 European Commission, 'Turkey 2004 Progress Report', 10 June 2004), 18, https://www.ab.gov.tr/siteimages/birimler/kpb/tr_rep_20061998/2004_tr_rap.pdf.

73 European Council, 'Helsinki Meeting', Presidency Conclusions, Helsinki, 10 December 1999, https://www.europarl.europa.eu/summits/hel1_en.htm#:~:text=The%20European%20Council%20met%20in,stage%20in%20the%20enlargement%20process, article 12.

74 MFA Turkey, '"Turkish Accession Partnership" Prepared by EU Commission', 2 November 2000, https://www.mfa.gov.tr/_turkish-accession-partnership_-prepared-by-eu-commission-_br__un-official-translation__br_no_211-_november-8_-2000.en.mfa.

75 T.C. Resmi Gazete, 'Avrupa Birliği Müktesebatının Üstlenilmesine İlişkin Türkiye Ulusal Programının Uygulanması, Koordinasyonu ve İzlenmesine Dair Karar', Pub. L. no. 2001/2129 (2001), https://www.resmigazete.gov.tr/eskiler/2001/03/20010324M1-1.pdf.

eliminating norms that do not comply with the European Convention on Human Rights (ECHR), further enhancing freedoms, lifting language bans, actualizing freedom of thought and expression, ensuring the right to a fair trial in accordance with article 6 of the ECHR, abolishing or restricting the death penalty in line with Protocol no. 6 of the ECHR, emphasizing the individual's right to seek justice, foreseeing measures in addition to the closure penalties for political parties, and basing compliance with the European Union on international agreements in cases of conflicts between domestic and international law.[76]

A new civil law was legislated in November 2001 and entered into force in January 2002 that primarily amended Turkish family law to establish gender equality in marriage, in addition to the law of inheritance, the law of persons, the law of property, and the law of obligations. The amendment abandoned the patriarchal status of the 'head of the family' and ordered equal sharing of property acquired during a marriage to protect women from remaining unrecognized during a divorce. Children born out of wedlock gained equal inheritance rights as the registered children. Women gained the right to use their own surnames beside the surname of their husband. The new civil law was seen as a milestone by Turkish civil society. These reforms faced serious obstruction by the conservatives in the parliament, but the changes were finally adopted by persuading the opposition to support them as a part of Turkey's candidacy bid.

Among the reforms, the most surprising one was the abolition of the death penalty, which was believed to be almost impossible due to the opposition of the Nationalist Movement Party (Milliyetçi Hareket Partisi, MHP), for whom withdrawal of the penalty to be applied to the terrorist leader Öcalan would be a betrayal. The August 2002 package incorporated Protocol no. 6 of the ECHR, restricting application of the death penalty (except for 'acts committed in time of war' or of 'imminent threat of war'). It is an unwritten rule that all EU member state sign and ratify Protocol no. 6. Turkey had not executed a prisoner since 1984, yet, capital punishment was still in the Penal Code. The amendment converted death penalties into life imprisonments. It also ratified Protocol no. 13, prohibiting the death penalty without excluding time of war or imminent war threats. The Anti-Terror Law prohibited broadcasting other than in the Turkish language. This law was amended to clear the way for broadcasting in languages other than Turkish. This was a revolutionary step in the human rights history of Turkey, where the

76 H. Tahsin Fendoğlu, '2001 Anayasa Değişikliği Bağlamında Temel Hak ve Özgürlüklerin Sınırlanması AY. Md 13', *Anayasa Yargısı* 18, no. 1 (2002): 111–49.

Kurdish language was demonized and prohibited from being used in the public sphere until this legal revision.

Another issues was that Turkey had never adopted the two major UN human rights covenants: the International Covenant on Civil and Political Rights (ICCPR, 1966) and the International Covenant on Economic, Social and Cultural Rights (ICESCR, 1966). It finally did so in 2000. The reason for the delay was that article 27 of the ICCPR recognized the existence of ethnic, religious, or linguistic minorities and their cultural, religious, and linguistic rights. Turkey avoided adopting this covenant due to reservations whether those rights would be used for spreading terror. In a similar manner, the ICESCR's article 13, which recognizes the right to education, binds the parties to enable this right for all nations and all racial, ethnic, or religious groups. The terror anxieties precluded adoption of these two covenants until 2000, when the EU finally persuaded Turkey to sign them. In 2003 ratification took place.

The European Charter of Local Self-government was adopted in 1985. Turkey signed it in 1988 and ratified it in 1991. This treaty was approached with suspicions due to autonomy discussions. After it was seen that the provisions did not allow for political, cultural, ethnic, or geographical autonomy but was only concerned with local populations, it was adopted.

Finally, the International Convention on the Elimination of All Forms of Racial Discrimination (ICERD) was adopted in the UN General Assembly (UNGA) in 1965 and came into effect in 1969. Turkey signed the treaty in 1972 and the parliament ratified it twenty years later, in 2002.

Turkey's adoption and ratification of international human rights treaties started in 1985. Although some treaties were formerly signed, the parliament did not hurry ratification. What provoked the parliament to take action to adopt and ratify such treaties was the prospect of EU candidacy (and then membership). As a result of the 1980 coup d'état hundreds of thousands of people were subjected to severe torture, beatings, humiliation, and starvation under custody. Thousands were tried in the martial law courts where the death penalty was demanded; more than five hundred were sentenced to death and fifty of those were executed.[77] The Turkish government ratified the Convention against Torture and Other Cruel, Inhuman or Degrading Treatment or Punishment (CAT, 1984) on 2 August 1988, after all the ill-treatment had already occurred.

77 Human Rights Association, 'İHD: No to Coups!', 11 September 2023, https://ihd.org.tr/en/ihd-no-to-coups/.

When the strong junta control over civil activism began to lessen, women's organizations started to raise their voices for improved rights and against sex-based discrimination. The Convention on the Elimination of All Forms of Discrimination against Women (CEDAW) was adopted in 1979 and came into force in 1981; Turkey accessed it on 25 July 1985. The liberalization movement within Turkey required better inclusion of women. On the other hand, the Turkish Civil Code was not able to adopt CEDAW. Thus, Turkey's accession was realized with broad reservations due to clashes with the civil law. Nonetheless, it withdrew the reservations in 1999 and then in 2008.[78] Turkey signed the European Social Charter, which guarantees fundamental social and economic rights complementary to the ECHR, on the day it was opened to signature, on 18 October 1961. However, it ratified the charter in 1989.

The ratification delay was also observed on the Convention on the Rights of the Child (CRC), which was adopted by the UN General Assembly in 1989 and signed by Turkey in 1990. The parliament ratified the CRC in December 1994 and it entered into force in April 1995.

Turkey ratified ICERD in April 2002 by introducing one reservation (to article 22) to the convention, according to which Turkey can only be referred to the International Court of Justice (ICJ) with its consent. Then, in July 2002, Turkey signed the European Agreement Relating to Persons Participating in Proceedings of the European Court of Human Rights.

As for the rights of migrants, the UN General Assembly adopted the International Convention on the Protection of the Rights of All Migrant Workers and Members of Their Families in 18 December 1990. Turkey signed it in 1999. The ratification and entry into force were respectively in June and July 2004.

The accession process to the European Union has been a significant motivational factor for the advancement of human rights in Turkey. Historically, Turkey exhibited reluctance in engaging with international human rights instruments, a hesitation that persisted for decades, primarily due to the politically repressive environment instigated by the 1980 military coup. This environment stifled the development of a vibrant civil society, essential for championing human rights reforms. The market-oriented liberalization initiated by Prime Minister Turgut Özal in the 1980s focused primarily on

78 On 30 September 1999 Turkey notified withdrawal of its reservations on article 15, paras. 2 and 4, on article 16, para. 1, subparas. (c), (d), (f), and (g)). On 29 January 2008 it withdrew the reservation on article 9, para. 1. The reservation on article 29, para. 1, still persists. This provision sets forth that disputes under this treaty will be settled by the ICJ.

economic objectives rather than on expanding civil liberties. Therefore, the surge in ratifying or acceding to international human rights treaties during the 1990s was largely influenced by external pressures rather than domestic advocacy. While these developments were generally welcomed by civil society, which had higher aspirations, it is clear that the government's actions in the human rights domain were responses to external incentives rather than to internal demands for reform.

Although the Helsinki Conclusions stimulated reforms in Turkey, its economy was overwhelmed by high inflation, and thus high interest rates and ever-growing debts prevented the realization of reforms until after 2001. Turkey's candidacy process, since the very beginning, has been primarily based on human rights–related matters, besides the stalemated political questions, such as the Cyprus issue and relations with Greece. The Union's priorities concerning Turkey's accession have been on rights-related matters, thus the reforms were rights-oriented. When the economy was hit by the 2001 financial shock that caused the Turkish lira to fall and the stock market to crash, the government had to give priority to economic adjustments. As a result, the chief political reforms could only be realized from 2001 onwards. The major improvement elements expected by the Union, as set forth in the accession partnership documentation, were: the enhancement of minority rights; the improvement of fundamental rights such as freedom of association, expression, and communication; the inviolability of the domicile; gender equality; removal of the death penalty from the Penal Code; transparency and accountability to prevent violations such as abuse and torture; and the strengthening of democracy and the civilian authority by the reduction (eradication) of the role of the military in politics through the National Security Council and in the judiciary through the State Security Courts (Devlet Güvenlik Mahkemesi, DGM). After the economic adjustments, the coalition started to pay more attention to fulfilment of these criteria.

Until the general elections on 3 November 2002, the coalition legislated three reform packages. In this framework, the government introduced new human rights institutions in 2001. First, the Directorate of Human Rights (İnsan Hakları Başkanlığı) was established under the Prime Minister's Office to coordinate between human rights–related institutions, providing them with trainings, monitoring the implementation of the relevant regulations, evaluating the outcomes, and making recommendations for improving the infrastructure. Second, the Supreme Board of Human Rights (İnsan Hakları Üst Kurulu) was established as one of the main service units of the Prime Ministry. Its duties were shaped around harmonizing human rights regulations with international treaties and standards.[79] Third, besides human rights institutionalization, the August 2002 legislation adopted a judicial reform that cleared the way for the right of retrial when the ECtHR determined that a violation of the ECHR has occurred due to an unfair trial. The Council welcomed the reforms and encouraged further fulfilment of the Copenhagen criteria, as indicated in the progress report.

Font argues that the Helsinki Summit was the first time the Council assumed a proactive and relatively more cooperative role than the traditional containment strategy.[80] Özbudun evaluates this new role as initiating the Union's 'carrot effect' over Turkey to influence its democratization process.[81] The motivator of the courageous reforms realized in the first decade of AKP rule can be traced back to this Council decision. From 1999 until the early 2010s Turkey enacted reforms that improved its democratization in order to meet the Union's standards. Civil society was also quite supportive of this process.[82] Although Turkey had signed a number of international human rights treaties decades earlier, such as in the late 1960s and the 1970s, they were not ratified. The ratification process of certain UN conventions started to take place with the motivation of the Helsinki Summit conclusions.

79 Ahmet Saraç, 'Türkiye'de İnsan Hakları Resmi Örgütlenmesi', *Türk İdare Dergisi*, no. 435 (2002): 157–76.

80 Nuria Font, 'Why the European Union Gave Turkey the Green Light', *Journal of Contemporary European Studies* 14, no. 2 (2006): 197–212, at 199–200.

81 Özbudun, *The Constitutional System of Turkey*, 154–55.

82 Müftüler Baç, 'Turkey's Political Reforms and the Impact of the European Union', 21.

# 5. Human Rights in Turkey during the AKP Rule and EU Perspectives

**Abstract:** This chapter analyses the evolution of human rights in Turkey under the AKP's rule (2002–24) and the shifting dynamics of EU–Turkey relations. It examines three major phases: the early reform era (2002–5), the plateau period (2005–13), and the authoritarian retrenchment phase (2013–24). It assesses key developments in the rule of law, judicial independence, media freedoms, and migration policy, highlighting how EU conditionality initially drove reforms before losing traction amid democratic backsliding. Adopting a neo-Gramscian lens, the chapter explores how domestic and international hegemonic struggles shaped the trajectory of rights protection in Turkey. It concludes that while the EU once functioned as a transformative force, its normative influence has eroded, giving way to a more transactional, fragmented mode of engagement.

**Keywords:** Migration, AKP–EU relations, buffer state, human rights, conditionality, democratic backsliding

Since the Justice and Development Party (AKP) came to power in 2002, the trajectory of Turkey's human rights landscape and its relations with the European Union have become deeply intertwined. Human rights, democratization, and governance standards have remained central elements in the evolving, often contentious, dialogue between the two sides. These developments are not only political in nature but are also reflections of broader struggles over the production of order, legitimacy, and hegemony as themes central to a neo-Gramscian understanding of international relations.

Initially, Turkey's EU accession process functioned as a powerful instrument of external influence, encouraging ambitious reforms aligned with the Copenhagen criteria. Much like the transformative experiences of Central and Eastern European states, Turkey's early reform agenda between 1999

Bayar, Tuğba. *The Rise and Relapse of European Human Rights in Turkey: The AKP Era, 2002–2024*. Amsterdam University Press/Central European University Press, 2025.
DOI 10.5117/9789048573813_CH05

and 2005 reflected a strategic attempt to internalize democratic norms and secure its place within the European order. During this phase, the EU's political conditionality operated as a mechanism of consensual hegemony, fostering alignment without overt coercion.

However, the relationship proved fragile. By the mid-2000s, doubts within the EU regarding Turkey's full membership prospects, compounded by unresolved issues such as Cyprus and the migration crisis, began to undermine the credibility of EU conditionality. Internally, Turkey's political trajectory shifted: the AKP's early reformism gave way to increasing centralization of power, culminating in a visible retreat from democratic norms after events such as the Gezi Park protests in 2013, the failed coup attempt in 2016, and the transition to a presidential regime in 2017. As the EU's ability to exercise normative influence waned, the dynamics between the EU and Turkey came to reflect a more contested and crisis-prone hegemonic relationship.

This chapter examines the evolution of human rights in Turkey during the AKP era, analysing how the interplay between domestic political transformations and shifting external pressures from the EU reshaped the landscape. It charts the initial phase of reform, the subsequent stagnation, and the later period of authoritarian consolidation, while critically reflecting on the limits of the EU's transformative power in the context of changing hegemonic orders.

## The Reform Era, 2002–5: Harmonization Packages and Democratization Efforts

The series of harmonization packages adopted by Turkey as part of its European Union accession process for addressing the political criteria significantly reshaped its legal and institutional framework, aligning it more closely with EU standards. The First Harmonization Package, effective from 19 February 2002, introduced crucial reforms to the Penal Code, Anti-Terror Law, and the Code of Criminal Procedure, among others, aimed at expanding freedom of expression, reducing pre-trial detention periods, and enhancing the protection of prisoner rights. This package, for instance, reduced the maximum sentences for offenses under article 159 of the Penal Code and repealed certain restrictive provisions in the Anti-Terror Law, thereby reducing constraints on freedom of thought and expression.

The Second Harmonization Package, which came into force on 9 April 2002, further liberalized laws pertaining to freedom of expression, freedom of association, and freedom of peaceful assembly. It included amendments to the Press Law, the Law on Political Parties, and the Law on Meetings and Demonstration Marches, effectively lowering barriers to more open political and civil engagement. These amendments facilitated a more inclusive and participatory public sphere and mitigated previous limitations on public communication and organization.

Subsequent packages continued this trend of liberalization and reform. For instance, the Third Harmonization Package abolished the death penalty, marking a significant shift in Turkey's human rights stance, particularly towards aligning with the Charter of Fundamental Rights of the European Union. This package also included provisions for retrial based on European Court of Human Rights decisions, thereby integrating European human rights jurisprudence into Turkish law more directly and ensuring greater legal recourse for rights violations.

The Fourth Harmonization Package focused on broadening the freedom of association, strengthening safeguards against torture, and improving the conditions and rights of prisoners. It introduced legislative changes that emphasized the urgency and prioritization of prosecuting cases of torture and mistreatment, reflecting Turkey's commitment to aligning its human rights practices with those of the EU.

Each of these packages not only addressed specific areas of law but collectively represented a comprehensive effort by Turkey to reform its judicial and administrative structures in accordance with European norms. This systematic approach to reform, influenced by the EU conditionality, demonstrated a clear trajectory towards enhancing democratic governance, judicial independence, and respect for human rights, despite challenges and criticisms related to the depth and consistency of implementation. These efforts underscored the transformative impact of EU integration processes on candidate countries, aiming to solidify the rule of law, judicial fairness, and the protection of fundamental freedoms.

In September 2003, the Turkish government established the Reform Monitoring Group (Reform İzleme Grubu, RİG), a high-profile committee tasked with ensuring the effective implementation of legislative reforms crucial for EU accession. Chaired by Abdullah Gül, then deputy prime minister and minister of foreign affairs, the group included key ministers such as Cemil Çiçek, minister of justice, Abdülkadir Aksu, minister of the interior, and Ali Babacan, state minister and chief negotiator from June 2005. The Prime Ministry's Secretariat General for EU Affairs provided secretarial services to the group, underscoring the bureaucratic support for EU-related activities.

The Reform Monitoring Group's Information Gathering Sub-Committee, led by the secretary general for EU affairs, actively monitored the implementation of decisions and prepared topics for discussion within the group. This sub-committee's role was crucial in maintaining continuous oversight and coordination of Turkey's reform efforts.

EU accession remained a standing item on the Council of Ministers' agenda, reflecting the government's commitment to integration with the EU. In a significant move on 3 June 2005, State Minister Ali Babacan was appointed as the chief negotiator for EU negotiations, signalling a focused approach to managing Turkey's accession talks.

Furthermore, Turkey's National Programme for the Adoption of the Acquis, first issued in March 2001 and subsequently updated in June 2003, outlined the country's strategy for aligning its legislation and institutional capacity with EU standards. The ongoing monitoring of this programme was managed through detailed tables tracking legislative priorities.

On 17 April 2007, Turkey launched its Programme for Alignment with the Acquis covering the period from 2007 to 2013. This programme, comprising primary and secondary legislation across thirty-three chapters of accession negotiations, was subject to rigorous monitoring to ensure compliance and effectiveness. Recognizing the dynamic nature of EU requirements, the programme was designed to be amendable as needed, with the Reform Monitoring Group continuing its oversight within the political criteria domain. This structured mechanism underscores Turkey's structured and methodical approach to its EU accession process.

In 2004, Turkey continued to align its legal and institutional frameworks with international standards, notably through ratifying significant human rights treaties. Protocol no. 6 to the European Convention on Human Rights, which concerns the abolition of the death penalty, was ratified and took effect in December 2003. Additionally, Turkey ratified the International Covenant on Civil and Political Rights and the International Covenant on Economic, Social and Cultural Rights, both of which came into force by the end of 2003. This period also saw the entry into force of the Council of Europe Criminal Law Convention on Corruption.

According to the Corruption Perception Index of Transparency International, Turkey ranks 115 out of 180 with a score of thirty-four perception points, this year, with a loss of two points since last year (see fig. 1). The global corruption barometer shows that 8 per cent of public service users paid bribes in the previous twelve months.

The implementation of the Law on the Right to Information, enhancing transparency and public access to information, a fundamental aspect of democratic governance, occurred in 2004. Additionally, Turkey continued

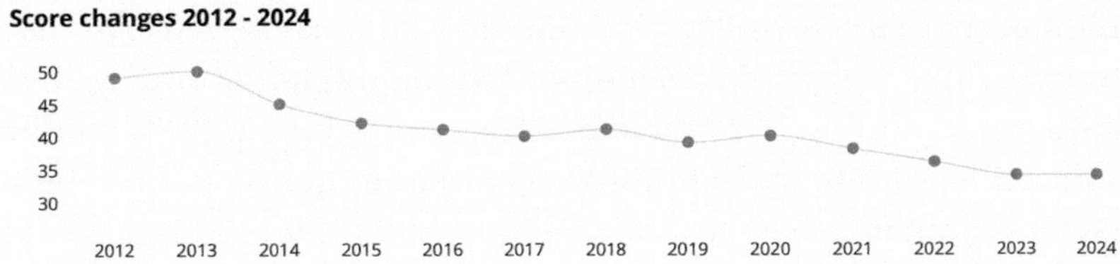


Figure 1. Corruption Perceptions Index scores from 2012 to 2024. Source: Transparency International.[1]

to reform its association and foundation laws to facilitate more effective and principled interactions with public institutions.

In summary, these reforms across 2004 and into 2005 reflect Turkey's ongoing efforts to enhance human rights protections, judicial fairness, and adherence to international norms, representing significant strides in its commitment to democratic reforms and the rule of law. These measures not only align with European Union accession criteria but also demonstrate Turkey's dedication to improving its governance and legal systems in concert with its obligations under various international frameworks.

## The Plateau Era, 2005–13

The period between 2005 and 2013 represents a critical plateau phase in Turkey's trajectory of political and legal reforms, particularly regarding human rights and migration policies. Following an initial era of dynamic reforms driven by EU accession aspirations, this period witnessed a slowing momentum, characterized by selective adaptation and stabilization of previous changes without deeper structural transformation. From a neo-Gramscian perspective, this phase reflects the consolidation of a passive revolution. While institutional and legal frameworks formally aligned with EU standards, the deeper hegemonic relations, the balance between domestic power structures and external pressures remained largely intact. Reformist rhetoric persisted, but substantive democratization and rights protection were uneven and instrumentalized. Turkey's interaction with the EU thus moved from a transformative engagement to a strategic and often

1 Transparency International, 'Our Work in Türkiye: Corruption Perceptions Index', accessed 20 October 2024, https://www.transparency.org/en/countries/türkiye.

transactional relationship, marking the limits of normative power when confronted with entrenched political interests and emerging regional crises.

In 2006, Turkey's Ninth Harmonization Package was introduced by Abdullah Gül, deputy prime minister and minister of foreign affairs, marking significant legislative and administrative reforms aimed at accelerating Turkey's alignment with international standards. This package focused on expediting the adoption of both draft legislation and international agreements and on enhancing administrative measures. Key legislative proposals included the Law on the Court of Audit, laws on administrative legal procedures, the establishment of a political ethics commission, and fundamental principles for elections and electoral rolls. Additionally, reforms targeted laws related to foundations, settlement, private education, and the ombudsman.

The Law on Foundations, pivotal for non-discriminatory provisions, was approved but returned by the president for further revision. Similarly, the new Law on Settlement, addressing equality for Roma, was enacted. Reforms in education removed discriminatory practices against foreign educators and deputy directors in schools. The Law on Ombudsman was approved, though some articles faced constitutional scrutiny.

Significant reforms also included the abolition of military courts' jurisdiction over civilians during peacetime, except for collective military crimes. This move was crucial for aligning with European human rights standards, ensuring civilian cases, especially those involving compulsory military service, were tried in civilian courts. Moreover, the package included the ratification of important international conventions, such as the UN Convention against Corruption and several human rights protocols, demonstrating Turkey's commitment to global standards.

Administratively, the Human Rights Presidency of the Prime Ministry was restructured, and efforts to coordinate anti-corruption measures were enhanced. The Prime Ministry's Circular no. 2006/32 also emphasized transparency and good governance, aligning domestic policies with international anti-corruption strategies.

Overall, 2006 was marked by significant strides in legislative reforms and international treaty ratifications, enhancing Turkey's legal framework in line with its European Union accession goals and broader international obligations. These reforms reflected a comprehensive approach to improving governance, human rights, and administrative efficacy within Turkey.

Actually, the period from 2005 to 2013 witnessed a deceleration in Turkey's reformative zeal. During these years, while Turkey continued to implement courageous reforms, the enthusiasm waned due to a combination of EU member states' reluctance to fully embrace Turkey's membership and contentious debates over a 'privileged partnership' instead of full EU membership. Issues such as the ongoing Cyprus question further complicated the accession talks, dampening the reform momentum. The EU's influence, while largely positive in the early stages, began to show mixed outcomes in its impact on Turkey's judicial reforms. Unlike the clear successes in Central and Eastern Europe, the EU's leverage and political conditionality did not exert the same effectiveness in Turkey, at least not with the enduring impact observed prior to those countries' accession.

Turkey had undergone a substantial transformation, often referred to by observers as a 'silent revolution' that has notably accelerated in recent years in line with the EU accession process. This transformation encompassed widespread reforms across various sectors, with a significant focus on meeting the Copenhagen criteria. The reforms had not only broadened individual rights and freedoms but have also been crucial in enhancing economic stability and welfare, reflecting a positive trend in Turkey's societal and economic benchmarks.

The reforms aimed to elevate the standards of living for the Turkish public to the highest international norms, with the Turkish populace actively driving these changes. The process had fostered a more open environment for public discourse, enabling civil society to express opinions and demands freely, thus enhancing transparency in discussing national issues.

Implementing such comprehensive reforms in a country as large as Turkey takes time. These reforms necessitate a cultural shift in understanding, thinking, and institutional behaviour, which can only be achieved through continuous education and new structural reforms. The transformation towards a new institutional culture involves changing longstanding practices and attitudes, a gradual process that Turkey is committed to pursuing.

The broader political context of the EU also played a crucial role in this trajectory. The EU's evolving political role aimed to address global challenges like security and globalization. Turkey's potential EU membership was seen as beneficial for its broader geopolitical implications, in particular.

However, from 2013 to the present, Turkey has experienced a noticeable backslide in democratic practices, veering towards authoritarianism with a significant regression in the rule of law and human rights. The erosion of checks and balances, coupled with institutional restructuring, has facilitated this authoritarian drift. This backsliding mirrors, albeit under different circumstances, the democratic erosion observed in some Central and Eastern European countries post-EU accession, where political costs of adaptation were high due to internal political struggles.

Theoretically, the EU could have played a more decisive role in curbing or reversing Turkey's authoritarian tendencies by leveraging various incentives. These incentives have historically proven effective in promoting reforms in other candidate countries. However, in recent years, the EU has prioritized employing these incentives primarily to secure Turkey's cooperation in managing the flow of migrants to EU territories, rather than forcefully advocating for continued democratic reforms. This strategic choice reflects a broader recalibration of EU–Turkey relations, where immediate geopolitical and security concerns have overshadowed the EU's foundational commitment to promoting democracy and human rights. Consequently, while Turkey's initial reform period showcased the potential for EU-induced transformation, the subsequent phases have highlighted the limitations and challenges of sustaining such reforms in the face of complex domestic and international political landscapes.

The trajectory towards authoritarianism in Turkey has been marked by a gradual weakening of the legislative and oversight capabilities of the Turkish parliament. Despite the orderly conduct of the 2024 local elections, which ostensibly respected the popular will, the overarching presidential system has diluted the power of the parliament, limiting its ability to hold the executive branch accountable. Most regulatory authorities are now linked directly to the presidency, which has not only centralized authority but also politicized public administration to a significant extent. This centralization is most evident in the government's continued pressure on opposition mayors, thereby undermining the foundations of local democracy.

Moreover, civil society organizations in Turkey find themselves operating within an increasingly restrictive environment, facing numerous constraints that include continuous governmental pressure. Despite these challenges, civil society has remained resilient, actively participating in civic life and making crucial contributions across various sectors. However, the need for more robust mechanisms to ensure that independent civil societies are consulted on new legislation and policies is clear, as this would enhance democratic engagement and ensure a broader representation of societal interests in the legislative process.

In terms of public administration reform, Turkey remains caught between minimal preparation and a moderate level of readiness, with little to no progress noted in recent periods. The European Commission has repeatedly emphasized the necessity for Turkey to adopt comprehensive strategies that align with EU principles, particularly in public administration and financial management. This includes the introduction of merit-based recruitment and promotions, particularly for senior positions, and a review of the policymaking process to ensure it is inclusive and evidence-based.

Judicial independence and the rule of law continue to be areas of significant concern. The judiciary is subject to undue pressures from the authorities, which undermines its independence and the overall quality of judicial processes. The European Commission stresses the need for profound judicial reforms that would enhance the functioning and autonomy of the judicial system, including aligning with the judgements of the European Court of Human Rights, which Turkey has occasionally refused to implement.

The fundamental rights situation in Turkey remains a major issue of concern. The legal framework provides general guarantees for the respect of human and fundamental rights; however, the actual legislation and its enforcement require significant adjustments to align with the European Convention on Human Rights and case law. The ongoing trials and convictions of journalists, academics, and various defenders of human rights for purportedly supporting terrorism underscore the pressing issues within the Turkish legal and judicial framework.

Addressing the challenges in the area of freedom of expression is particularly urgent. The implementation of criminal laws related to national security and counterterrorism continues to hinder freedom of expression and diverges from the standards set by the European Convention on Human Rights as well as the jurisprudence of the ECtHR. The European Commission has called for revisions in the criminal legislation, notably the Anti-Terror Law and the Penal Code, to ensure these are in proportion and do not unduly curtail freedom of expression.

In the domain of migration and security, Turkey has shown a commendable effort in hosting and supporting a substantial refugee population. Nonetheless, the country faces ongoing challenges, including the need to resume return operations from the Greek islands and improve overall coordination and execution of border management strategies. These efforts are crucial for managing the persistent flow of irregular migrants and addressing associated security concerns. The reluctance of EU member states to accept migrants, coupled with a predominantly securitized approach to migration within the EU, has led to the externalization of migration management solutions. In this context, Turkey has assumed a proactive role in preventing the onward movement of migrants towards Europe. To facilitate the retention of these migrants within its borders, Turkey enacted the Law on Foreigners and International Protection in 2014. This legislation mirrors the European *acquis* in matters of migration and asylum, reflecting a significant alignment with European standards and expectations in addressing migration challenges.

The analysis in this section of the thesis will delve into the intricacies of these challenges and the broader implications they have for the relationship between the EU and Turkey. By examining the evolution of this relationship through the lens of international regimes theories, the discussion aims to offer a nuanced understanding of the political, legal, and social dynamics at play. Furthermore, it will explore potential pathways that could foster improvements in human rights and democratic governance, benefiting both Turkey and the European Union in their shared aspirations for a more stable and democratic region.

This comprehensive examination not only highlights the current challenges but also underscores the opportunities for reform and collaboration that could enhance the quality of EU–Turkey relations in the face of increasing complexities in global and regional politics.

## The Retrenchment of Human Rights, 2013–24

The phase of democratic backsliding in Turkey can be interpreted through a neo-Gramscian lens as a period marked by an intensifying crisis of hegemony, wherein the ruling bloc sought to consolidate its dominance through authoritarian restructuring rather than broad societal consent. The initial cracks appeared with the Gezi Park protests in 2013, which represented a significant rupture between the ruling AKP and diverse segments of civil society. The failed coup attempt in July 2016 then served as a catalyst for a profound reconfiguration of the state, allowing the executive to enact what Gramsci termed a passive revolution, a top-down transformation consolidating a new hegemonic project under conditions of emergency.

Amidst the deepening organic crisis that ruptured the historic compromise underpinning Turkey's earlier Europeanization project, the AKP actively sought to reconstruct a new historic bloc by reconfiguring both domestic and international alliances beyond the traditional Western liberal order. In response to the waning credibility of the EU accession framework and the mounting external normative pressures, the government pursued a strategy of counter-hegemonic bloc formation, turning towards alternative centres of economic and political power. Financial dependency was partially recalibrated through strengthened partnerships with Gulf states such as Qatar and Saudi Arabia, which supplied much-needed monetary support to bolster Turkey's fragile economy. Militarily, the acquisition of the Russian S-400 missile system signalled not merely a tactical manoeuvre but an intentional disruption of NATO-aligned security structures, thereby asserting an embryonic strategic autonomy. Ankara also engaged in symbolic and practical overtures towards Eurasian initiatives, including expressions of interest in the Shanghai Cooperation Organisation and partnerships within the Belt and Road Initiative, thereby gesturing towards a reorientation of Turkey's geopolitical identity. Discursively, this reconfiguration was legitimated through narratives of national sovereignty, civilizational independence, and 'precious loneliness' ('*değerli yalnızlık*'), signalling a conscious attempt to reforge social consent around a post-Western, sovereigntist vision. Collectively, these moves reflected a coherent project of passive revolution at the international level, seeking to secure the AKP's domestic hegemony by embedding Turkey within an emerging multipolar order less constrained by liberal-democratic norms.

The 2017 constitutional referendum, conducted under a prolonged state of emergency and marred by procedural irregularities such as the acceptance of unstamped ballots, institutionalized this transformation. The resulting shift to a presidential system fundamentally altered Turkey's political architecture: the legislature was rendered increasingly inactive, the executive amassed disproportionate powers, and the judiciary's independence was systematically eroded. President Erdoğan, first elected by direct popular vote in 2014, was re-elected in 2018 under the new constitutional order. Although constitutional provisions stipulated that a president could serve only two terms unless early elections were called, Erdoğan's eligibility for re-election was upheld, illustrating how legal interpretations were increasingly subordinated to political expediency.

The 2019 local elections dealt a significant blow to the AKP's hegemonic project, with opposition victories in key metropolitan areas such as Istanbul and Ankara. In response, the government resorted to coercive and administrative measures to maintain control, including the dismissal of elected mayors in south-eastern Anatolia and their replacement with trustees, the unilateral withdrawal from the Istanbul Convention (Convention on Preventing and Combating Violence against Women and Domestic Violence), the effective seizure of control over the EU–Turkey migration deal, and the symbolic reconversion of Hagia Sophia from a museum into a mosque. These actions reflect a strategy of *transformismo*, the selective incorporation or neutralization of opposition elements, to reconstitute the regime's fragile hegemony in the face of growing societal dissent.

In parallel, the European Union recalibrated its stance towards Turkey. From 2016 onwards, the EU increasingly prioritized migration management over the promotion of human rights and democratic norms. Designating Turkey as a safe third country, despite clear deficiencies in meeting the EU's own legal criteria enabled the externalization of border control responsibilities to Ankara, at the cost of undermining the Union's normative commitments. The EU's shifting position thus contributed to the external legitimation of Turkey's internal authoritarian drift.

The onset of the COVID-19 pandemic further aggravated Turkey's socio-economic vulnerabilities, providing additional justification for the executive to centralize authority. The shortcomings of this hyper-presidential system were laid bare during the devastating 2023 Kahramanmaraş earthquakes, where restrictions on communication platforms such as Twitter, delays in delivering emergency aid, and widespread infrastructural failures revealed the regime's inability to effectively manage national crises despite its extensive powers.

Viewed through a neo-Gramscian framework, this period is characterized by a deepening democratic deficit, the politicization of the judiciary, the contraction of civil liberties, particularly freedom of expression, media freedoms, and freedom of association, and a notable deterioration in the human rights conditions for migrants and refugees. Rather than securing a stable and legitimate hegemonic order, the Turkish government has increasingly relied on mechanisms of authoritarian statism, whereby the state assumes an ever more autonomous and coercive role vis-à-vis society. This authoritarian consolidation reflects the regime's ongoing struggle to resolve its crisis of authority not through the building of consent, but through the narrowing of political space and the intensification of state control.

## The Democracy Deficit

Gramsci's concept of hegemony offers a crucial framework for understanding the dynamics of democracy and human rights, especially in the context of Turkey under the AKP. Unlike liberal democratic theories that emphasize the direct implementation of human rights through institutional mechanisms, Gramsci stresses the importance of political and ideological consent. The state, according to Gramsci, does not only govern through coercion but also through the consent of its citizens, which is shaped by a complex web of institutions, cultural norms, and political processes. In the case of Turkey, the AKP's governance has been characterized by a dual approach: On the one hand, it has promoted democratic reforms to secure consent from key societal groups; on the other, it has systematically undermined democratic institutions in order to consolidate state power.

Gramsci's theory of the passive revolution is particularly relevant in understanding the shifts in Turkish democracy since the early 2000s. Rather than a radical rupture with the past, Turkey has experienced a gradual transformation, where the AKP has redefined democratic structures to align with its own vision of governance. These changes, while initially framed as democratizing reforms, have increasingly served the purpose of consolidating the AKP's hegemony over the political field. The reforms introduced by the AKP, such as the dismantling of military influence, the reduction of the role of the National Security Council, and judicial reforms, were framed as part of the EU accession process but also allowed the AKP to consolidate control over key state institutions.

In this framework, democracy is not simply the adoption of liberal principles but is constantly shaped by the struggle over the control of the state apparatus. Gramsci's emphasis on the 'war of position' helps explain how the AKP, over time, has navigated between offering reforms to gain legitimacy both domestically and internationally, while simultaneously securing its position in the state by weakening opposition and civil society structures that might challenge its authority. The tension between reform and authoritarian consolidation under the AKP reflects the ongoing process of hegemony-building, in which the state's ability to govern is not solely based on force but on its capacity to manage consent and control public discourse.

In Turkey, as elsewhere, democratization processes have unfolded not as linear progress but as contested terrains shaped by competing social forces, institutional struggles, and shifting hegemonies. As Fuat Keyman observes, Turkish politics from the mid-1990s onward reveal two contrasting periods, each shaped by competing political projects and shifting hegemonic alignments. Between 1995 and 2000, Turkey was defined by a state-centric and security-oriented model, marked by democratic deficits, human rights abuses, a weak rule of law, economic instability, and crises of legitimacy. Identity-based conflicts, such as Islamic revivalism and the Kurdish question, together with pervasive corruption and clientelism, reinforced the fragility of this order. Turkey has undergone substantial transformations in its political, economic, and cultural spheres. This era has been characterized by efforts towards democratization and its consolidation, restructuring state–economy relations to foster sustainable growth, and ambitious reforms to activate and democratize Turkish foreign policy. Additionally, significant strides have been made towards establishing a rights-based citizenship regime and addressing regional, economic, political, and cultural disparities.[2] He argues that this transition was facilitated by Turkey's Europeanization efforts. During this period, Turkey's candidacy was accepted, and membership negotiations appeared imminent.

In contrast, the early 2000s witnessed a partial reconfiguration of Turkey's political, economic, and cultural spheres. Democratic reforms, market restructuring, and a rights-based discourse began to reshape the political landscape, underpinned by Turkey's Europeanization process. However, these transformations were not merely technical adaptations to EU norms; they were embedded in struggles over the direction of state power, societal inclusion, and the redefinition of citizenship. The EU's conditionality functioned both as a catalyst for reform and as an external influence on Turkey's contested democratization trajectory, as Ankara's candidacy status and accession negotiations gained momentum.

When the Justice and Development Party (AKP) assumed power in November 2002, Turkey was classified as an electoral democracy. In its early terms, the AKP government undertook significant reforms that dismantled key elements of Turkey's tutelary democracy, long protected by military and bureaucratic elites. These reforms included curtailing the National Security Council's influence over politics, abolishing military courts' jurisdiction over civilians, and removing military figures from influential advisory bodies such as the Radio and Television Supreme Council (RTÜK). The death penalty was abolished, and formal improvements were made in the areas of gender equality and minority rights.

While these changes were largely motivated by the requirements of EU accession, they also formed part of a deeper hegemonic reorganization. Drawing from Gramscian insights, these reforms can be interpreted as a case of passive revolution. It is a top-down process, a controlled transformation designed to defuse popular demands for deeper democratization while simultaneously reinforcing a new bloc of political power. Rather than fundamentally transforming power relations, the AKP selectively adopted democratic norms to neutralize old centres of opposition and reconstitute hegemony under its own leadership.

Consequently, Turkey was portrayed internationally as a model of successful democratization in a Muslim-majority, middle-income country.[3] However,

2 E. Fuat Keyman and Senem Aydın Düzgit, 'Europeanization, Democratization and Human Rights in Turkey', in *Turkey and the European Union: Prospects for a Difficult Encounter*, ed. E. LaGro and K.E. Jørgensen (London: Palgrave Macmillan, 2007), 69–89.

3 Paul Kubicek, 'Debating the Merits of the "Turkish Model" for Democratization in the Middle East', *Alternatives: Turkish Journal of International Relations* 12, no. 3 (2013): 66–80; Stefano M. Torelli, 'The Rise and Fall of the Turkish Model for the Middle East', in *Turkey's Relations with*

the judicial and political reforms undertaken by Erdoğan's AKP not only enhanced Turkey's economic performance and formal democratic indicators but also served to entrench the party's dominance. These measures helped broaden the AKP's social base, particularly among a public that had initially viewed the party with scepticism due to its founders' roots in the political Islamist National View (Millî Görüş) tradition.

The democratic backsliding that intensified after 2013 can be interpreted through the Gramscian lens of passive revolution, wherein initial reformist openings were gradually neutralized through the reassertion of coercive state power. The authoritarian response to the Gezi Park protests revealed the limits of the earlier consent-based hegemony and marked the beginning of a shift towards a more overtly coercive mode of governance. Framing the 17–25 December 2013 Corruption and Bribery Operation as a judicial coup, the AKP initiated a structural reconfiguration of the judiciary, enhancing executive control over ostensibly independent institutions. This manoeuvre mirrored Gramsci's notion of Caesarism, as the balance of political forces broke down and leadership became increasingly personalized.

Following the failed coup attempt of 15 July 2016, the regime institutionalized a state of exception, enabling Erdoğan to govern by decree and suspend ordinary constitutional guarantees. The 2017 constitutional referendum formalized this centralization of power, dismantling the residual architecture of parliamentary democracy and codifying executive supremacy. The subsequent autocratic survival strategies, including the withdrawal from the Istanbul Convention by presidential decree and the replacement of elected municipal leaders with government-appointed trustees,[4] further exemplified the closing of political space and the progressive hollowing out of democratic forms. In this trajectory, Turkey's political evolution reflects not merely an episodic authoritarian turn but a broader counter-revolutionary project aimed at stabilizing an emerging authoritarian capitalist order under the ideological cover of electoral legitimacy.

The breakdown of democratic institutions in Turkey has many roots. The first one is the elimination of the military elements from civilian politics did not only elevate democracy but also removed the tutelary elements that were behaving as the protector of republican, secular values. The elimination of

*the Middle East: Political Encounters after the Arab Spring*, ed. Hüseyin Işıksal and Oğuzhan Göksel, 53–64 (Springer, 2018).

4 Tuğba Bayar, 'Turkey's Withdrawal from Istanbul Convention: International Human Rights Regime vis-à-vis Authoritarian Survival', *Turkish Studies* 25, no. 1 (2024): 22–42.

one group of veto player enabled the AKP to go in an authoritarian direction will less resistance. In addition to the democratic reforms undertaken as a part of the harmonization packages with the EU, there had been military overthrow conspiracies in the second half of the 2000s (2007–10), known as Ergenekon and Balyoz, which were later named as terrorist organizations in the indictment. The members were spotted as the high-ranking members of the army to active duty and retired ones. They were accused of attempting to remove the government, violently.[5] The general consensus is that the gap created by the removal of almost 10 per cent of the high-ranking officers was filled by placing the FETÖ-related Gülenist personnel. This claim is mentioned by various politicians and journalists, such as Turhan Çömez[6] of Good Party (İyi Parti, İP), former CHP member Muharrem İnce[7] and Ümit Özdağ[8] of Victory Party (Zafer Partisi, ZP) and a prominent journalist, Fikret Bila.[9] The 2016 failed coup was then, according to the aforementioned allegations, carried out by the FETÖ members who had replaced the secular officers.

The Gezi Park protests, originating in May 2013 as a localized demonstration against urban development plans, escalated through social media into a widespread challenge to the government. This peaceful movement, characterized by its diverse participant base engaging in peaceful, pacifist sit-ins and standing protests, rapidly transformed into a nationwide expression of dissent against the policies of the AKP government.[10] Prime Minister Erdoğan derogatorily labelled the protesters as 'looters' ('*çapulcular*'), insinuating manipulation by foreign entities, and viewed the demonstrations as a direct threat to the survival of the AKP's governance.[11] The protests were elaborated in the National Security Council, as a national security

5 BBC, 'Ergenekon Davasında Karar Açıklandı: Hüküm Sonrası Kim Ne Dedi?', 1 July 2019, https://www.bbc.com/turkce/haberler-turkiye-48830230.

6 Gazete Duvar, 'Turhan Çömez ve Mustafa Yeneroğlu Arasında "Balyoz-Ergenekon" Polemiği', 20 April 2023, https://www.gazeteduvar.com.tr/turhan-comez-ve-mustafa-yeneroglu-arasinda-balyoz-ergenekon-polemigi-haber-1614506.

7 Veryansın TV, 'Ümit Özdağ ve Muharrem İnce'den Mustafa Yeneroğlu'nun "Ergenekon-Balyoz" Sözlerine Tepki', 20 April 2023, https://www.veryansintv.com/umit-ozdag-ve-muharrem-inceden-mustafa-yeneroglunun-ergenekon-balyoz-sozlerine-tepki.

8 Ibid.

9 Fikret Bila, 'Yüreğim Yanıyor Vicdanım Sızlıyor', *Hürriyet*, 8 December 2016, https://www.hurriyet.com.tr/yazarlar/fikret-bila/yuregim-yaniyor-vicdanim-sizliyor-40190131.

10 Stavroula Chrona and Cristiano Bee, 'Right to Public Space and Right to Democracy: The Role of Social Media in Gezi Park', *Research and Policy on Turkey* 2, no. 1 (2017): 49–61.

11 Taptuk Erkoc, 'Taksim Gezi Park Protests: Birth and Backlash of a Political Sphere', *Journal of Global Faultlines* 1, no. 2 (2013): 43–46, at 45.

topic.[12] The state's response was marked by severe police brutality aimed at suppressing the uprising. Erdoğan said that he had given the order to the police.[13] The arbitrary denial of the right to peaceful assembly culminated in abusive use of force by the police to cause a tragic outcome, with eight fatalities, nearly ten thousand injuries, and three thousand arrests. The law enforcement unites were not held responsible for their actions.[14]

Erdoğan consistently portrayed the Gezi Park incident as a foreign conspiracy aimed at destabilizing his government. This narrative culminated in the trial and subsequent life imprisonment of Osman Kavala, a prominent Turkish businessman and philanthropist. He was accused of orchestrating and financially supporting the 2013 Gezi Park protests in an alleged attempt to forcibly overthrow the government. As detailed earlier, the European Court of Human Rights reviewed the Kavala case and ordered his release. However, Turkey's refusal to comply with this ECtHR verdict continues to strain relations between the Council of Europe and Turkey, highlighting significant concerns regarding adherence to international judicial decisions within the country.

The deterioration of democracy in Turkey intensified with the declaration and subsequent extension of the state of emergency, which was a response to the coup attempt on 15 July 2016. The state of emergency lasted for two years and marked a significant shift towards autocratization. This period saw the executive branch significantly empowered, effectively sidelining the legislative branch and circumventing traditional legal procedures and checks. This shift allowed President Erdoğan to govern increasingly through decrees, consolidating power in a presidential system while substantially undermining the democratic framework of the state. In the aftermath, the government led by Erdoğan pledged a democratization package to address both the demands of the protesters and the violations that had occurred.

Analysing various datasets reveals that Turkey achieved its peak democratization between 2004 and 2006. Subsequently, this upward trend plateaued until 2013, which marked the onset of democratic backsliding, intensifying markedly from 2016 onward. Rather than being explained solely by the decline of European Union transformative leverage or the responsiveness of the incumbent government, this trajectory can be better understood through

12 NTV, 'Gezi Olayları MGK'da', 26 June 2013, https://www.ntv.com.tr/turkiye/gezi-olaylari-mgkda,xKVaowHyJEix_byG9LwAYg.

13 Amnesty International, *Gezi Park Protests: Brutal Denial of the Right to Peaceful Assembly in Turkey* (London: Amnesty International, 2013), 9, https://www.amnesty.org/en/documents/EUR44/022/2013/en/.

14 Ibid., 35–39.

a Gramscian lens: the gradual formation of a counter-hegemonic project by the ruling party. As the Justice and Development Party consolidated its rule, it progressively constructed an alternative normative and institutional order that contested the liberal democratic norms previously championed during the Europeanization phase. While empirical studies on EU conditionality suggest that reforms tend to stall after the opening of accession negotiations, Turkey's experience stands out for the scale and depth of its democratic regression, culminating in the emergence of a hybrid regime.

The harsh measures undertaken in response to the failed coup of 2016, followed by the conversion of the parliamentary system to a presidential one, dismantling the core structures of checks and balances, inflicted severe damage on Turkey's democratic institutions. This structural transformation aligned with the AKP's counter-hegemonic agenda, which replaced constitutionalism and Europeanization with a more centralized, majoritarian vision of governance. As a result, Turkey transitioned into a hybrid regime, often characterized as an electoral autocracy,[15] moving further away from democratic standards while maintaining the formal trappings of multiparty elections.

The early 2000s witnessed the Justice and Development Party securing broad legitimacy through a combination of economic growth, expansive democratization reforms aligned with the European Union accession process, and a discourse of inclusivity aimed at various social groups. This period corresponded to a classical phase of hegemonic construction, where consent was manufactured not merely through electoral victories but through substantive socio-economic and political reforms.

However, by the mid-2010s, this hegemonic project entered a plateau phase. Economic stagnation, rising authoritarian tendencies, and an increasing reliance on Islamist-conservative values as the dominant societal framework signalled a shift from consent-based legitimacy towards coercive strategies of counter-hegemonic consolidation. Rather than sustaining broad-based legitimacy, the AKP progressively institutionalized a majoritarian conception of governance that marginalized pluralistic and democratic spaces.

The opposition's success in the 2019 local elections, where Ekrem İmamoğlu of CHP in Istanbul, Mansur Yavaş of CHP in Ankara, and Tunç Soyer of CHP in İzmir captured critical metropolitan municipalities, constituted a significant rupture in AKP's counter-hegemonic strategy. Having

15 Steven Levitsky, *Competitive Authoritarianism: Hybrid Regimes after the Cold War* (Cambridge: Cambridge University Press, 2010), 14–16.

controlled the major urban centres for over two decades, the electoral defeat triggered a crisis of legitimacy for the AKP. In response, the party escalated authoritarian survival[16] tactics, such as appointing state trustees to municipalities in the eastern provinces and unilaterally withdrawing from the Istanbul Convention without parliamentary consultation.[17] These actions revealed a deepening reliance on coercive state apparatuses over societal consent.

From a neo-Gramscian perspective, the AKP's post-2016 trajectory highlights the erosion of pluralism, the entrenchment of an overarching Islamist-conservative doctrine, and the instrumentalization of judicial and political institutions to suppress alternative discourses. The prolonged state of emergency and the adoption of the presidential system further insulated the ruling bloc from democratic contestation, undermining the very basis of the initial hegemony built through reform and economic performance.

### *The Prolonged State of Emergency*

A state of emergency, also referred to as a state of exception, is considered a sovereign power of the state. Departing from the principle that extraordinary circumstances require extraordinary solutions, this power is employed as a response to exceptional occurrences, with the primary aim of enabling a return to normality. Extra-normality is mostly associated with defence and security-related areas. The emergency power allows the state to deploy extrajudicial terms and to suspend certain human rights, such as declaring curfews or prohibiting gatherings, for a brief time period. Legislation is replaced by executive decrees, justified under the principle of safeguarding public welfare.

However, from a neo-Gramscian perspective, states of emergency are not neutral instruments but rather mechanisms through which ruling blocs attempt to preserve or reconstitute hegemony in times of crisis. Exceptional measures, while formally temporary, often serve to reconfigure the balance of power in favour of dominant interests, suspending pluralistic contestation under the guise of necessity. As such, the prolonged state of emergency in Turkey must be understood not only as a security response but as a strategic project to restructure civil and political life around the ruling party's evolving counter-hegemonic vision.

16 Oksan Bayulgen, Ekim Arbatli, and Sercan Canbolat, 'Elite Survival Strategies and Authoritarian Reversal in Turkey', *Polity* 50, no. 3 (2018): 333–65.

17 Bayar, 'Turkey's withdrawal from Istanbul Convention'.

The 1982 Turkish constitution deals with the state of emergency in articles 10, 15, 17, 18, 119–22, and 125. As stated under article 119, a state of emergency may be declared by the president of the Republic, regionally or nationwide, in the event of threats against national security, or in the event of a natural disaster, outbreak of dangerous epidemic diseases, or a dangerous economic crisis. The decision is promulgated in the official gazette and then submitted for the approval of the Turkish Grand National Assembly, which can reduce or extend the period or lift the state of emergency.

After the military coup of 12 September 1980, the first nationwide state of emergency was implemented since the 2016 coup attempt. After 1980, the first emergency regime was proclaimed by the cabinet led by Prime Minister Turgut Özal in 1987, as a response to the increase in terror activities. The emergency regime encompassed thirteen cities in eastern and south-eastern Anatolia and lasted until 1999, when the terrorist leader Abdullah Öcalan was captured. The state of emergency was first declared to cover Bingöl, Diyarbakır, Elazığ, Hakkari, Mardin, Siirt, Tunceli, and Van. Adıyaman, Bitlis, and Muş were added as neighbouring cities. Lastly, the region covered by the emergency was expanded to include Batman and Şırnak. This period of extrajudicial implementations still faced unenlightened allegations of civilian killings, exile, torture, and unsolved murders.[18]

Following the breakdown of the Kurdish opening process in Turkey, the events in Kobane occurred in 2014. Daesh had laid siege to the Syrian city Kobane, which is also known as Ayn'el-Arab. The city is heavily inhabited by Syrian Kurds, who resisted the Daesh attack. Turkey allowed those fleeing the conflict into the country, but did not allow Kurds to leave Turkey to provide the city with support against the terrorists. In line with this prevention policy, Turkish governors in south-eastern Anatolia declared curfews.

The state of emergency was declared on 20 July 2016, on the fifth day following the 15 July 2016 coup d'état attempt by the terrorist organization FETÖ, the Gülenist movement. The Turkish Grand National Assembly was on summer recess, yet it approved the emergency decision as soon as it was put for a vote after the government had consulted the National Security Council and had published the notice in the official gazette. The emergency rule was for three months and was subsequently prolonged for seven periods of three months each. It ended two years later, on 21 July 2018. The assessment of the seriousness of the conditions to decide upon prolongation is left to the given country's authorities, as stated in *Brannigan and McBride v. The*

18 BBC, 'Türkiye'de Olağanüstü Hâllerin Tarihi', 21 July 2016, https://www.bbc.com/turkce/haberler-turkiye-36852284.

*United Kingdom*, decided by the ECtHR in 1993.[19] The Turkish authorities justified the prolongations by the presence of FETÖ terrorist organization's members and their activities.[20]

On 21 July 2016 the secretary general of the COE and the secretary-general of the UN were notified that the post-coup measures may result in derogations.[21] According to the ECHR, (article 15) and the International Covenant on Civil and Political Rights (ICCPR, 1996, article 27), the derogation mechanism permits reducing the scope of the obligations created by international human rights instruments.[22] The core rights are not subjected to derogations, such as the right to life and the prohibition of torture. These rights are protected from derogation by article 15, para. 2, of the constitution, by article 15, para. 2, of the ECHR, and by article 4, para. 2, of the ICCPR.

The emergency regime relieves government officials and those meeting the duties as per the executive decrees from fulfilling particular international and national obligations that arise from international agreements and from their municipal laws. The very first decree stripped the executioners of this decree of their individual legal, administrative, financial, and penal responsibilities.[23] With a further decree the impunity was expanded to include those civilians who played roles in resisting against the coup attempt and against other events following the attempt.[24]

The separation of the three powers of the state, the executive, legislative, and the judiciary, is impeded by transferring some of them directly to the executive. The empowerment of the executive is the most significant due to the loss of political and legal control, which has the potential to lead the abandonment of the rule of law. This is particularly the case in countries, as in Turkey, where a single-party rule persists.

Under the emergency, Erdoğan used his authority to issue decrees, as endorsed by article 121 of the constitution. He published thirty-six emergency decrees during the emergency period of 2016–18. Under the decrees at least 125,678 civil servants (such as administrative staff, academics, teachers,

19 Venice Commission, 'Turkey: Opinion on Emergency Decree Laws Nos. 667–676 Adopted Following the Failed Coup of 15 July 2016', Opinion (865/2016) (Strasbourg: Council of Europe, 12 December 2016), article 43, https://www.venice.coe.int/webforms/documents/default.aspx?pdffile=CDL-ad(2016)037-e.

20 Ibid., article 42.

21 Ibid., articles 31–32.

22 Ibid., article 33.

23 T.C. Resmi Gazete, 'Olağanüstü Hal Kapsamında Alınan Tedbirlere İlişkin Kanun Hükmünde Kararname', KHK/667 § (2016), https://www.resmigazete.gov.tr/eskiler/2016/07/20160723-8.htm.

24 'Olağanüstü Hal Kapsaminda Bazı Düzenlemeler Yapılması Hakkında Kanun Hükmünde Kararname', KHK/696 § (2017), https://www.resmigazete.gov.tr/eskiler/2017/12/20171224-22.htm.

judges and prosecutors, actresses/actors, and regisseurs) were dismissed from public service, 270 students were discharged from universities, and 3,213 armed forces personnel were stripped of their ranks for being FETÖ members.[25] The dismissals were made public by attaching lists of names to the decrees as an appendix. The dismissed individuals lost their passports and gun licenses immediately. Moreover, 204 media outlets, such as newspapers, radio stations, television channels, publishers, journals, and news agencies were closed.[26] Besides media institutions, more than 3,750 legal persons were also closed, such as NGOs, federations, confederations, foundations, trade unions, military high schools, private health institutions, private education institutions, and private universities.[27] Corporate activities of banks, companies, and commercial enterprises were taken over.[28] During the state of emergency, eighty-six trustees were appointed to oust eighty-six municipalities.[29] Legislative changes were assumed concerning security, intelligence, and communications. A new criterion was set for entering into public service, which was to pass a security investigation prior to the assumption of the duty. The state of emergency decrees also introduced new measures concerning social security and social rights such as disciplinary punishments for periods left out of social security coverage, instatement, and the roles of watchmen (*bekçi*), village governors (*muhtar*), etc., with Decrees 674, 676, 680, 681, 690, 694, 696, 678, and 696.

The constitutionality of the aforementioned decrees is still subject to debates. The main opposition, the Republican Peoples Party (CHP), asked the Constitutional Court in 2016 to cancel the decrees. The CHP argued that some of the decrees were not related to the struggle against FETÖ. The court rejected the request, stating that it was not responsible for reviewing the validity of decrees. This ruling was issued despite a decision of the Constitutional Court from 1992 that cancelled a number of decrees by

25 Gizem Sade, '15 Temmuz Darbe Girişimi Sonrasında Kaç Kişi Görevinden Ihraç Edildi, Kaç Kişi Tutuklandı?', *EuroNews*, 15 July 2020, https://tr.euronews.com/2020/07/15/verilerle-15-temmuz-sonras-ve-ohal-sureci.

26 Ibid.

27 Ali Yıldız, 'Did Turkey's Recent Emergency Decrees Derogate from the Absolute Rights?', *Verfassungsblog*, 28 September 2019, https://verfassungsblog.de/did-turkeys-recent-emergency-decrees-derogate-from-the-absolute-rights/.

28 İsmet Akça et al., *When the State of Emergency Becomes the Norm: The Impact of Executive Decrees on Turkish Legislation* (Heinrich Böll Stiftung, 2018), 111, https://tr.boell.org/sites/default/files/ohal_rapor_ing.final_version.pdf.

29 Zeynep Altıok, 'OHAL Bilançosu Hak Ihlalleri Raporu' (Ankara: CHP, 12 January 2018), https://content.chp.org.tr/file/33743.pdf.

stating that 'decrees must only contain matters that relate to the essence of the emergency conditions'.[30]

The 2017 constitutional referendum was also held during state of emergency conditions. Although the Turkish constitution does not forbid amending the constitution during a state of emergency, it is politically very complicated.[31] In particular, due to the severe suppression of the media and the large number of detentions, the emergency offered the potential to prohibit free expressions and discussions that form public opinion which lead to an 'unlevel playing field for the two sides of the campaigns and undermined safeguards for the integrity of the election'.[32] The European Commission stated in its 2018 Turkey Progress Report that 'the amendments were assessed by the Venice Commission as lacking sufficient checks and balances as well as endangering the separation of powers between the executive and the judiciary'.[33]

The reaction of the EU concerning the post-coup measures in Turkey was to call on the Turkish authorities to observe the highest human rights standards possible and to question the measures taken as to their necessity and proportionality. Additionally, the Union emphasized the suspension of key procedural rights under the state of emergency, especially in regards to the level of transparency that should be established when examining allegations of wrongdoing by civil servants to ensure a healthy due process. The European Commission underlined the significance of respect for the separation of powers since individual criminal responsibility should be determined in the light of an independent judiciary and the right of the accused to a fair trial. Another important criticism was about the suppression of human rights defenders, opposition voices, and Kurds by exploiting the post-coup measures that led to serious human rights violations such as the ill-treatment or torture of detainees.

The Commission criticized the further extension of the pre-trial detention period to thirty days without access to a judge, a decision contrary to ECtHR case law. Moreover, the number of cases submitted by Turkish citizens against the Turkish state demonstrated a significant increase in 2017, reaching approximately 30,000 cases, in which violations occurred as

30 Onur Erem, 'OHAL Sona Erdi: İki Yıllık Sürecin Bilançosu', *BBC*, 19 July 2018, https://www.bbc.com/turkce/haberler-turkiye-44799489.

31 The constitutional amendments during state of emergency and martial law are prohibited in some countries, such as Estonia, Lithuania, Portugal, Romania, Spain, and Ukraine.

32 European Commission, 'Turkey 2018 Progress Report', 17 April 2018, 4, https://www.ab.gov.tr/siteimages/kapbtablolar/20180417-turkey-report.pdf.

33 Ibid., 4.

a result of the implementation of the state of emergency. The court declared inadmissibility on the grounds of non-exhaustion of domestic remedies. The establishment of the Inquiry Committee in January 2017 prevented complainants from completing their domestic trajectory until the final verdict. The majority of the cases seen by the court concerned the right to fair trial, liberty and security, freedom of expression, freedom of assembly and association, as well as the length of the proceedings.[34]

During the post-coup struggle against the Gülenist movement, Turkey had reached out to a number of EU member states with particular demands, such as for the closure of schools and other institutions established by FETÖ. The EU was already sceptical of those schools owing to their efforts for the re-Islamization of Turkey.[35] The schools were then seized by the Turkish government.[36]

The broadness and collective nature of the measures that concerned the Union involved the vagueness of the criteria used to confirm membership in FETÖ as well as the opaqueness surrounding the evidence and the procedures that were followed. The decrees taken under the state of emergency also came under the scrutiny of the Commission when the main opposition party CHP appealed them to the Constitutional Court as decrees not relevant to the post-coup measures. The 2016 Turkey Progress Report denoted that both bipartite and tripartite social dialogue was weak in the country and that it had further weakened under the post-coup conditions. The decrees were criticized in the progress report, which noted that the parliament's role in the law-making process was limited significantly, so that 'the parliamentary oversight of the executive remained weak'.[37] The Commission stated that the prosecutions of journalists, writers, and social media users for insulting the president of the Republic or defamation was creating a hostile environment for freedom of expression, which was not in line with the emerging European consensus. The establishment by decree of a new body with wide powers to enforce restrictions on freedom

34 European Commission, 'Turkey: Supporting Fundamental Rights in Turkey', Instrument for Pre-Accession Assistance (IPA II) 2014–20, 4, accessed 1 September 2023, https://neighbourhood-enlargement.ec.europa.eu/document/download/8f5bf356-1fed-4c95-8110-ccd1436f3c2c_en?filename=ad_fr.pdf.

35 Mara Bizzotto, 'Consolidation of the Islamic Gülen Movement within the EU', European Parliament, Parliamentary Question, 22 September 2011, https://www.europarl.europa.eu/doceo/document/E-7-2011-008665_EN.html.

36 Türkiye Maarif Vakfı, 'FETÖ'nün Yurt Dışındaki 218 Okulu Maarif Vakfı'nda', 17 July 2019, https://turkiyemaarif.org/news/fetonun-yurt-disindaki-218-okulu-maarif-vakfinda.

37 European Commission, 'Turkey 2016 Progress Report', 11 September 2016, 10, https://www.ab.gov.tr/files/pub/2016_progress_report_en.pdf..

of communications – the Information and Communications Technologies Authority (Bilgi Teknolojileri ve İletişim Kurumu, BTK) – also attracted the attention of the EU. Additionally, it was indicated that the overall deteriorating situation harmed the business environment. Finally, the appointing of trustees to the municipalities in eastern and south-eastern Anatolia was held under the lens by the Commission.

During the 728 days of the state of emergency in Turkey, thirty-two presidential decrees were published. Seventy newspapers, twenty magazines, thirty publishing and distribution companies, thirty-three television channels, and thirty-four radio stations were shut down or faced closure orders. Approximately 125,800 people were dismissed from public service. Out of the initial 1,128 academics who signed the declaration known as 'Academics for Peace' ('Barış için Akademisyenler'), 148 faced legal proceedings. Additionally, 7,080 individuals were dismissed from universities. In addition to the closure of numerous schools allegedly linked to FETÖ or the Gülenist movement, sixty-four private course centres, 847 student dormitories, forty-seven private healthcare centres, fifteen foundation universities, and 145 foundations were also shut down.[38]

The extensive use of presidential decrees during the prolonged state of emergency, alongside mass dismissals, media closures, and systematic suppression of dissenting academic voices, demonstrates how emergency governance became an instrument for reshaping the political field in Turkey. In Gramscian terms, the AKP, faced with the erosion of its initial consent-based hegemony rooted in democratic reform and economic performance, resorted increasingly to coercive mechanisms to secure its continued dominance. The state of emergency thus functioned not merely as a response to security threats but as a strategic tool in the party's counter-hegemonic project. It dismantled pluralistic spaces, restructured civil society, and insulated the ruling bloc from democratic contestation. By concentrating power through extraordinary legal measures, the AKP aimed to rebuild a new form of legitimacy based on control rather than consensus, accelerating the erosion of human rights protections that once underpinned Turkey's democratization trajectory.

### *The Presidential System and the Transformation of Executive Power*

During the state of emergency, one significant development was the transition to the 'Turkish type' presidential system as a result of a referendum

38 Zehra Yıldız, '7 Kez Uzatıldı, 2 Yıl Sürdü: OHAL'in Bilançosu', *EuroNews*, 18 July 2018, https://tr.euronews.com/2018/07/18/7-kez-uzatildi-2-yil-surdu-ohal-in-bilancosu.

held on 16 April 2017. The transition to the presidential system in Turkey cannot be understood merely as a structural reorganization of political institutions. It must be situated within a broader neo-Gramscian framework of hegemonic transformation. From this perspective, the constitutional changes of 2017 represent a deliberate counter-hegemonic strategy aimed at consolidating executive power, reshaping political society, and neutralizing mechanisms of horizontal accountability. In neo-Gramscian terms, the presidential system serves as an institutional tool for establishing a new historic bloc, one that fuses state power with dominant social forces under the leadership of the executive. Rather than reinforcing the classical liberal principle of separation of powers, the reforms eroded parliamentary autonomy, expanded executive prerogatives, and recalibrated the balance of power to favour the ruling bloc's continued dominance. This shift reflected not only a reconfiguration of political authority but also a fundamental rearticulation of the societal consensus underpinning Turkey's political order, moving it further away from the European constitutionalist tradition towards a form of competitive authoritarianism legitimized through electoral mechanisms.

The state of emergency declared following the 15 July 2016 coup attempt and the executive decrees issued until the referendum of 2017 significantly contributed to the transformation process of the government system. The fact that only four of these state of emergency decrees was debated and enacted into law by the Turkish Grand National Assembly, while the rest were implemented without being subjected to the oversight of the legislative body or the Constitutional Court, demonstrates that these decrees operated outside the bounds of political and judicial scrutiny.[39]

The AKP government leveraged longstanding criticisms of the 1982 constitution to advocate for constitutional amendments introducing a presidential system, framing the reforms as a means to liberate the elected legislature and executive from the influence of military, bureaucratic, and judicial elites. Moreover, the AKP government criticized the pre-AKP governments often that they were coalitions and thus they were politically instable. Erdoğan initially portrayed the proposed amendments as a step towards democratization, political stability, promising greater political participation, an improved economy, political stability, and a stronger rule of law. However, the presidential system ultimately pushed economy

39 İsmet Akça et al., *Olağanlaşan OHAL: Khk'larin Yasal Mevzuat Üzerindeki Etkileri* (Heinrich Böll Stiftung, 2018), https://tr.boell.org/tr/2018/01/10/olaganlasan-ohal-khklarin-yasal-mevzuat-uezerindeki-etkileri.

into a worse condition[40] and introduced reinforced authoritarian elements aligning the political system with the conservative, moral, and religious values of the majority, contrasting it with previous constitutions, which Erdoğan criticized as Western imports disconnected from local traditions.

The transition from the parliamentarian system to the 'Turkish-style' presidential system,[41] as the AKP elites call it, took place by a referendum on 16 April 2017. As a result, Erdoğan was swept into power with the approval of 57.41 per cent of the votes. Although presidential systems around the world are based on the principle of separation of powers, in the Turkish-style presidential system the president directly appoints the vice presidents and ministers without requiring parliamentary approval, which has inevitably corroded the autonomy and legislative authority of the parliament. These changes caused unavoidable corrosion of the powers of the parliament.

The duties and powers of the parliament concerning budgetary functions were also limited to a great extent. In the event of a conflict between the president and the parliament over the budget and the parliament's failure to approve the budget, the president has been granted the authority to bypass the parliament. With the constitutional amendments enacted, the parliament lost two of its principal powers and was been reduced to an institution with the authority to enact, amend, and repeal laws.

The presidential system does not dissociate the president from their political party, as is required by the constitution (article 18).[42] With the constitutional amendment voted in the referendum, the provision in article 101 of the constitution was removed, which stated that '[i]f elected president, their affiliation with any political party shall be severed', thereby paving the way for a partisan presidency. As a result, Erdoğan kept his position as the leader of the AKP. Under such conditions, it is unrealistic to expect that an elected president will assume a nonpartisan and impartial identity that transcends political parties. According to the new system, the president who is also the leader of a political party and thus has the ability to determine the parliamentary candidates of their party. In other words, the president can exercise significant influence in shaping a substantial portion of the legislative body. Therefore, the president has the power to dominate the

40 T24, 'Cumhurbaşkanı, "Bu Kardeşinize Yetkiyi Verin, Şunla Bunla Nasıl Uğraşılır Göreceksiniz" Demişti; TL, 50 Günde Yüzde 25 Değer Kaybetti', Ağustos 2018, https://t24.com.tr/haber/cumhurbaskani-bu-kardesinize-yetkiyi-verin-sunla-bunla-nasil-ugrasilir-goreceksiniz-demisti-tl-50-gunde-yuzde-25-deger-kaybetti,675523.

41 Türey Köse, '"Türk Tipi Başkanlık" TBMM Genel Kurulu'nda', *BBC Türkçe*, 8 January 2017, https://www.bbc.com/turkce/haberler-turkiye-38529200.

42 Law no. 6771.

parliament, which limits the representative function of the parliament to transfer the sovereignty from the subjects of the nation to the parliament. It also contradicts the principle of separation of powers.

The constitutional amendments also expanded the number of parliamentarians from 550 to 600, yet simultaneously raised procedural thresholds that weakened the legislature's effectiveness. At least 200 members must now be present for proposals to be debated, and a simple majority of 151 votes is required to pass a law. However, if the president vetoes a law, the parliament must secure an absolute majority with 301 votes to override it, as opposed to the previous system, where a simple re-signature of the proposing deputies sufficed. This transformation redefined the presidential veto from a procedural delay into a substantive legislative hurdle.

Beyond the veto mechanism, the president held extensive decree powers, especially during states of emergency, further concentrating authority in the executive branch. The cumulative effect of these constitutional revisions reflects a paradigmatic shift: from a parliamentary system with horizontal accountability[43] towards a model of 'executive aggrandizement'.[44] This process, often associated with theories of authoritarian constitutionalism,[45] illustrates how formal legal mechanisms are utilized not to enhance democratic governance, but to systematically dismantle checks and balances under the veneer of constitutional change.

Presidential decrees have also supplanted the legislative decrees formerly issued by the Council of Ministers, significantly reducing judicial oversight. Unlike their predecessors, presidential decrees cannot be contested before the Council of State, even by individuals adversely affected by their provisions, thereby consolidating executive authority and limiting avenues for judicial review. Furthermore, oversight mechanisms traditionally available to the parliament were weakened. The oral inquiry power, for example, was eliminated and replaced by a written inquiry, further restricting the legislative branch's ability to hold the executive accountable. These structural changes illustrate a pronounced shift in power dynamics, consolidating executive dominance at the expense of legislative autonomy and judicial scrutiny.

The president wielded extensive authority over state institutions, consolidating significant control across various domains. The president held

43 Guillermo A. O'Donnell, 'Horizontal Accountability in New Democracies', *Journal of Democracy* 9, no. 3 (1998): 112–26.

44 Nancy Bermeo, 'On Democratic Backsliding', *Journal of Democracy* 27, no. 1 (2016): 5–19, at 6, 10–13.

45 Mark Tushnet, 'Authoritarian Constitutionalism', *Cornell Law Review* 100 (2014): 391–462.

exclusive power to appoint all ministers and senior civil servants within every governmental department. Furthermore, the president oversaw all central agencies that exercise direct control over key sectors, including the bureaucracy, the military, the economy, the media, and civil society. This concentration of power significantly enhanced the executive's influence over institutional structures and public life.

Additionally, local government was also subjected to the personalization and centralization of power, a trend that predated the transition to the presidential system. This process intensified following the 2016 coup attempt, when a state of emergency decree granted the government authority to replace elected mayors, particularly in the Kurdish-dominated eastern/south-eastern regions, with trustees appointed by the minister of the interior. By the time local elections were held in March 2019, a total of ninety-five mayors had been removed from office, further eroding local democratic governance.

The judiciary has also been affected by the concentrated power of the president. The president appoints central judicial councils, the Council of Judges and Prosecutors (Hakimler Savcılar Kurulu, HSK). The president appoints the majority of the members to these councils. The HSK has thirteen members (which was twenty-two in the parliamentary system) and the president appoints six of the members. The remaining seven members are appointed by the parliament. HSK has the power to appoint, promote, investigate, or penalize judges and prosecutors. This indicated the president's direct control over the entire judiciary. Out of the fifteen members of the Constitutional Court, the president appoints twelve and the parliament appoints three. Another judicial council, the Radio and Television Supreme Council (Radyo ve Televizyon Üst Kurulu, RTÜK), is also significant. With the regulation introduced under article 17 of Emergency Decree Law no. 680, RTÜK, has been granted the authority to suspend broadcasts that violate its bans and regulations for a day. In cases of repeated violations, the suspension may extend up to five days for a second offense, fifteen days for a third, and may ultimately result in the revocation of the broadcast license upon a fourth violation.[46] The fact that this authority can be exercised beyond the state of emergency represents a severe blow to press freedom and constitutes a disproportionate restriction on the right to access information.

Erdoğan became the first Turkish president to publicly dismiss a ruling of the Turkish Constitutional Court. His ally, the leader of the Nationalist Movement Party (Milliyetçi Hareket Partisi, MHP), Devlet Bahçeli, called

46 Akça et al., Olağanlaşan OHAL.

for the closure of the Constitutional Court.[47] The non-implementation of the ECtHR rulings can also be seen in this framework. Once the president began to speak out on judicial decisions, judges and prosecutors became hesitant to give independent decisions.

The consolidation of presidential authority, as institutionalized through the constitutional reforms, has fundamentally altered the political structure in Turkey by embedding executive dominance within the state's fabric. Rather than ensuring impartial governance, the system has facilitated the emergence of a new hegemonic project, wherein the presidency operates not as a neutral arbiter but as the central node of a reconfigured historic bloc. This transformation has systematically weakened democratic institutions and eroded the mechanisms of accountability essential for the protection of human rights. In neo-Gramscian terms, the presidential system thus marks the entrenchment of a counter-hegemonic order that prioritizes the reproduction of executive power over the sustenance of pluralism, legality, and democratic contestation.

## The Judiciary and the Rule of Law

*I swear upon my honour and integrity, before the great Turkish nation, to safeguard the existence and independence of the state, the indivisible integrity of the country and the nation, and the absolute sovereignty of the nation; to remain loyal to the supremacy of law, to the democratic and secular republic, and to Atatürk's principles and reforms; not to deviate from the ideal according to which everyone is entitled to enjoy human rights and fundamental freedoms under the notion of peace and prosperity in society, national solidarity and justice, and loyalty to the constitution.*

– The oath that members of the Turkish Grand National Assembly take when assuming office.[48]

The oath taken by members of the Turkish parliament, as stipulated in article 81 of the Turkish constitution, encapsulates the profound commitment to uphold the core tenets of the nation's governance and democratic integrity. This oath is not merely a formality but a solemn vow to preserve

47 EuroNews, 'Bahçeli: Anayasa Mahkemesi Ya Kapatılmalı Ya Da Yeniden Yapılandırılmalı', 14 November 2023, https://tr.euronews.com/2023/11/14/bahceli-anayasa-mahkemesi-ya-kapatilmali-ya-da-yeniden-yapilandirilmali.

48 Republic of Turkey, 'The Constitution of the Turkish Republic (November 7, 1982)', article 81.

the existence and independence of the state, and the indivisible integrity of the country and its people. Central to this pledge is the commitment to the supremacy of law, which underpins the principle of the rule of law. This principle is crucial as it ensures that all members of society, including those in positions of power, are equally subject to the law and that their actions are governed by law. The emphasis on adherence to a democratic and secular republic, alongside Atatürk's principles and reforms, highlights the legislative dedication to a governance structure that balances traditional values with progressive reforms. The oath also reflects a dedication to human rights and fundamental freedoms, aligning with universal democratic values that promote peace, prosperity, national solidarity, and justice. Through this oath, Turkish legislators affirm their unwavering commitment to these ideals, recognizing that the judiciary's role is not only to interpret and apply the law but also to act as a guardian of these constitutional principles, ensuring that the governance remains within the ambit of the law, thus securing the democratic fabric of the nation. This reinforces the judiciary's critical role in maintaining the rule of law, which is indispensable for the stability and continuity of democracy in Turkey.

The Council of Europe (COE) delineates its mission as promoting democracy, human rights, and the rule of law throughout Europe and beyond. By setting common standards and policies, the COE plays a pivotal role in shaping the rule of law, while also identifying and addressing potential threats to its integrity. This emphasis on the rule of law underlines the COE's commitment to establishing a consistent and harmonized approach across member states, ensuring that the principles of fairness, equality, and justice are upheld. Through its efforts, the COE contributes significantly to the stabilization and enhancement of democratic governance, reinforcing the fundamental principles that support civil society and governmental accountability across the continent.

The rule of law, conceptually, embodies a fundamental principle of governance whereby all individuals, entities, and institutions, both public and private, including the state, are subject to laws that are transparently promulgated, uniformly enforced, and impartially adjudicated in accordance with international human rights norms and standards. This principle mandates adherence to several core tenets: the supremacy of law, equality before the law, accountability under the law, fairness in the application of the law, the separation of powers, inclusivity in decision-making, legal certainty, the avoidance of arbitrariness, and both procedural and legal transparency. These components collectively ensure that the rule of law not only upholds justice but also fortifies the mechanisms of democracy and governance.

A critical examination of Turkey's adherence to the rule of law and judicial standards reveals significant concerns, stagnation, and even backsliding in the judiciary. Despite the announcement of successive judicial reform packages, fundamental deficiencies in judicial functioning persist unaddressed. From a neo-Gramscian perspective, following Cox's conceptualization of institutions as integral components of hegemonic orders, the subordination of the judiciary in Turkey reflects a deliberate attempt to reshape the state apparatus to consolidate executive hegemony. Rather than serving as an autonomous arena for mediating power and safeguarding rights, the judiciary increasingly functions as part of a hegemonic apparatus designed to reproduce and stabilize the prevailing power configuration. Consequently, the continuous pressures exerted by the executive not only undermine the quality and impartiality of judicial proceedings but also foreclose the possibilities for democratic contestation and the maintenance of a genuine rule of law.

The influence of politics over the Turkish judicial environment and thus the loss of is independence and impartiality are observable. For example, the selection processes of the Council of Judges and Prosecutors (Hakimler Savcılar Kurulu, HSK) demonstrates the influence of the executive and takes its toll on the autonomy of the judiciary. Additionally, the diminishing respect for fundamental rights in entire judicial proceedings stresses the importance of the principles of individual criminal responsibility and legal certainty, as well as the rights to a fair trial and defence.

There are also systemic issues affecting the legislative functions of the Turkish parliament, which diluted the legislature's role in governance as a result of the presidential system. This dilution manifests in limited oversight capabilities and a lack of necessary tools for holding the government accountable, thereby exacerbating the erosion of democratic functions and the rule of law.

Furthermore, Turkey's rule of law extends to its actions on the international stage, notably its reluctance to implement decisions by the European Court of Human Rights (ECtHR). This reluctance signals a troubling disregard for international judicial mechanisms and raises concerns about Turkey's commitment to upholding the rule of law and human rights obligations as stipulated in its international commitments.

In the broader context of the rule of law, Turkey's disregard extends beyond international mechanisms to its own constitutional framework. Notably, the government under the Justice and Development Party (AKP) had repeatedly neglected decisions of the Turkish Constitutional Court. This was starkly highlighted in 2016 when President Erdoğan openly declared his lack of respect for the Constitutional Court's verdicts.[49] This disregard was further compounded by comments from the government's ally, the leader of the ultra-nationalist Nationalist Movement Party (Milliyetçi Hareket Partisi, MHP), Devlet Bahçeli, who called for the closure or restructuring of the Constitutional Court[50] following another of its decisions.[51] Such actions underscore a troubling trend of undermining judicial independence and highlight a broader erosion of the rule of law within Turkey, raising serious concerns about its commitment to upholding not only international human rights obligations but also its own constitutional mandates.

In summary, the current state of the rule of law in Turkey is marked by systemic challenges and a significant need for profound judicial reforms. From a neo-Gramscian perspective, the erosion of judicial independence reflects not merely institutional decay but an active restructuring of the judiciary to sustain a new hegemonic order centred around executive dominance. The subordination of legal norms to political expediency undermines the judiciary's traditional role as a counterbalance to power, transforming it into a mechanism of passive consent rather than active contestation.

Aligning the judiciary with European standards remains crucial not only for advancing Turkey's EU accession aspirations but also for restoring the integrity of democratic institutions and safeguarding principles of justice and equity. However, the government's persistent disregard for decisions made by the Constitutional Court, most notably in the case of Can Atalay, whose constitutional rights to liberty and political participation were twice upheld yet effectively ignored, illustrates how judicial conflict has become a site of hegemonic struggle. As the Court of Cassation openly defies the Constitutional Court's rulings, it exposes the deeper transformation of the judiciary from an independent arbiter into a fractured apparatus caught within competing political and hegemonic projects. This discord underscores that the crisis of the rule of law in Turkey today is not an anomaly but a symptom of a broader hegemonic reconfiguration.

### *The EU Criteria and the Internal Dynamics of the Rule of Law in Turkey*

The Copenhagen criteria form a cornerstone of the European Union's enlargement policy, setting four essential conditions that countries must

49 BBC, 'Erdoğan: AYM'nin Kararına Saygı Duymuyorum', 28 February 2016, https://www.bbc.com/turkce/haberler/2016/02/160228_erdogan_dundar_aym.

50 EuroNews, 'Bahçeli: Anayasa Mahkemesi Ya Kapatılmalı Ya Da Yeniden Yapılandırılmalı'.

51 BBC, 'Erdoğan'dan Yargıtay'ın AYM kararıyla ilgili açıklama: "Bu tartışmada taraf değil hakem konumundayız"', 10 November 2023, https://www.bbc.com/turkce/articles/cjrp8xgr79lo.

meet to qualify for EU membership. Established by the European Council in Copenhagen in 1993 and further elaborated in 1995 by the European Council in Madrid, these criteria underscore the paramount importance of stable institutions that guarantee not only democracy and human rights but also the rule of law. From a neo-Gramscian perspective, the rule of law functions as a key element of the broader hegemonic project that the EU seeks to extend, stabilizing liberal democratic norms across candidate countries as part of consolidating a normative order.

The rule of law is fundamental, requiring prospective members to demonstrate a robust judicial system that upholds laws consistently and impartially, ensuring fairness and justice for all individuals. This includes the protection of minorities and the maintenance of legal standards aligned with EU norms. However, beyond formal compliance, neo-Gramscian theory emphasizes that the deeper transformation sought through these criteria involves the internalization of liberal-democratic legal consciousness, not merely the adoption of technical reforms. Moreover, the criteria mandate a functioning market economy and the capacity to contend with the competitive pressures and market dynamics within the EU, tying legal reforms to economic liberalization as mutually reinforcing aspects of hegemonic integration. The comprehensive adherence to these criteria ensures that new members are prepared for the responsibilities and benefits of the EU, aligning with its political, economic, and monetary union aims.

When Erdoğan's Justice and Development Party (AKP) assumed power in 2002, it embarked on a series of ambitious reforms aimed at meeting the European Union's Copenhagen criteria for accession. This era was characterized by accelerated reforms across various sectors, with significant emphasis on judicial reforms to align Turkey more closely with EU standards. The parliament enacted comprehensive reforms of the Civil and Penal Codes, which not only harmonized Turkish laws with the EU *acquis* but also recognized the supremacy of the European Court of Human Rights (ECtHR) over domestic courts.

The EU's *acquis communautaire* provides a comprehensive legal framework that compels candidate countries to implement judicial reforms, particularly those enhancing judicial independence. These reforms aimed to reduce the executive's influence over the judiciary, highlighted by the 2010 and 2017 constitutional referendums that focused on revising the judiciary's structure thereby minimizing political control over the judiciary as exercised mostly through judicial councils, such as the High Council of Judges and Prosecutors (Hakimler Savcılar Yüksek Kurulu, HSYK).

A pressing concern for the European Union has been the coexistence of military and civilian authority within Turkey, a situation deemed incompatible with the healthy functioning of a democracy. Historically, Turkish democracy has experienced significant disruptions when military interventions overthrew democratically elected governments, notably during the coup d'états in 1960, 1970, and 1980. These episodes not only led to the execution of elected leaders and widespread human rights abuses, including torture and cruel, inhuman treatment, but also the systematic dismantling of democratic governance. Therefore, the democratization initiatives commencing in 1999 prioritized the diminution of the military influence in politics. This adjustment was not only a stipulation of the EU but also a domestic imperative, reflecting a broader consensus on the need to realign the military's role to ensure the consolidation of democratic institutions.

In order to reduce the role of the army within politics, initially, the number of civilians in the National Security Council (Milli Güvenlik Kurulu, MGK) were increased. The MGK is one of the outcomes of the 1960 coup d'état. It was established pursuant to article 111 of the 1961 constitution.[52] The MGK was preserved under article 118 of the 1982 constitution.[53] By the amendment of the constitution on 3 October 2001, the structure of the MGK was altered. The deputy prime ministers and the minister of justice were included as members of the Council. The Council's meeting frequency was changed from once a month to once every two months. The decisions of the MGK were formerly considered as the priority of the government. By the 2001 amendments, the MGK decisions gained a recommended status. Lastly, the chief of general staff could propose extraordinary meetings of the MGK, which was removed by the amendment.[54]

State Security Courts (Devlet Güvenlik Mahkemesi, DGM) were special courts established by Law no. 2845, 'On the Establishment and Trial Procedures of State Security Courts', which was enacted on 16 June 1983, during the period when the military junta was in power. The involvement of military judges in the DGMs, which adjudicated civilian cases, was deemed a violation of the ECHR, due to the denial of the right to have cases heard by an independent and impartial tribunal. This view was substantiated

52 It was established by Law no. 129 on 11 December 1962.

53 After the 1980 coup d'état a new constitution was adopted and the MGK was then established under Law no. 2945.

54 *T.C. Milli Güvenlik Kurulu Genel Sekreterliği*, 'Milli Güvenlik Kurulu ve Milli Güvenlik Kurulu Genel Sekreterliği Hakkında Genel Bilgi', 2018, https://www.mgk.gov.tr/index.php/kurumsal/hakkimizda.

by the ECtHR, which issued rulings against Turkey in 1998 and 1999, citing breaches of fair trial principles.[55] In a move towards alignment with European judicial standards, Turkey excised military judges from these courts in 1999 and completely dissolved the DGMs by 2004. This period also witnessed significant judicial reforms, including the establishment of the Justice Academy in 2003, the introduction of Heavy Felony Courts that same year, and the enactment of a new Penal Code and Criminal Procedures Code in 2004 and 2005, respectively, further solidifying the reform trajectory in the judicial domain.[56]

Further measures were implemented as part of the eighth harmonization package, adopted on 14 July 2004, aimed at curtailing the military's influence in civilian politics. This package specifically revoked the authority of the general staff to appoint members to the Higher Education Council (Yüksek Öğrenim Kurulu, YÖK).[57] The amendment of article 160 of the constitution in 2004 introduced auditing of the military expenditure for enhanced transparency, which led to the passing of Law no. 6085 on Turkish Court of Accounts (Sayıştay Yasası) on 3 December 2010. Until 2010, the decisions of the Supreme Military Council (Yüksek Askeri Şura, YAŞ) were not subject to judicial review, which was amended so that decisions over discharging staff were subject to judicial review.[58]

Apart from those reforms devised to reduce the role of the military in civil politics, a significant amendment on 7 May 2004 to article 90 of Turkey's 1982 constitution ensured the supremacy of international agreements, particularly European legislation, over domestic law.[59] The zenith of these judicial reforms came in 2009 with the adoption of a new Judicial Reform Strategy by the Ministry of Justice, which outlined necessary changes to meet EU criteria for judicial independence.[60]

During the adoption of harmonization packages, between 2002 and 2005, that concern mostly the fulfilment of the political criteria, several legal reforms were enacted. The Law on the Establishment, Duties, and

55 See ECtHR, *Abdullah Altun v. Turkey*, no. 24561/94, 19 January 2007.

56 Hürriyet, 'DGM Yerine Ağır Ceza', 12 May 2004, https://www.hurriyet.com.tr/gundem/dgm-yerine-agir-ceza-38603002.

57 Secretariat General for EU Affairs, 'Political Reforms in Turkey' (Ankara, 2007), https://www.ab.gov.tr/files/pub/prt.pdf.

58 NTV, 'YAŞ Kararlarına Yargı Yolu Açılıyor', 9 April 2010, https://www.ntv.com.tr/turkiye/yas-kararlarina-yargi-yolu-aciliyor,IRIrqxd5PU6EOO10WFLhDQ.

59 Türk Anayasa Hukuku Sitesi, 'Türkiye Cumhuriyeti Anayasasının Bazı Maddelerinin Değiştirilmesi Hakkında Kanun', 7 May 2004, md. 7, https://www.anayasa.gen.tr/5170sk.htm.

60 Adalet Bakanlığı, 'Yargı Reformu Stratejisi, 2009', 2009, https://sgb.adalet.gov.tr/Resimler/SayfaDokuman/23122019163043Yargi-Reformu-Stratejisi.pdf.

Trial Procedures of Juvenile Courts was revised to mandate the creation of juvenile courts in districts with populations exceeding 100,000 within metropolitan areas. This law reflects Turkey's commitment to tailoring its judicial processes to better serve vulnerable populations, such as juveniles. Moreover, the Prime Minister's Office issued directives to ensure gender equality in public service recruitment, emphasizing adherence to constitutional provisions and international commitments.

Significant adjustments were made to broadcasting regulations, allowing for programmes in languages and dialects traditionally used by Turkish citizens, thus broadening media freedom and cultural expression. This change was part of a broader reform encapsulated in the new Press Law, which came into force in June 2004, enhancing freedom of the press in line with European human rights standards.

The 2010 constitutional referendum was particularly transformative. It reformed the Constitutional Court by granting Turkish citizens the right to make individual applications to the court if they believed that government decisions, laws, or their implementation infringed upon their basic rights and freedoms.[61] This amendment significantly enhanced the court's role as a veto player against the executive branch. These reforms from 1999 to around 2013 and 2014 illustrate the profound impact of EU policy conditionality on promoting judicial independence in Turkey, with the EU's evaluations and recommendations in its progress reports and other documents from the Council of Europe serving as key reference points. The Commission acknowledged the progress made in fulfilling the significant requirements related to the judiciary and fundamental rights.[62] The Commission called Turkey to make more efforts in improvement of the protection of the personal data and military justice.

In Turkey, four fundamental legal reforms have been enacted as part of the alignment process with the European Union, commonly referred to as 'judicial packages'. A judicial package is legislation that changes a state's fundamental legal statutes in order to complete the harmonization process with European Union norms in the judicial area. The four fundamental legal reforms consist of three laws and one decree having the force of law, from 2011 to 2013.

61 T.C. Anayasa Mahkemesi, 'Bireysel Başvuru', accessed 7 November 2023, https://www.anayasa.gov.tr/tr/mahkeme/gorev-ve-yetkileri/bireysel-basvuru/.

62 European Commission, 'Turkey 2014 Progress Report', 8 October 2014), 3, https://www.ab.gov.tr/files/IlerlemeRaporlari/2014_progress_report.pdf.

The first judicial package,[63] which was officially entitled 'Law on Amendments to Certain Laws for the Acceleration of Judicial Services', was adopted on 31 March 2011 and consisted of seventeen laws. As stated in the preamble of the law, this package aimed to 'accelerate state services and justice, ensuring their swift, efficient, and economical execution, reduce the workload of the courts, and prevent the loss of time and effort in judicial activities'.

The second judicial package[64] was entitled 'Decree-Law on the Amendment and Adoption of the Decree-Law on the Organization and Duties of the Ministry of Justice, and on Amending Certain Laws and Decree-Laws' and was adopted 'to contribute to the more effective and efficient administration of justice services'. It consisted of forty-four articles, but numerous of these articles of this decree-law were annulled by the Constitutional Court. The second package led to the establishment of the Human Rights Department within the Directorate General of International Relations and Foreign Law at the Ministry of Justice. Other amendments concern the Council of State Law, the Supreme Court of Appeals Law, the Judges and Prosecutors Law, the Justice Academy Law, and the Law on the Council of Judges and Prosecutors.

The third judicial package,[65] entitled 'Law on Making Amendments to Some Laws for the Purpose of Enhancing Judicial Services and Deferring Trials and Penalties for Crimes Committed through Press and Broadcasting', was adopted on 2 July 2012. This package consists of 107 articles and three temporary provisions. In was formulated after acknowledging the increasing workload on therefore slowing pace of the judiciary. As a result, the judiciary, most of the time, exceeds the 'reasonable time' element, as accepted by the constitution and the ECHR. Exceeding of the time limits caused Turkey to be sentenced to pay compensation under the ECtHR. The package amended the law on bankruptcy, criminal law, and administrative judicial legislation in order to expedite judicial processes. It also addressed the need to legislate protections for fundamental rights such as freedom of expression and privacy.

The fourth judicial package was enacted on 11 April 2013 under the title 'Law on Making Amendments to Some Laws in the Context of Human Rights and Freedom of Expression'. It focused primarily on changes within the context of human rights and comprised twenty-seven articles. This package includes amendments to the Anti-Terror Law (ATL) and certain articles in the Turkish Penal Code (TPC). The objective of the fourth judicial

63 The first judicial package is also known as Law no. 6217.

64 The second judicial package is also known as Decree no. 650.

65 The third judicial package is also known as Law no. 6352.

package was to provide relief concerning ECtHR rulings that were under supervision by the Committee of Ministers of the Council of Europe which had been finalized but not yet implemented. For example, one amendment (ATL, article 6) states that those who print and publish the declarations and statements of terrorist organizations, engage in their propaganda, or participate in illegal meetings and demonstrations, will not be punished for the crime of membership in a terrorist organization. Another amendment states that the decisions finalized by the European Court of Human Rights regarding violations will be acknowledged as grounds for retrial in proceedings before the Military Supreme Administrative Court. Another amendment confirmed that a statute of limitations would not apply to crimes of torture.

The reforms started to face stagnation and then reversal from 2013 until today. The Gezi Park protests in Istanbul caused the first authoritarian reaction of the AKP government. Beginning with the 2015 Turkey Progress Report, the European Commission has emphasized that the principle of separation of powers was being compromised, with judges and prosecutors facing significant political pressure that threatened the independence of the judiciary. The coup d'état attempt of the FETÖ terrorist organization and the prolonged state of emergency declared as a reaction to the coup created numerous unwanted changes in the judiciary and the rule of law. As a response to the intense discussions on the death penalty, the EU Commission president Jean-Claude Juncker said, 'Turkey is in no position to become a European Union member any time soon and all negotiations for it to join will stop immediately if it reintroduces the death penalty'.

In the Commission's Turkey progress reports from 2018 on, serious backsliding in the judiciary and in fundamental rights was noted. The turn from the parliamentary system into the presidential system by the 2017 constitutional referendum caused a deterioration in the separation of powers and curbed the effectiveness of the legislation. The broken checks and balances caused weakening in accountability and transparency, which possibly fostered corruption. Notably, following the coup d'état attempt on 15 July 2016, legislative changes enacted under the state of emergency decrees adversely impacted progress in the judicial sector. There had been a marked regression in the rule of law since 2016, which directly undermined the independence and impartiality of the judiciary in practice.

The politicized judiciary in Turkey has been exploited by the government as a tool against the opposition voices, particularly journalists and others who can influence the public, academics, and civil society. The recent detention of Turkish mountaineer Nasuh Mahruki presents a vivid example of the politicization of the judiciary. Mahruki is the founder of the Turkish Search and Rescue Association (AKUT) and one of the heroes of the 1999 Istanbul earthquake, He was detained on 20 November 2024 for allegedly 'publicly spreading misleading information' and 'insulting judicial bodies' in a social media post. In his post he criticized the Supreme Electoral Council (Yüksek Seçim Kurulu, YSK) by posting the following:

> Great Turkish nation, be vigilant. The government and YSK are setting up a scheme to steal the elections one last time. The Chamber of Computer Engineers must oversee an early presidential election to ensure transparency. Without monitoring, they will steal our votes, replace them with fake ones, and unlawfully win again. This would mark the end of the Republic of Turkey in a manner worse than your worst nightmares.[66]

The Istanbul Chief Public Prosecutor's Office's Press Crimes Investigation Bureau launched an investigation against Mahruki. Allowing his statement at the courthouse, authorities referred Mahruki to the Criminal Court of Peace for arrest. The court subsequently ordered his detention. He was then released on 6 December 2024. His detention and then arrest was perceived as a threat against the opposition that criticized the AKP.

With the systemic erosion of the integrity of the judicial system, the multitude of ongoing legal proceedings against Turkish journalists, academics, politicians of the opposition, civil society leaders, and activists starkly illustrates the politicization of the judiciary and corrosion of the rule of law. These judicial processes exhibit recurring patterns that not only reveal their underlying political motives but also demonstrate strategic manipulations aimed at circumventing the principles of due process and fair trial. This widespread judicial malpractice undermines the autonomy and transparency of the judiciary and highlights the instrumental use of legal mechanisms to suppress dissent and maintain political control.

The case against Ekrem İmamoğlu, the mayor of Istanbul and a member of the Republican People's Party (CHP), is another remarkable case to demonstrate the politicization of the judiciary. İmamoğlu was prosecuted on allegations of insulting members of the High Election Board by calling them 'fools'. There is a possibility that the appellate court may uphold the prison sentence and the 'political ban' imposed on him in this case.

66 Duvar English, 'Turkish Court Arrests Former Rescue Association Chair for "Spreading Disinformation"', 21 November 2024, https://www.duvarenglish.com/turkish-court-arrests-former-rescue-association-chair-for-spreading-disinformation-news-65284.

In November 2019, shortly after the election when he was elected to become the mayor of the Istanbul metropolitan municipality, İmamoğlu was invited to speak at the Congress of Local and Regional Authorities in Strasbourg, France. At that time, Süleyman Soylu, the then minister of the interior and an AKP member from Istanbul in the parliament, criticized İmamoğlu by stating, 'I am addressing the fool who goes to the European Parliament to complain about Turkey. This nation will make you pay the price.' In response, İmamoğlu retorted, 'Those who cancelled the election on 31 March are the true fools. They should focus on that and consider where we stand in the eyes of the world, especially in Europe, after what happened.'[67]

Subsequently, members of Turkey's Supreme Election Council (YSK), which organizes elections in the country, claimed they were insulted and aggrieved by İmamoğlu's remarks and filed a formal complaint with the Istanbul Anatolian Chief Public Prosecutor's Office. The office drafted an indictment accusing İmamoğlu of 'publicly insulting public officials because of their duties' and sought a prison sentence ranging from one year, three months, and fifteen days to four years and one month for him. The case was tried, and resulted in İmamoğlu being sentenced to two years, seven months, and fifteen days in prison along with a political ban. The appeal continues to be heard in the Regional Courts of Justice (İstinaf Mahkemesi), which act as the appellate courts in Turkey.[68]

Due to his widespread popularity, Ekrem İmamoğlu is considered a potential candidate for the upcoming Turkish presidential elections. The decision regarding his political ban, currently pending in the appeals court, hangs over him like the sword of Damocles, casting a shadow over his political future.

The European Commission has expressed concerns about 'extensive changes to the structures and compositions of high courts', which deviate from European standards,[69] including involuntary transfers of judges and prosecutors against their will[70] and protracted legal proceedings.[71] Additionally, the Commission has reported multiple times that perceptions of corruption remain elevated and there has been no progress in addressing the gaps in Turkey's anti-corruption framework. Among the dismissal of civil servants pursuant to being a member to the FETÖ terrorist organization,

67 Ayşe Sayın, 'Ekrem İmamoğlu'na Ceza Onanırsa CHP'de Hangi Adımlar Atılacak?', *BBC Türkçe*, 10 October 2024, https://www.bbc.com/turkce/articles/c5yov2z5r78o.

68 Ibid.

69 European Commission, 'Turkey 2016 Progress Report', 6.

70 Ibid., 18.

71 Ibid., 20.

the Venice Commission warned that 'every decision ordering the dismissal of a judge needs to be individual and reasoned, must refer to verifiable evidence'.[72] Under the AKP government, particularly due to the autocratic turn, the executive and legislative branches gained the habit of publicly commenting on ongoing judicial cases, which was noted by the Commission.[73] The non-transparent selection of the candidate judges and prosecutors has been creating concerns over the professionalism of the process and whether the recruitment criteria is merit based, objective, uniform, competitive and pre-established.[74]

While the judiciary is politicized and used to silence and suppress opposition elements, the everyday reality often revealed in media reports, where perpetrators of harassment, rape, assault, and femicide crimes possess extensive criminal records yet remain at liberty, points to a selective and instrumentalized application of the law. From a neo-Gramscian lens, this phenomenon illustrates how legal institutions, rather than serving a universalistic function of justice, are increasingly restructured to protect the prevailing political hegemony, criminalizing dissent while tolerating socially disruptive behaviours that do not threaten the dominant bloc.

The fact that individuals with such criminal records are not imprisoned, whereas detention centres are filled with those convicted for thought crimes, is a significant indicator of the erosion occurring within the legal system. Rather than embodying the impartial rule of law envisaged by the Copenhagen criteria, the Turkish judiciary today reflects a transformation of law into a mechanism of selective repression and passive consent, serving to reinforce rather than challenge the incumbent power structures.

### *International Implications of Turkey's Rule of Law and Judiciary Backsliding*

In 2002 three sets of reform packages were adopted in February, March, and August. The third reform package of August 2002 provided for the retrial of persons whose convictions have been found by the ECtHR to be in violation of the ECHR.[75] The permit for retrials paved the way for the retrial of the parliament members of the Kurdish party known as the Democracy Party (DEP), who were sentenced to imprisonment, by the

72 Ibid., 24.

73 Ibid., 25.

74 European Commission, 'Turkey 2019 Progress Report', 29 May 2019), 24, https://www.ab.gov.tr/siteimages/resimler/20190529-turkey-report(1).pdf.

75 European Commission, 'Turkey 2003 Progress Report', 19 May 2003), 13, https://www.ab.gov.tr/siteimages/birimler/kpb/tr_rep_20061998/2003_tr_rap.pdf.

Ankara State Security Court, for assisting and supporting membership in an armed gang pursuant to article 168 of the Penal Code, after dissolution of the DEP by the Constitutional Court on 16 June 1994. The applicants lodged their complaint to the ECtHR that they had not had a fair trial in the Constitutional Court in so far as their rights of defence had been restricted during those proceedings. They considered this to amount to a violation of article 6, para. 1, of the convention.[76] The ECtHR ordered the retrial of the applicants in Turkey. The conviction was rejected in Turkey. Yet, with an amendment the path to reconviction was allowed and consequently, the applicants were freed. In this regard, the case of Leyla Zana and colleagues (the ECtHR case is also known as *Sadak and Others v. Turkey*) is deemed to be symbolic, as also mentioned by the Commission in the 2004 Turkey Progress Report.[77]

The broken rule of law's first international signal was given when the pastor for the İzmir Diriliş (Resurrection) Church,[78] Andrew Brunson, living in Turkey for more than twenty years, was taken into custody. Brunson had filed an application to renew his residence visa in April 2016. He was taken into custody when he was called to the local police station on 7 October 2016 for a routine meeting to discuss his visa extension. He was convicted of FETÖ-related terror crimes: political or military espionage and support of a terrorist organization. His access to a lawyer was denied. His detention caused a diplomatic crisis between Washington and Ankara. President Donald Trump tweeted that Brunson was being held 'hostage' in Turkey.[79] The US authorities imposed financial sanctions on Turkey and finally Brunson was released in October 2018 and deported to the US with his family. President Erdoğan stated multiple times that he could not meddle with Turkey's judicial independence and that only the courts would decide Brunson's fate.[80] Conversely, he said in 2017 that Turkey could free the pastor if the United States handed over Fetullah Gülen, living in Pennsylvania.[81]

76 ECtHR, *Sadak and Others v. Turkey*, no. 29900/96, 29901/96, 29902/96, and 29903/96, 11 June 2002.

77 European Commission, 'Turkey 2004 Progress Report', 16.

78 The evangelical Presbyterian congregation in the city of Izmir, with a small community.

79 Tara Mckelvey, 'US–Turkey Row: Pastor a "Pawn in Personal Feud"', *BBC*, 19 August 2018, https://www.bbc.com/news/world-us-canada-45237372.

80 BBC, 'Andrew Brunson: Trump Meets US Pastor Freed by Turkey', 13 October 2018, https://www.bbc.com/news/world-europe-45842735.

81 Reuters, 'Turkey's Erdogan Links Fate of Detained U.S. Pastor to Wanted Cleric Gulen', 29 September 2017, https://www.reuters.com/article/world/turkeys-erdogan-links-fate-of-detained-us-pastor-to-wanted-cleric-gulen-idUSKCN1C31IJ/.

The Brunson incident was followed by another similar case: the pre-trial detention of Deniz Yücel, the Turkish correspondent of the German daily newspaper *Die Welt*. He was detained on 14 February 2017 for spreading PKK/KCK and FETÖ propaganda and of stirring enmity. During his detention, Erdoğan called him a 'spy', a 'terrorist', and even a 'spy terrorist', and in answer to a question, Erdoğan said that Yücel would never ever be released: 'It will never happen, not as long as I am in this position.'[82] However, Yücel was released on 16 February 2018, and he returned to Germany.

These two incidents, marked by Erdoğan's outspoken involvement in the charges and the detainment-and-release scenarios, underscore significant concerns regarding the arbitrary nature of the judicial system and the prevailing influence of political forces on judicial decisions. Moreover, each case serves as a clear example of the national judiciary being exploited as a tool in foreign relations by the AKP government, strategically deployed to negotiate specific issues or secure advantages.

Since Turkey recognized the individual applications in 1987 and the compulsory jurisdiction of the European Court of Human Rights (ECtHR) in 1990, Turkey has emerged as the predominant source of applications to the court, a testament to the frequent violations of the rights enshrined in the European Convention on Human Rights (ECHR) within its jurisdiction. This high volume of cases indicates significant challenges within the Turkish judicial system to provide adequate remedies for these violations. As of 1 January 2024, Turkey accounts for 23,400 of the 68,450 pending applications before the ECtHR, constituting 34.2 per cent of all cases,[83] a clear indication of ongoing human rights challenges. In the 2023 annual review of violation rulings by the ECtHR across twenty-five countries, Turkey was ranked third, following Russia and Ukraine, with a total of seventy-two rulings. This statistical context underscores the systemic issues within Turkey's adherence to the standards set forth by the ECHR highlighting both the domestic and international implications of its human rights record.

The European Court of Human Rights has played an instrumental role in advancing human rights in Turkey. In response to the court's directives, the Turkish government has enacted several legislative reforms to align more closely with the European Convention on Human Rights. Notably, during

82 Diken, 'Erdoğan Tutuklu Die Welt Muhabiri İçin "Ant İçti": Ben Olduğum Sürece Asla İade Yok', 14 April 2017, https://www.diken.com.tr/erdogan-tutuklu-die-welt-muhabiri-icin-ant-icti-ben-oldugum-surece-asla-iade-yok/.

83 ECHR, 'Statistical Reports – Pending Applications', 31 October 2024, https://www.echr.coe.int/statistical-reports.

the constitutional amendments of 2004, a significant revision was made to article 90, titled 'Ratification of International Treaties'. The amendment stipulated that in instances of conflict between international agreements concerning fundamental rights and freedoms that have been duly enacted and domestic laws on the same subject, the provisions of the international agreements would take precedence.[84] This amendment effectively elevated the status of international treaties, making them supranational over domestic laws in matters of fundamental rights and freedoms.[85]

The rulings rendered by the ECtHR has led numerous amendments in Turkish laws for the improvement of freedom of expression. In 2001, in conjunction with the EU accession process, amendments were made to article 26 of the constitution that removed barriers to the use of languages other than Turkish. On 3 October 2002, within the framework of the Third Harmonization Package, legal obstacles to providing education in languages and dialects other than Turkish, as well as to broadcasting in languages and dialects other than Turkish on radio and TV, were also abolished.[86]

Turkey's Constitutional Court has adjudicated on the dissolution of forty political parties over the history of the Republic. The shutting down of nineteen political parties since 1982 has been another element of tension between the ECtHR and Turkey.[87] To a great extent, the jurisprudence of the ECtHR on party closure cases is based on applications from Turkey. The ECtHR found that in six out of seven cases it reviewed concerning Turkey, the decision to ban the political party violated the European Convention on Human Rights. For instance, after the closure of the United Communist Party of Turkey (Türkiye Birleşik Komünist Partisi, TBKP) led the interpretation of the court (in para. 27) that article 11 of the ECHR, which holds that everyone has the right to freedom of peaceful assembly and to freedom of association with others, is absolute even for the political parties that the national authority's claim was attempting to subvert the constitutional order.[88] Numerous Kurdish and Islamist parties were abolished on the grounds of separatist activities and activities against secularism. The ECtHR criticized the Turkish state multiple times for its rigid and restrictive interpretation of the 'territorial unity of the state' and constitutional provisions on secularism. Among all the applications from Turkey, the only decision of the court in

84 Secretariat General for EU Affairs, 'Political Reforms in Turkey'.

85 Özbudun and Türkmen, 'Impact of the ECtHR Rulings on Turkey's Democratization', 987.

86 Ibid., 988.

87 Can, 'The Motion before Turkey's Constitutional Court to Ban the Pro-Kurdish HDP'.

88 ECtHR, *United Communist Party of Turkey and others v. Turkey*, no. 133/1996/752/951, 30 January 1998.

favour of the Turkish state was in the case of the Welfare Party ban. The jurisdiction was based on the public statements of several party members and particularly the spokesman of the party that incited the use of force against their opponents.[89]

The penal law reform on domestic violence is another outcome of the ECtHR rulings. The main sources of the amendments have been, predominantly, *Opuz v. Turkey* (2009), but also *Huseyin Pasali and Others v. Türkiye* (2020). In *Opuz*, Turkey became the first country to address criminal domestic violence in the family. The case motivated Turkey to assume a role in the formulation of the COE's Convention on Preventing and Combating Violence against Women and Domestic Violence, also known as the Istanbul Convention. Turkey was also the first signatory to the convention. During the democratization process, Turkey undertaking ambitious reforms also include the replacement of Law no. 4320 with the Law to Protect Family and Prevent Violence against Women (Law no. 6284, 2012), which was formulated in line with the provisions of Istanbul Convention. Although Turkey withdrew from the Istanbul Convention in 2021, Law no. 6284 is still in force.

Another element that attracted attention regarding the rule of law in Turkey is its conformity with ECtHR rulings. The Union warned Turkey to ensure the conformity of the decisions of the Constitutional Court with ECtHR rulings. When the lower courts started to deny the verdicts of the Constitutional Court, the European Commission addressed Turkey to ensure the conformity of the lower courts with the ECtHR jurisprudence. Turkey's non-compliance with the European Court of Human Rights rulings, especially in the high-profile cases of Selahattin Demirtaş and Osman Kavala, heightened concerns about the judiciary's commitment to international and European legal standards.

Osman Kavala, a businessman and civil society activist, was detained in October 2017 due to accusations of participation in the 2013 Gezi Park protests and the 2016 attempted coup. The charges against Kavala, which labelled him as a traitor, alleging his involvement in attempts to overthrow the Turkish government during the 2013 protests and the coup attempt. The charges against him included attempting to overthrow the government and engaging in political and military espionage. Although repeatedly acquitted and re-arrested on different charges, his detention has been marked by unsubstantiated judicial reasoning and controversial decisions. On 25 April 2022, Kavala was convicted of attempting to overthrow the

89 ECtHR, *Refah Partisi (the Welfare Party) and Others v. Turkey*, no. 41340/98, 41342/98, 41343/98, and 41344/98, 13 February 2003.

government and sentenced to aggravated life imprisonment, though this judgement remains subject to appeal within the Turkish judicial system.

In its judgement of 10 December 2019, the European Court of Human Rights determined that the detention of Kavala on charges under article 312 (attempt to overthrow the government) and article 309 (attempt to overthrow the constitutional order) of the Turkish Penal Code was arbitrary. The court found this detention to be in violation of article 5, para. 1(c), and article 5, para. 3, of the European Convention on Human Rights (ECHR), emphasizing that Kavala's imprisonment stemmed from his exercise of rights protected under the ECHR. The ECtHR concluded that the Turkish authorities had failed to demonstrate a 'reasonable suspicion' that Osman Kavala had committed any criminal offense warranting his deprivation of liberty.[90]

After examining the entirety of the criminal proceedings brought against Osman Kavala up to the 2019 ruling, which included extensive alleged facts and evidence, the court further found that the Turkish authorities had acted with an ulterior motive. Specifically, it held that the prosecution sought to silence Kavala as a human rights defender, constituting a violation of article 18 of the ECHR in conjunction with article 5, para. 1, of the ECHR. Given the arbitrary and bad faith nature of his detention, the court ruled that any continuation of Kavala's pretrial detention would result in further violations of his rights under the ECHR and contravene Turkey's legal obligations under article 46, para. 1, of the ECHR to comply with ECtHR judgements. Accordingly, the court ordered the Turkish authorities to immediately release Kavala and terminate his detention. Despite this binding judgement, Kavala was not released. Erdoğan reacted to the ECtHR ruling by stating: 'We do not recognize those who do not recognize our court rulings.'[91]

The case of Osman Kavala has become a focal point for examining Turkey's compliance with European human rights standards and the enforcement mechanisms of the European Court of Human Rights. In its landmark 2019 judgement, the ECtHR found Kavala's detention arbitrary and in violation of article 5, para. 1(c), article 5, para. 3, and article 18 of the European Convention on Human Rights. The court underscored that his imprisonment lacked a reasonable suspicion of criminal activity and was pursued with the ulterior motive of silencing him as a human rights defender. Despite the court's unequivocal order for Kavala's immediate release, the Turkish

90 ECtHR, *Kavala v. Turkey*, no. 28749/18, 5 November 2020.

91 EuroNews, 'Erdoğan'dan Osman Kavala Açıklaması: Bizim Mahkeme Kararlarımızı Tanımayanı Biz de Tanımayız', 2 March 2022, https://tr.euronews.com/2022/02/03/erdogan-dan-osman-kavala-ac-klamas-bizim-mahkeme-kararlar-m-z-tan-mayan-biz-de-tan-may-z.

authorities have failed to comply, triggering infringement proceedings, a rare mechanism within the Council of Europe.[92]

Infringement proceedings, governed by article 46, para. 4, of the ECHR, allows the Committee of Ministers to refer cases back to the ECtHR when a state fails to execute its judgements. Initiated in Kavala's case in 2022, the proceedings have been accompanied by strong criticisms from both domestic and international actors, including bar associations, civil society organizations, and the European Parliament. The Turkish government contends that Kavala's current detention relates to new charges and proceedings; however, these are based on the same evidence previously rejected by the ECtHR as insufficient. This refusal to abide by the court's decisions has not only strained Turkey's relations with the Council of Europe but also raised broader concerns about the integrity and independence of the Turkish judiciary.

The Grand Chamber of the ECtHR will deliver its judgement on the infringement proceedings, which will have immediate and binding legal consequences for Turkey. This includes requiring domestic courts to align with the ruling and mandating the Committee of Ministers to oversee its implementation. The Kavala case thus underscores the ongoing challenges within the European human rights framework in ensuring compliance from member states and highlights the tension between domestic sovereignty and international legal obligations.

Another non-implementation case is about the jurisdiction of Selahattin Demirtaş. The prolonged detention of Demirtaş, former co-chair of Turkey's pro-Kurdish rights political party, the People's Democratic Party (Halkların Demokrasi Partisi, HDP), represents a critical infringement of human rights and an alarming erosion of the rule of law in Turkey. The Grand Chamber of the European Court of Human Rights ruled in 2020 that his detention was politically motivated and intended to curtail his political activities, a rare violation of article 18 of the European Convention on Human Rights (ECHR).[93] The Turkish authorities have consistently failed to comply with the court's judgement. Instead, they have employed tactics to circumvent the binding ruling, including reliance on new evidence stemming from alleged events over seven years ago, which remains vague and lacks substantiation. This defiance undermines the ECHR system, as well as democratic pluralism and political freedoms in Turkey.

The joint submission by prominent human rights organizations, including the Turkey Human Rights Litigation Support Project (TLSP), ARTICLE 19,

92 Ibid.

93 ECtHR, *Selahattin Demirtaş v. Turkey (no. 2)*, no. 14305/17, 22 December 2020.

Human Rights Watch (HRW), the International Commission of Jurists (ICJ), and the International Federation for Human Rights (FIDH), calls on the Committee of Ministers of the Council of Europe (CM) to insist on Demirtaş's immediate release and to consider initiating infringement proceedings under article 46, para. 4, of the ECHR.

The submission underscores the continued abuse of the judicial system to silence political opposition and limit freedom of expression, highlighting a broader pattern of state persecution against dissenting voices. These organizations argue that the Turkish government's refusal to comply with the ECtHR ruling not only extends the violation of Demirtaş's rights but also severely compromises the integrity of the European human rights framework. To ensure accountability and uphold the rule of law, the CM is urged to apply all necessary measures to enforce compliance with the ECtHR judgement and safeguard the democratic principles enshrined in the ECHR.[94]

The European Union's scrutiny of Turkey's judiciary and the rule of law reveals a complex landscape marked by significant challenges and unmet expectations. The European Commission's Turkey 2024 Progress Report underscores a persistent stagnation in the advancement of judicial reforms and the rule of law, positioning Turkey at an early stage of preparation with no progress noted on key issues previously identified. Fundamental concerns linger regarding the functioning of the judiciary, which continues to be characterized by a lack of independence and impartiality. This situation is exacerbated by the Turkish government's sustained influence over the judiciary, with high-level executive pressures unduly affecting judges and prosecutors. Such pressures compromise the judiciary's ability to function independently and degrade the quality of judicial processes, directly contravening the principles upheld by the European Union.

The EU's expectations for Turkey in this realm are clear and rooted in its foundational values of democracy, human rights, and the rule of law. The Commission advocates for a comprehensive overhaul of Turkey's judicial framework to align with European standards, emphasizing the need for genuine reform efforts that address the systemic shortcomings. Specifically, the EU calls for the establishment of mechanisms that bolster the separation of powers, enhance judicial independence, and ensure that all

94 International Commission of Jurists, 'Turkey: End Abuse of Criminal Proceedings against Selahattin Demirtaş', accessed 23 February 2024, https://www.icj.org/resource/turkey-end-abuse-of-criminal-proceedings-against-selahattin-demirtas/.

court proceedings uphold fundamental rights, particularly the rights of defendants and victims within the criminal justice system.

Moreover, the EU criticizes the continued non-implementation of European Court of Human Rights' rulings by Turkey, viewing it as indicative of broader systemic issues within the Turkish legal and institutional framework. The EU's concerns are compounded by Turkey's refusal to implement decisions that are crucial for safeguarding human rights and maintaining judicial integrity. This refusal not only undermines the authority of the ECtHR but also signals Turkey's reluctance to fully commit to the norms and standards expected of a candidate country aligned with the EU's legal and democratic ethos.

In summary, the EU perceives Turkey's judiciary and adherence to the rule of law as areas fraught with challenges that necessitate urgent and substantial reforms. The European Union expects Turkey to undertake rigorous and sincere improvements to fulfil the criteria for accession and align more closely with European judicial standards. However, viewed through a neo-Gramscian lens, the EU's expectations are not neutral expectations or purely technical or legalistic; they are embedded in a broader strategy of stabilizing a transnational liberal-democratic order, within which rule of law reforms serve as key instruments of political and economic convergence.

Without such reforms, Turkey's aspirations for deeper integration with the EU will likely remain unfulfilled, as the rule of law is a cornerstone of the Union's normative hegemony and a prerequisite for any potential member state. Until the mid-2010s, the high willingness of the Turkish government and the credibility of the EU as a normative actor paved the way for a rapid reform process to improve the rule of law in Turkey. These efforts, driven by a momentary alignment of internal and external hegemonic projects, succeeded in diminishing the role of the military and in introducing measures that enhanced transparency and accountability in the judiciary. However, the subsequent weakening of EU leverage, combined with the rise of counter-hegemonic forces within Turkey, contributed to a regression that reflects deeper tensions between competing conceptions of sovereignty, governance, and legal order.

### *Ever-Repeating Death Penalty Reinstatement Discussions in Turkey*

The debate over the death penalty remains a contentious issue worldwide, reflecting broader questions about justice, human rights, and governance. Globally, support for the abolition of the death penalty has been steadily increasing, with more than two-thirds of all countries abolishing it in law or practice. Despite this trend, retentionist states like Iran, China, and

Saudi Arabia continue to impose the death penalty, often in ways that violate international standards. In Turkey, the death penalty was abolished nearly two decades ago, yet discussions about its reinstatement resurface periodically, particularly following emotionally charged events. The debates raise significant legal, political, and moral questions. These discussions do not only reveal domestic political and social dynamics but also highlight Turkey's obligations under international law. This section elaborates on the issue through the lenses of international law, constitutional constraints, political implications, and practical challenges, highlighting the broader ramifications of such a policy shift.

The discussions surrounding the death penalty in Turkey can also be seen as a tool of populist rhetoric, frequently employed to polarize society. These debates create a dichotomy between supporters of the death penalty and those who oppose it. Opponents are often stigmatized as sympathizers of criminals, such as traitors, rapists, terrorists, or arsonists responsible for forest fires, reinforcing a narrative that delegitimizes dissent. This tactic allows the government to strengthen its base by framing the opposition as morally and politically aligned with society's adversaries.

When Erdoğan and the Justice and Development Party (AKP) assumed office in 2002, they made significant efforts to distance themselves from the political Islamist National View (Millî Görüş) tradition, which had deep roots in radical Islam and anti-Western sentiment. Erdoğan's 2003 declaration that the party had moved beyond this ideology marked a shift towards a pro-European agenda. During these early years, meeting the Copenhagen criteria was among the AKP's top priorities. The EU candidacy served as an anchor for democratic reforms, particularly in expanding rights and freedoms.

However, as domestic resistance and political challenges emerged, most notably during the Gezi Park protests in 2013, the AKP's rhetoric began shifting towards a more anti-Western and anti-European tone. Statements by European leaders suggesting that Turkey would never become a full EU member, or offering alternatives such as a 'privileged partnership', significantly dampened the Turkish government's enthusiasm for alignment with European standards. This loss of hope weakened the EU's function as a normative anchor for Turkey, particularly in areas such as human rights.

Simultaneously, disputes between Turkey and the EU escalated over issues such as Cyprus, anti-terror legislation, and minority rights, including the Kurdish issue. These tensions coincided with the AKP government's increasingly authoritarian stance, characterized by rhetoric and policies that directly contradicted European norms. Against this backdrop, discussions about reinstating the death penalty further illustrate Turkey's deviation from European values, serving as a populist instrument that exacerbates domestic divisions while straining relations with the EU.

The European Union was strongly opposed to the death penalty and deemed it as cruel and inhuman. The abolition of the death penalty caused a normative expansion of the right to life. Contrary to the arguments of the retentionist countries, empirical evidence proves that capital punishment does not act as a deterrent to crime and it affects disadvantaged groups, such as the poor and minorities, disproportionately. The prohibition of torture is recognized in international law as a *jus cogens* (peremptory) norm, a fundamental principle of international law that allows no derogation under any circumstances.

The abolition of the death penalty in Europe was an achievement of the Council of Europe, with which the European Union shares its founding values – democracy, human rights, and the rule of law – which were mobilized by the same founding fathers. Overlapping membership is another significant association between the COE and the EU. The intense cooperation between these two intergovernmental organizations is visible when it is comprehended that every country that has joined the EU has first become a member of the Council of Europe and they both share the vision of a death penalty–free Europe.

Global support for the abolition of the death penalty has been steadily increasing, with more than two-thirds of all countries having abolished it either in law or in practice. Notably, in 2023, the number of countries carrying out executions reached a historic low,[95] despite a significant rise in executions in certain states, such as Iran, which has been sentencing political prisoners, ethnic minorities, and foreign nationals.[96] According to the latest statistics, the highest number of executions were carried out in Iran, China, Saudi Arabia, Somalia, and the US. Iran is responsible for 74 per cent of all recorded executions.[97] Public opinion surveys carried out in the US show that popular support for capital punishment is decreasing and Americans believe the death penalty is being applied more unfairly (50 per cent) than fairly (47 per cent). The diminishing trend is even visible

95 Death Penalty Information Center, 'The Death Penalty in 2023: Year End Report', 1 December 2023, https://deathpenaltyinfo.org/facts-and-research/dpic-reports/dpic-year-end-reports/the-death-penalty-in-2023-year-end-report.

96 Human Rights Watch, 'Iran: Flurry of New Death Sentences', 14 September 2024, https://www.hrw.org/news/2024/11/20/iran-flurry-new-death-sentences.

97 Council of Europe Newsroom, 'Joint Statement on Death Penalty', 9 October 2024, https://www.coe.int/en/web/portal/-/european-and-world-day-against-the-death-penalty-10-october-2024.

in retentionist states, particularly in Africa, which have amended their legislation to limit its scope.[98] Studies show that the death penalty does not diminish criminal rates to make societies safer. In fact, the misuse of the punishment in an arbitrary, unlawful, or indiscriminate way has irreversible negative social consequences.

International law has been progressively restricting the use of the death penalty and the European system can be deemed as the flag carrier for this effort. Turkey has also abolished the death penalty as a result of the European initiative. Public international law has developed in a way to prohibit capital punishment in order to prevent its irreversible outcomes. The international standards are devised to limit the use of capital punishment in the narrowest possible way. In other words, international law imposes a threshold of the 'most serious crimes' as in article 6 of the International Covenant on Civil and Political Rights (ICCPR, 1966). The ICCPR also prohibits carrying out capital punishment on pregnant women and on imposing it for crimes committed by persons below eighteen years of age. It guarantees the right of those sentenced to death to seek a pardon or commutation of the sentence, which may be granted in all cases. The ICCPR also urges its signatories to abolish capital punishment (article 6, para. 6). In 1984, the Economic and Social Council (ECOSOC) reiterated the 'most serious crimes' standard in a resolution (Annex, article 1) endorsed by the UN General Assembly.[99] The resolution underlined the necessity of clear and convincing evidence for the verdict, and it also prohibited the use of capital punishment on new mothers and those who have become insane (Annex, article 3).

The 'most serious crimes' concept does not have a clear definition and is open to wide interpretation. Observation of how it has been implemented hint that these crimes include drug-related offences, crimes against the state and military codes, and murder crimes (terrorism, in particular). Yet, it is well-known that states like Iran impose the death penalty for reasons such as pre-marital consensual sex.

From 1920 to 1984, 712 people were executed, including fifteen women. The penalty was carried out under the Law of Treason (Hıyanet-i Vataniye Kanunu). In 1925 the scope of the penalty was broadened. When the death penalty was regularized under the criminal law (repealed article 765), the

98 Parliamentary Assembly, '"The Death Penalty Does Not Make Society Safer", Says General Rapporteur', 10 September 2024, https://pace.coe.int/en/news/9638.

99 ECOSOC, 'Safeguards Guaranteeing Protection of the Rights of Those Facing the Death Penalty', Pub. L. no. 1984/50 (1984), https://www.unodc.org/documents/commissions/CCPCJ/Crime_Resolutions/1980-1989/1984/ECOSOC_Resolution_1984-50.pdf.

crimes that allowed for capital punishment were numerous, including drug trafficking, murder, kidnapping, and rape in addition to treason and state-centred crimes such as (incitement to) armed rebellion against the government, crimes against the constitution, disclosure of information related to state security, disclosure of prohibited material during wartime, disclosure of discoveries, inventions, and innovations that must remain confidential for national security, citizens' participation in war against the state, inciting a foreign state to declare war against Turkey, recruiting soldiers and engaging them in hostile activities, destruction of military facilities, destruction of documents related to national security, espionage against the state, preventing the members of the Council of Ministers from performing their duties by force, armed rebellion against the government, and assassination of the president.

Among the victims of this penalty, the execution of six people has left a mark in the political history of Turkey. The outcome of the 27 May 1960 coup d'état was the execution of Prime Minister Adnan Menderes, Minister of Foreign Affairs Fatin Rüştü Zorlu, and Minister of Finance Hasan Polatkan; in 1972 three revolutionaries (Deniz Gezmiş, Yusuf Aslan, and Hüseyin İnan) were executed after the 12 March 1971 Memorandum.

The death penalty has not been practiced in Turkey for forty years and was formally ended twenty-four years ago. The amendment that also abolished the death penalty is known as the Eighth Harmonization Package. It was adopted on 14 July 2004. Capital punishment was then replaced by an aggravated life sentence. Currently, debates over the reinstatement of capital punishment resurface periodically in Turkey, often spurred by emotionally charged events. These discussions tend to gain public traction following incidents such as child abuse cases, large-scale wildfires, terrorist attacks, and, notably, the 2016 coup attempt, which reignited widespread calls for its reintroduction. President Erdoğan has repeatedly affirmed his readiness to restore the death penalty, a stance that has garnered the support of the Nationalist Movement Party (Milliyetçi Hareket Partisi, MHP), which has expressed its willingness to back such an initiative if pursued.[100]

The discourse on capital punishment has not been confined to 2016 but continues to resurface through statements from the ruling Justice and Development Party (AKP) leadership. For instance, in 2020, Mustafa Şentop, the former speaker of the Turkish Grand National Assembly, remarked: 'I believe that the death penalty could be considered for crimes of premeditated

100 Bianet, 'Bahçeli: AKP İdama Hazırsa Biz de Varız', 19 July 2016, https://bianet.org/haber/bahceli-akp-idama-hazirsa-biz-de-variz-176885.

murder and sexual offenses committed against minors and women.'[101] In 2022, Erdoğan called for the reconsideration of death penalty for those who ignite wildfires.[102] This persistent rhetoric underscores the enduring political and societal tensions surrounding the issue.

It can be argued that there is a strong relationship between regime type and the practice of capital punishment. The majority of states implementing the death penalty are authoritarian, with Japan and the US standing out as exceptions among well-established democracies. This trend underscores how the use of capital punishment often aligns with broader patterns of repression and limited political freedoms. On 20 December 2023, the government of the Maldives announced its intention to reinstate the death penalty, followed more recently in November 2024 by a similar declaration from Burkina Faso's military junta. These cases reflect how non-democratic regimes may leverage capital punishment as a tool to consolidate authority or signal their commitment to law-and-order politics.

In this sense, the revival of death penalty discussions in Turkey can also be interpreted as part of its broader democratic backsliding. Since the failed coup attempt in 2016, Turkey has experienced an erosion of democratic norms, characterized by increased authoritarianism, restrictions on freedoms, and a concentration of power in the executive branch. The rhetoric surrounding the reinstatement of the death penalty in Turkey not only echoes these broader shifts but also raises questions about its alignment with international norms and obligations. This trajectory places Turkey closer to authoritarian regimes that rely on capital punishment as a mechanism of control.

The reaction of the EU was voiced by the EU High Representative for Foreign Affairs, Frederica Mogherini, that Turkey 'is bound by its commitments under the European Convention on Human Rights and as a member of the Council of Europe not to reintroduce the death penalty. No country can become an EU member state if it introduces the death penalty.'[103] She was echoed by Jean-Claude Junker, the president of the European Commission,

101 Sinan Uslu, Ali Kemal Akan, and Adem Balta, 'TBMM Başkanı Şentop: Taammüden Adam Öldürme ve Cinsel Suçlarla Ilgili Idam Cezasının Düşünülebileceği Kanaatindeyim', 29 September 2023, https://www.aa.com.tr/tr/politika/tbmm-baskani-sentop-taammuden-adam-oldurme-ve-cinsel-suclarla-ilgili-idam-cezasinin-dusunulebilecegi-kanaatindeyim/1989509.

102 EuroNews, 'Turkey Re-evaluating Death Penalty after Erdogan's Wildfires Comment – Minister', 26 June 2022, https://www.euronews.com/2022/06/26/uk-climate-wildfires-turkey.

103 Reuters, 'EU Reminds Turkey It Bound by Treaty Not to Use Death Penalty', 18 July 2016, https://www.reuters.com/article/world/eu-reminds-turkey-it-bound-by-treaty-not-to-use-death-penalty-idUSKCN0ZY10F/.

who said: 'If Turkey should bring back the death penalty, we will immediately stop the negotiation process.' In his speech he also underlined that he does not believe Turkey will become an EU member in the near or long term because of the current circumstances in the country; which indicated the political chaos including both the coup d'état attempt and the coping methods of the government.[104]

As indicated by Mogherini, the reinstatement of the death penalty is fundamentally a matter of national law. States legislate or amend their laws in line with the hierarchy of norms within their legal system. The systems around the world vary. For example, in countries where the judicial system is based on the common law, judicial precedents (*stare decisis*) come before other sources, and in countries where the judicial system is based on sharia, neither the constitution nor the law, decrees, or other regulations can contradict the Qur'an.

As for the Turkish system, first comes the Turkish constitution. In the second place are international agreements. Pursuant to article 90 of the constitution, the ratification of treaties concluded with foreign states and international organizations is subject to the ratification of the Turkish Grand National Assembly. International treaties duly put into effect have the force of law. In case of a conflict between national laws and international treaties duly put into effect, concerning fundamental rights and freedoms, international treaties prevail.[105] However, the constitution is silent about any possible conflict between international human-rights conventions and the constitution itself.[106]

Discussions about reinstating the death penalty in Turkey are typically limited to the Turkish Penal Code. Those engaging in the debate often approach the issue solely from a punitive perspective, either deliberately or inadvertently neglecting the right to life as enshrined in human rights treaties. However, it is equally essential to evaluate the possibility of reinstating capital punishment from the perspective of the international instruments

104 Hale Türkeş, 'Death Penalty Will End Turkey's EU Bid, Says Juncker', *AA*, 25 July 2016, https://www.aa.com.tr/en/europe/death-penalty-will-end-turkeys-eu-bid-says-juncker/615091.

105 In the Turkish hierarchy of norms, the subsequent order is, respectively, presidential decrees during a state of emergency, presidential decrees, regulations (*yönetmelik*), directives (*yönerge*), notifications/communiqués (*tebliğ*), circulars (*genelge*), and instructions or mandates (*talimat*).

106 Zühtü Arslan, 'The Status of the International Law in the Turkish Constitution', Constitutional Court of the Republic of Türkiye, 23 November 2022, https://www.anayasa.gov.tr/en/president/former-presidents-speeches/zuhtu-arslan/speeches/the-status-of-the-international-law-in-the-turkish-constitution/.

to which Turkey is legally bound, as these obligations significantly constrain its ability to reintroduce the death penalty.

Turkey banned capital punishment in three steps. First came the Third Harmonization Package and ECHR Protocol nos. 6 and 13. The abolition of the death penalty in Turkey was initiated through the this package, enacted on 3 August 2002, which effectively eliminated the practice. The DSP–MHP–ANAP coalition government abolished the death penalty with the exception of crimes committed 'in cases of war or imminent threat of war'. On 29 June 1999, the same year when Turkey received its EU candidacy status, the terrorist leader Abdullah Öcalan was sentenced to death for the crime of 'founding and leading an armed terrorist organization'. However, following the abolition of the death penalty, this sentence was commuted to aggravated life imprisonment.

The COE introduced additional protocols to the ECHR for further legal strengthening of the protection of fundamental rights. Protocol no. 6 was adopted on 28 April 1983, which entered into force on 1 March 1985, and was signed by Turkey on 15 January 2003, becoming legally binding on 1 December 2003. This protocol banned capital punishment during peacetime. In 2004, the death penalty was fully removed from Turkey's legal framework, without distinction between wartime and peacetime. This was realized when Turkey adopted COE's Protocol no. 13 to the European Convention on Human Rights, further consolidating its commitment to the prohibition of capital punishment by abolishing it during wartime. As a result, under these protocols Turkey further cemented its legal obligations against the reinstatement of capital punishment.

Turkey is legally bound by the International Covenant on Civil and Political Rights (ICCPR) and the European Convention on Human Rights (ECHR), along with its protocols, which collectively mandate the abolition of the death penalty. They guarantee the right to life and prohibit torture, inhuman, or degrading treatment. Reinstating capital punishment would require Turkey to withdraw from these international instruments. However, the ICCPR does not provide a withdrawal mechanism. For instance, when North Korea (DPRK) attempted to withdraw from the ICCPR in a notification dated 23 August 1997, the United Nations rejected the withdrawal. Consequently, Turkey remains firmly bound by these international legal frameworks, which preclude any reinstatement of the death penalty.

The absence of a denunciation or withdrawal provision underscores the rigidity of international human rights law, leaving states with little flexibility to deviate from established human rights norms once ratified. The ICCPR, together with the International Covenant on Economic, Social and Cultural Rights and the Universal Declaration of Human Rights, constitute the International Bill of Human Rights. The lack of a withdrawal provision ensures a strict legal and political commitment for guaranteeing fundamental human rights.

There is no legal obstacle preventing Turkey from withdrawing from the European Convention on Human Rights (ECHR) or its protocols. However, reflecting on Russia's exclusion from the Council of Europe (COE) illustrates the potential consequences of such actions. Russia's exclusion was based on article 8 of the Statute of the COE, which states:

> Any member of the Council of Europe which has seriously violated Article 3 may be suspended from its rights of representation and requested by the Committee of Ministers to withdraw under Article 7. If such member does not comply with this request, the Committee may decide that it has ceased to be a member of the Council as from such date as the Committee may determine.

Article 3, in turn, requires that all COE members 'accept the principles of the rule of law and of the enjoyment by all persons within its jurisdiction of human rights and fundamental freedoms, and collaborate sincerely and effectively in the realization of the aim of the Council'. Given this framework, the reinstatement of the death penalty in Turkey would likely constitute a violation of these principles, thereby endangering its membership in the COE.

Similarly, Turkey's EU candidacy could face significant risks due to the EU's staunch opposition to the death penalty. The efforts were initiated by the COE. In one resolution of the Parliamentary Assembly of the COE (PACE), the Council started to consider the attitude of applicant states towards the death penalty when deciding on their admission as full members to the COE.[107] In other words, abolishing the death penalty (legally and practically) became a prerequisite for COE membership, which is a de facto prerequisite for membership in the EU. The resolution also recommended the Committee of Ministers of the COE to draw up an additional protocol abolishing the death penalty both in peacetime and in wartime.

The EU has consistently advocated for the abolition of capital punishment: 'The EU reaffirms its strong and unequivocal opposition to the use of the death penalty at all times and under all circumstances.' This stance is further enshrined in the Charter of Fundamental Rights of the European Union,

107 Parliamentary Assembly, 'Abolition of Capital Punishment', Recommendation 1246 (1994), https://pace.coe.int/en/files/16455.

article 2, which explicitly states: '(i). Everyone has the right to life. (ii) No one shall be condemned to the death penalty, or executed.' The protocols to the ECHR and the Charter of Fundamental Rights demonstrate that the abolition of capital punishment is a core value for both institutions. Therefore, Turkey's reinstatement of the death penalty would not only jeopardize its COE membership but could also critically undermine its bid for EU membership, as it would signal a departure from the shared human rights principles that form the foundation of these organizations.

Beyond international obligations, domestic constitutional provisions also impose significant barriers to reinstating the death penalty. The domestic impediments are thrown out of focus when politicians and journalists concentrate on the nature of the crimes that death penalty proponents argue warrant the penalty, such as child molestation or acts causing significant harm to national resources, such as setting forest fires or committing large-scale acts of terror.

The process of amending the Turkish constitution to reintroduce the death penalty is itself a highly complex and multifaceted undertaking. The Turkish Grand National Assembly (Türkiye Büyük Millet Meclisi, TBMM) currently consists of 600 members. For a constitutional amendment to be proposed, the initiative must be backed by at least 200 members. Once proposed, the amendment requires the approval of at least 360 members, representing a three-fifths majority of the assembly, for adoption. Even under the current rule of the single-party government in Turkey, the number of the supporting parliament members totals only 314 (267 from AKP and 47 from MHP). However, this is only the first hurdle in the process. Should the president choose to veto the amendment and send it back to the Turkish Grand National Assembly for reconsideration, the assembly would need to adopt the amendment again with a two-thirds majority (400 parliament members) for it to move forward.

Even after clearing these legislative thresholds, the president retains the discretion to submit the amendment to a national referendum. In such a referendum, a simple majority, defined as 50 per cent of the votes plus one, is required for the constitutional amendment to be ratified. These procedural hurdles illustrate the significant political and institutional challenges associated with attempting to reinstate the death penalty through constitutional reform in Turkey, further complicating an issue already fraught with international legal implications.

Article 148 of the Turkish constitution explicitly guarantees the protection of fundamental rights and freedoms within the framework of the European Convention on Human Rights (ECHR). This constitutional provision underscores Turkey's commitment to upholding the principles and obligations enshrined in the ECHR, ensuring that these rights are safeguarded at the national level. Furthermore, article 90 of the constitution, which addresses the ratification of international treaties, reinforces the supremacy of international legal instruments in cases of conflict with domestic laws. The article stipulates: 'In the case of a conflict between international agreements, duly put into effect, concerning fundamental rights and freedoms and the laws due to differences in provisions on the same matter, the provisions of international agreements shall prevail.'

This constitutional framework firmly establishes that international agreements, particularly those related to fundamental rights and freedoms, take precedence over conflicting domestic legislation. Consequently, any attempt to reinstate the death penalty in Turkey would be in direct contradiction with the ECHR and its associated protocols, which unequivocally prohibit the use of capital punishment. Given the constitutional mandate that international agreements supersede municipal laws, the reintroduction of the death penalty would not only violate Turkey's international legal obligations but also contravene the supremacy clause embedded within its own constitutional structure. This legal conflict highlights the inherent barriers and significant challenges to any such legislative endeavour.

In addition to legal and constitutional challenges, reinstating the death penalty would have severe diplomatic and practical consequences, particularly in the context of extradition. Reinstating capital punishment in Turkey would present a significant barrier to the extradition of fugitive criminals to the country. For the majority of abolitionist states, the prohibition on the death penalty is not only a legal stance but also a moral imperative. These countries consider it ethically unacceptable to facilitate the execution of an individual, even indirectly. As a result, the extradition of individuals who may face the death penalty has become a globally contentious issue, often drawing substantial criticism and opposition.

This issue holds particular relevance for Turkey, especially in the context of its efforts to address the activities of the Gülenist terrorist organization FETÖ. Since the attempted coup on 15 July 2016, Justice Minister Yılmaz Tunç has revealed that Turkey has formally requested the extradition of 1,271 individuals accused of involvement with FETÖ.[108] However, should Turkey reinstate capital punishment, it is highly likely that these extradition requests would

108 Daily Sabah, 'Fight against FETÖ Prevails 7 Years after Coup Attempt in Türkiye', 13 July 2023, https://www.dailysabah.com/politics/fight-against-feto-prevails-7-years-after-coup-attempt-in-turkiye/news.

face even stronger resistance from abolitionist states, rendering the Turkish state unable to bring these fugitives to justice within its own legal system.

In this sense, the reintroduction of the death penalty would not only undermine Turkey's international standing but also prove counterproductive to its own interests. Such a move could effectively create legal and diplomatic obstacles that would hinder the pursuit of justice for crimes committed against the state, ultimately making the reinstatement of capital punishment a self-damaging act.

In conclusion, the recurring debates on reinstating the death penalty in Turkey are closely tied to the country's ongoing democratic backsliding and reflect a deeper contestation of hegemonic norms. The neo-Gramscian hegemony framework demonstrates that these discussions serve not merely as populist tools to rally domestic support, but as symbolic acts challenging the liberal international order and its human rights–based common sense. By invoking emotionally charged issues like capital punishment, the government fosters a nationalist narrative that reasserts state sovereignty against external legal and normative constraints.

Nevertheless, the practical realization of such debates remains highly improbable due to the significant legal and institutional barriers in place. Turkey's binding obligations under international treaties, such as the European Convention on Human Rights and the International Covenant on Civil and Political Rights, coupled with its constitutional framework, create formidable obstacles to the reintroduction of capital punishment. Any attempt to reinstate the death penalty would not only provoke international isolation, risking expulsion from the Council of Europe and fatally damaging its already fragile EU candidacy, but would also signify a decisive reorientation of Turkey's hegemonic alignment away from the liberal-democratic bloc.

Ultimately, the death penalty debates illuminate the broader tensions between Turkey's domestic counter-hegemonic narratives and its historical commitments to the norms of the European-centred international order. They reveal how moments of crisis are exploited to renegotiate national identity, redefine political legitimacy, and challenge existing structures of international hegemony.

## The Erosion of Expression, Media Freedoms, and Freedom of Association

The amendment of article 133 of the Turkish constitution in 1993 abolished the state monopoly in the radio and television broadcasting sector and led to the rapid proliferation of private radio and television stations that characterizes Turkish media today. The Radio and Television Supreme Council (Radyo ve Televizyon Üst Kurulu, RTÜK) was established by the enactment of Law no. 3984 on the Establishment and Broadcasts of Radio and Television in 1994. (It was abolished in 2011.)

Regarding media and press freedoms, the European Commission noted in its 'Turkey 1998 Regular Report' that both domestic and foreign publications, offering a diverse range of views and opinions, are broadly accessible in Turkey. Instances of government censorship of foreign publications are infrequent. Nonetheless, there have been occasional instances where Turkish newspapers faced censorship during the printing process.

The Commission also found that public criticism of the armed forces, as well as the peaceful advocacy of alternatives to the fundamental principles of the Turkish state, such as territorial integrity and secularism, can result in criminal charges. The narrow interpretation of the laws was resulting in the prosecution and conviction of elected politicians, besides journalists, activists, writers, trade unionists, and NGO members, for their statements, publications, or speeches that would not constitute a crime in EU member states.[109]

The Commission noted the frequent confiscation of newspapers, books, and films, primarily those providing coverage of events in south-eastern Turkey. These confiscations prevented the Turkish media from reporting on the Kurdish issue in an objective manner. Additionally, the 1998 report underlined the significant level of self-censorship that prevailed within the media, stemming from an acute awareness of the stringent enforcement of constitutional and legal boundaries on freedom of expression.[110]

The constitutional amendment enacted on 3 October 2001 abrogated the provision in article 28, para. 2, of the 1982 constitution, which stipulated that 'publications cannot be made in any language prohibited by law'. While some scholars argued that this amendment was unnecessary, given that the law prohibiting publications in languages other than Turkish had already been repealed on 12 April 1991,[111] the Commission regarded this amendment as a significant advancement. It underscored its importance as a concrete guarantee of freedom of expression, explicitly affirming the

109 European Commission, 'Turkey 1998 Regular Report'.

110 Ibid.

111 Kemal Gözler, '3 Ekim 2001 Tarihli Anayasa Değişikliği: Bir Abesle İştigal Örneği', *Anayasa Yargısı* 18, no. 1 (3AD).

legality of publications and the dissemination of opinions in writing and other media in languages other than Turkish.[112]

The restructuring of the media in Turkey happened in two steps. In the first step, the 2001 banking crisis was influential. The crisis led to the confiscation of some media assets by the Savings Deposit Insurance Fund (Tasarruf Mevduatı Sigorta Fonu, TMSF), which sold them on to new owners. The new owners were four major[113] and four minor[114] groups.[115]

The adoption of the RTÜK law in May 2002 introduced tight restrictions on freedom of expression and freedom of media by prohibiting broadcasts that violate the existence and independence of the Turkish Republic, the territorial and national integrity of the state, or the reforms and principles of Atatürk, or instigate the community to violence, terror, or ethnic discrimination. It introduced very high penalties. In that year, RTÜK imposed a record number of daily broadcast bans on radio and television channels. Moreover, one owner of a local television channel (Gün TV) was indicted for broadcasting a song in Kurdish and charged under the Anti-Terror Law.[116]

Freedom of expression has been one of the major areas of reform that has caused intense conflict between the reformist and conservative elements in Turkey.[117] Yet these conflicts have resulted in judicial reforms that led to a significant decrease in prosecutions over the aforementioned topics.

Among the chapters of the *acquis* subject to negotiation, chapter 10 on 'information and media' encompasses specific regulations governing electronic communications, information society services (including electronic commerce and conditional access services), and audio-visual services. In the domain of electronic communications, the *acquis* seeks to remove barriers to the effective functioning of the internal market for telecommunications services and networks, foster competition, and protect consumer interests, ensuring the universal availability of modern services. Regarding audio-visual policy, the *acquis* mandates legislative alignment with the Television without Frontiers Directive, which facilitates the free

112 European Commission, 'Turkey 2001 Progress Report', 13 November 2001, https://www.ab.gov.tr/siteimages/birimler/kpb/tr_rep_20061998/2001_tr_rap.pdf.

113 Doğan Group, Merkez Group, Çukurova Group, and Star (Uzan) Group.

114 İhlas Group, Doğuş Group, Samanyolu Group, and Aksoy Group.

115 Gözde Yılmaz, 'Europeanisation or De-Europeanisation? Media Freedom in Turkey (1999–2015)', in *Is Turkey De-Europeanising? Encounters with Europe in a Candidate Country*, ed. Alper Kaliber and Senem Aydin-Düzgit (Routledge, 2018), 147–62, at 150.

116 European Commission, 'Turkey 2002 Progress Report', 10 September 2002, https://www.ab.gov.tr/siteimages/birimler/kpb/tr_rep_20061998/2002_tr_rap.pdf.

117 Keyman and Düzgit, 'Europeanization, Democratization and Human Rights in Turkey', 78.

movement of television broadcasts within the European Union. Additionally, the *acquis* aims to establish a transparent, predictable, and efficient regulatory framework for public and private broadcasting, consistent with European standards. Furthermore, compliance requires the capability to participate in EU programmes such as Media Plus and Media Training.

In line with these EU standards, Turkey undertook a number of constitutional amendments which have also contributed to the enhancement of press freedom, further bolstered by the enactment of a new press law. This legislation eliminated punitive measures such as the closure of publications, suspension of distribution, and confiscation of printing equipment, marking a significant step towards safeguarding press rights. Nevertheless, the persistent and frequent prosecution of journalists remains an urgent concern, raising questions about the consistency and depth of these reforms in fostering genuine freedom of the press.[118]

Amendments to the Law on Public Meetings and Demonstrations have significantly eased restrictions on the exercise of freedom of association and peaceful assembly. The proposed Law on Associations, initially passed by parliament in July 2004 but subsequently vetoed by the president, holds substantial potential for limiting state interference in the activities of associations, if enacted. The establishment of new institutions, such as the Department for Associations, has facilitated the transfer of responsibilities previously managed by the police to civilian authorities. Additional measures have been implemented to curtail the systematic recording of meetings and demonstrations and to address and penalize the disproportionate use of force by security forces. However, reports indicate that human rights defenders, including human rights associations, continue to face harassment through judicial means, raising concerns about the consistent implementation of these reforms.[119]

The 2004 EU reform package introduced significant advancements in the realm of freedom of expression. Notably, the prohibition on radio and television broadcasting in languages other than Turkish was abolished, marking a critical step towards linguistic inclusivity. Additionally, the Press Law underwent substantial revisions, and amendments to the Penal Code were enacted to decriminalize expressions that conveyed information or offered critical perspectives, thereby fostering a more open and pluralistic public discourse.

118 European Commission, 'Turkey 2004 Progress Report', 17.
119 Ibid., 18.

Although the government was working hard to prepare judicial reforms in order to achieve harmonization with the EU standards, the AKP was also worried about its political survival. Thus, freedom of speech and expression was not meant for the opposition. Erdoğan's AKP has only undertaken reforms that do not affect the government or that worked to strengthen the political status of the party, such as the removal of the military elements from civilian institutions.

Erdoğan is known to be intolerant of any kind of criticism, political satire, political cartooning, or political imitation/impression directed at him. He made a complaint against a cartoonist, Musa Kart, in 2004 for a cartoon depicting him as a cat entangled in strings. The caption read 'İmam Hatip Liseleri' ('Islamic vocational high schools'), referring to the political problems Erdoğan was facing related to those schools. Erdoğan filed a claim for compensation and won it. In a similar manner, Erdoğan made a complaint against the satire magazine *Penguen* over an illustration on the cover of issue 127 (24 February 2005). Entitled 'Tayyipler Alemi' ('The world of Tayyips'), it depicted Erdoğan as diverse types of animals. The court rejected Erdoğan's claim for moral damages of 40,000 TL. At their graduation ceremony, students from the Middle East Technical University (METU) carried the cartoon on a banner, which resulted in them being detained in their homes by the police for a period.

According to the article 299 of the Turkish Penal Code, whoever insults the president of the Republic shall be sentenced to a penalty of imprisonment for one to four years; if the insult is perpetrated in public, then the sentence is increased by one-sixth. Prosecution for this offense is subject to the approval of the Minister of Justice. Due to its signatory status of the European Convention on Human Rights and the International Covenant on Civil and Political Rights, Turkey is legally bound to respect freedom of expression. However, article 299 is often employed to silence opposing voices and to render Erdoğan beyond debate and criticism.

While there were 132 cases in 2014, when Erdoğan was elected president for the first time, the number rose to 1,953 in 2015, 4,187 in 2016, and 6,033 in 2017.[120] In the three years following Erdoğan's election as president, 68,817 individuals were investigated for insulting the president. Between June 2017 and November 2018, thirty publishing houses and 116 media outlets were shut down. The accusation of 'insulting the president' increased fifteen-fold

120 Diken, 'Erdoğan'a Hakarette Üç Yıl: 68 Bin 817 Kişiye Soruşturma, 3 Bin 414 Kişiye Hapis', 12 November 2018, https://www.diken.com.tr/erdogana-hakarette-uc-yil-68-bin-817-sorusturma-3-bin-414-ceza/.

during Erdoğan's presidency compared to previous administrations. The prosecution numbers rocketed to the highest levels in 2018 following the institutionalization of the Turkish-style presidential system. In the first eleven months of 2018, seventy-four journalists were sentenced to a total of four hundred years in prison, and 26,115 individuals, including 168 children, were tried, with a total of 5,223 convictions.

Under previous Turkish presidents, cases of 'insulting the president' were relatively limited: there were 340 during Kenan Evren's tenure, 207 under Turgut Özal, 158 under Süleyman Demirel, 163 under Ahmet Necdet Sezer, and 848 during Abdullah Gül's presidency. However, during the first three years of Recep Tayyip Erdoğan's presidency, the number of such cases surged dramatically. Compared to the previous term, the total number of defendants accused of 'insulting the president' increased approximately thirteenfold, reaching a staggering 12,173. This sharp rise reflects a significant intensification in the use of legal mechanisms to address perceived criticism of the presidency, marking a notable shift in the political and legal landscape of Turkey.[121]

By 2007 'pro-governmental circles' started to become visible in the media environment.[122] The confiscated media assets of groups with debts were sold to groups with ties to governmental elites.[123] The new owners were not experienced in the media business, but rather in construction and trade. They were encouraged by Erdoğan. The newspapers owned by these groups attracted particular attention when all of them started to come out with identical headlines. This was seen to be clear evidence that the news was coming from one source. For example, when Erdoğan made statements about the military coup and consequent events and persecution in Egypt, seven Turkish newspapers used the same headline – 'One Day the Pharaoh Will Face Moses' – on 16 August 2013 (see fig. 2).

One other significant impediment to the development of freedom of expression in Turkey was article 301 of the new Penal Code (which was formerly article 159). It is known as the article on 'insulting Turkishness'. The article stipulates that a person who publicly degrades the Turkish nation, the Turkish Republic, the Turkish Grand National Assembly, the government of the Republic of Turkey, the judicial bodies of the state, the military, or the security organizations could be sentenced a penalty of imprisonment for a

121 Simge Akkaş, 'Cumhurbaşkanına Hakaretten Kaç Kişi Yargılanıyor?', *Doğruluk Payı*, 16 October 2019, https://www.dogrulukpayi.com/bulten/2018-yilinda-cumhurbaskanina-hakaretten-kac-kisi-sanik-oldu.

122 Yılmaz, 'Europeanisation or De-Europeanisation?', 150.

123 European Commission, 'Turkey 2004 Progress Report', 18.

Figure 2. Front pages of seven Turkish newspapers from 16 August 2013 displaying the identical headline: 'One Day the Pharaoh Will Face Moses'.

term of six months to two years. The article also states that the expression of an opinion for the purpose of criticism does not constitute an offence. In order to limit the employment of the article, another provision was later added, which states that the conduct of an investigation into such an offence is subject to the permission of the Minister of Justice.

Nobel laureate author Orhan Pamuk faced prosecution under article 301 for insulting Turkishness after stating in an interview published on 6 February 2005 in *Das Magazin*, a Swiss weekly, that 'one million Armenians and 30,000 Kurds were killed in these lands'.[124] The statement led the Turkish prosecutor's office to initiate legal proceedings against him, highlighting the contentious use of article 301 in cases involving discussions of sensitive historical and political issues. In January 2006, the Court of Cassation dismissed the case against the author, who was facing up to three years in prison, ruling that the Ministry of Justice's statement ('We lack the authority to grant permission for prosecution') could not be interpreted as an authorization to proceed with the trial.[125]

124 Erol Önderoğlu, 'Pamuks File at the Justice Ministry's Door', *Bianet*, 14 December 2005, https://bianet.org/haber/pamuks-file-at-the-justice-ministrys-door-71569.
125 Bianet, 'Orhan Pamuk'un 301 Davası Ortadan Kalktı', 3 August 2007, https://bianet.org/haber/orhan-pamukun-301-davasi-ortadan-kalkti-100513.

Hrant Dink, a Turkish-Armenian journalist for the Turkish newspaper *Agos*, was assassinated on 19 January 2007 in Istanbul after he was convicted of insulting Turkishness. Dink was convicted twice under article 301, once after a talk he had given in 2002, when he said he was an Armenian from Turkey; and a second time because of an op-ed he published in *Agos*. The words in the op-ed were twisted and taken out of context in order to convict him. The conviction made him a target and paved the way for his assassination.

In addition to reducing freedom of expression, article 301 also caused a disparity relating to making references to minority groups. For example, Erdoğan made a derogatory statement on television that went unpunished: 'Some have called me Georgian, and, excuse me, some have said much worse, calling me Armenian. I am Turkish.'[126] In this statement, Erdoğan used the names of other nations in a pejorative manner, however, he was not subject to any kind of prosecution under the Penal Code. In contrast, someone who used the word 'Turk' in a similarly derogative manner would be subject to conviction under article 301.

The aforementioned cases are noted in the Commission's progress reports, too, to highlight the necessity of adopting the article 10 of the ECHR on freedom of expression, which allows the exchange of opinions and information without interference by public authorities.

The current legal framework and its enforcement fail to ensure open and unrestricted expression online. In April 2023, coming up to a general election, one graphic designer, Mahir Akkoyun, printed stickers with Erdoğan's photo on them alongside references to the ever-growing inflation rates in the country. When the stickers became popular on social media he was accused of insulting the president and disrupting an election by creating disinformation. He was detained and then released.

The government has persistently engaged in frequent closures of websites and social media accounts that voice criticism of its policies. In August 2024, access to Instagram was reinstated following a nine-day ban, highlighting the recurrent limitations imposed on digital platforms. Meanwhile, the online gaming platform Roblox continues to be prohibited, exemplifying the broader constraints on digital expression. In 2004, when a young woman, Dilruba Kayserilioğlu, responded to questions regarding the Instagram ban in a street interview published on a YouTube channel, she was detained on the ground of insulting the president and inciting hatred and hostility among the public. She was then released.

126 Bianet, 'Erdoğan: Afedersin Ermeni Diyen Oldu', 6 August 2014, https://bianet.org/haber/erdogan-afedersin-ermeni-diyen-oldu-157616.

The trajectory of freedom of expression in Turkey, as delineated in the above analysis, reflects a complex interplay of progressive reforms and enduring challenges. While significant advancements have been made, such as the abolition of the state monopoly on radio and television broadcasting and the lifting of restrictions on publications in languages other than Turkish, these reforms coexist with persistent limitations that undermine genuine freedoms. For instance, the establishment of regulatory frameworks like the RTÜK law, initially aimed at harmonizing Turkey's media landscape with democratic principles has, in practice, imposed stringent penalties and restricted critical broadcasts, particularly on sensitive issues like Kurdish rights.

The influence of external factors, especially Turkey's EU accession process, has been pivotal in driving judicial reforms and enhancing press and media freedoms. However, viewing these developments through a neo-Gramscian hegemony lens suggests that the government's selective motivation for reform that prioritizes political survival over the promotion of democratic norms can be understood as a strategic effort to preserve a domestically constructed counter-hegemonic order. Instead of embracing reforms as genuine steps towards democratization, they were often instrumentalized to maintain and reassert political hegemony. This inconsistency is starkly visible in the government's willingness to suppress dissent through legal mechanisms such as article 299 of the Turkish Penal Code and the infamous article 301, which have been repeatedly employed to silence journalists, authors, and ordinary citizens for expressing dissenting views.

Additionally, the proliferation of pro-government media outlets and the instrumentalization of legal tools to suppress opposition have significantly impaired the pluralism necessary for a democratic society. In neo-Gramscian terms, the media landscape in Turkey illustrates how the dominant bloc consolidates its ideological leadership by marginalizing alternative discourses, thereby reshaping common sense to align with state-sanctioned narratives. The exponential rise in prosecutions for insulting the president, the closure of media outlets, and the weaponization of laws against perceived criticism collectively highlight a concerning erosion of freedom of expression and a strategic containment of oppositional counter-hegemonies.

While Turkey's commitments to international treaties, including the European Convention on Human Rights, have introduced a normative framework for protecting expression, the inconsistent implementation of these obligations reflects broader governance issues rooted in a contestation of hegemonic norms. The criminalization of dissent, restrictions on internet freedoms, and targeted actions against individuals and media platforms exemplify the state's active management of civil society spaces to sustain its hegemonic project.

In conclusion, Turkey's record on freedom of expression reveals an ongoing struggle between reformist aspirations, driven by external normative pressures, and authoritarian practices aimed at maintaining domestic hegemonic stability. The selective application of reforms, coupled with an expanding state apparatus aimed at curbing dissent, underscores the need for more robust mechanisms to safeguard these fundamental rights. As international scrutiny grows and domestic demands for democratic accountability persist, the government faces an intensifying tension between defending its established bloc and responding to emerging counter-hegemonic pressures. Only through consistent implementation of reforms and the removal of restrictive measures can Turkey hope to achieve the open, pluralistic society envisioned by its foundational democratic principles and international obligations.

## The Migration Dilemma

While this section gives particular attention to migration, it is not treated merely as a discrete policy field. Rather, migration is analysed as a key domain where human rights norms, international obligations, and domestic governance practices intersect. Turkey's handling of migration, asylum, and refugee protection offers a critical vantage point to assess broader patterns of democratic backsliding and human rights compliance under the AKP. Simultaneously, it highlights the EU's growing departure from its own proclaimed commitment to human rights and international law, particularly as it externalizes migration control to third countries.

The Turkish government has become a cornerstone of European migration policy, serving as a critical partner in managing migration flows towards the Union. Although chapter 24 on justice, freedom, and security, encompassing asylum and migration issues, remains unopened in Turkey's EU accession negotiations, alignment with the EU asylum *acquis* began as early as 2000. A pivotal moment was the adoption of the Turkish National Action Plan for the Adoption of the EU Acquis in the Field of Asylum and Migration in 2005, signalling Turkey's strategic accommodation to European standards under external normative pressures.

As set by the neo-Gramscian hegemony framework, Turkey's migration governance reflects a dynamic of passive revolution: limited reforms are undertaken under the influence of a dominant external order (the EU), without fundamentally altering domestic power structures or genuinely prioritizing the protection of human rights. The adoption of the Law on Foreigners and International Protection (LFIP) in 2014, replacing the restrictive 1994 regulation, marked formal convergence with European standards. Yet, this legal transformation did not translate into consistent rights protection, as persistent violations of the principle of non-refoulement and multiple condemnations by the European Court of Human Rights reveal.

Equally important, however, is the role of the European Union itself. The EU–Turkey Joint Action Plan of 2015 and the subsequent externalization of migration management to Turkey signify not merely a pragmatic cooperation but a broader trend of the EU's securitization of migration. By designating Turkey as a 'safe third country' despite clear evidence that Turkey does not meet the EU's own criteria for such status, the Union effectively compromises its human rights obligations under international and European law. Through this arrangement, the EU shifts its legal and ethical responsibilities onto Turkey, a country struggling with its own human rights challenges.

This asymmetrical cooperation reinforces a broader neo-Gramscian dynamic, according to which the EU, as the hegemonic actor, exports governance responsibilities while eroding its normative foundations. Turkey, for its part, internalizes selected aspects of European migration governance to secure political and economic gains, while selectively disregarding core human rights principles in practice. Migration policy thus serves as a critical field where both Turkey's authoritarian trajectory and the EU's normative decline are exposed.

### *The Evolution of the Asylum and Migration Acquis in the EU*

Article 14 of the Universal Declaration of Human Rights indicates that 'everyone has the right to seek and to enjoy in other countries asylum from persecution'. At the same time, states are sovereign entities that decide upon the conditions of entry at their borders. The contesting two approaches are regulated to a certain extent by the two major international instruments: the Refugee Convention (1951) and the Refugee Protocol (1967). The international instruments provide the definition of a refugee, outline their rights, and set the minimum standards of refugee protection. They also introduced one general principle of international law, which is a core principle of the global asylum regime: the non-refoulement that protects the refugee from being forcefully returned to the country of origin where persecution awaits them. These instruments were created as a response to the conditions resulting from World War II.

In the years from the nineteenth century until before World War II, the European continent emerged as a push region in terms of migration.

European populations left the continent for reasons that varied from ethnic discrimination to the search for better economic and living conditions. In time, however, economic, democratic, and intellectual developments on the continent became pull factors for migrants from other regions. Steady economic growth and industrial progress required workers. Hence, industry owners in European states followed migrant-friendly policies to tempt foreign workers (called *Gastarbeiter* – guest workers – in Germany). Europe took measures to limit migration to family reunifications only starting in the early 1970s, particularly after the oil crisis of 1973.

The dissolution of the Soviet Union in 1989 made another impact on migration within Europe. Thus, the Union made efforts for a common migration policy during the 1990s. In 1993, the Treaty of Maastricht introduced asylum/migration topics into the EU's institutional framework, within which the Commission was to cooperate with the Council and inform the parliament. It was aimed to form a shared structure to control the irregular migration movement throughout the outer borders of the Union. The structure was to be determined in an intergovernmental manner, via diplomatic negotiations, conferences, and cooperation.

The Dublin Convention was adopted on 15 June 1990 and first came into force on 1 September 1997. The Dublin Convention is considered the first EU initiative on refugees. The convention determines which EU member state will assess asylum and refuge applications made by third-country nationals. Under the Dublin Convention, the responsibility for evaluating whether an asylum seeker should be granted refugee status is assigned based on specific criteria. First, the member state where the asylum seeker's family members reside takes precedence. If no family connections exist, the responsibility shifts to the state that issued the asylum seeker a visa or residence permit. In the absence of these conditions, the state where the asylum seeker first entered the EU and lodged their application is deemed responsible. This responsible state will assess the application in accordance with the Refugee Convention (1951) and the Refugee Protocol (1967) to determine the applicant's eligibility for refugee status. This country is called as first safe country. These provisions are designed to address the issue of multiple asylum applications done by one applicant within the EU. The Dublin II Regulation was adopted in 2003 and Dublin III in 2013 to regulate which EU member will be responsible for the evaluation of the asylum application.

The adoption of the Schengen Agreement in 1990 (it entered into force in 1995) created a Schengen *acquis* that removed the intra-border checks among the signatory states and reinforced control on the external borders of the Schengen Zone. This agreement regulates the free roaming of citizens, residents, and tourists within the Schengen borders. The regulation facilitates the Union to share information for preventing, detecting, and struggling against transnational crimes, by creating an area without internal border controls.[127] In this sense, the agreement also facilitates the management of regular and irregular migration. The Schengen Borders Code allows the party states to reinstate border controls in case of foreseeable events constituting a serious threat to internal security. The suspension of the Schengen borders is possible with a prior notification and for a period up to thirty days. As for the cases that require immediate action, a member state may reintroduce border control for ten days without prior notification. The reintroduction can be prolonged for periods of up to twenty days, and the overall period of border control shall not exceed two months. According to the official data provided by the European Commission, between October 2006 and December 2024 party states temporarily reintroduced border controls at internal borders 455 times.[128]

The Maastricht Treaty, signed in 1992, marked a significant phase in the European Union's effort to establish a common migration policy. The removal of internal borders through the Schengen Agreement and the goal of a common market established by the Single European Act accelerated the treaty's ratification process. With the adoption of the Maastricht Treaty, the European Community was transformed into a Union. The treaty outlined the Union's objectives, including the elimination of internal borders, enhanced economic and social integration, the implementation of a common defence policy, the establishment of Union citizenship to protect the rights and interests of citizens of member states, and the strengthening of judicial and internal affairs cooperation. Key issues focused on in the treaty included preventing abuses of asylum procedures, reducing the number of asylum claims from third-country nationals, and combating irregular migration. It exempted operations conducted by the law enforcement agencies of the member states and measures deemed necessary for maintaining public order from scrutiny or oversight, paving the way for potential restrictions on the right to asylum under the pretext of security. Another significant aspect of the treaty is the establishment of the European Union citizenship. According

127 European Parliament and European Commission, 'Proposal on: Information Exchange between Law Enforcement Authorities of Member States', Pub. L. no. COM(2021) 782 final, 2021/0411(COD), accessed 12 November 2024, https://eur-lex.europa.eu/legal-content/EN/TXT/HTML/?uri=CELEX%3A52021PC0782.

128 European Commission, 'Temporary Reintroduction of Border Control', *Live, Work, Travel in the EU*, accessed 13 November 2023, https://home-affairs.ec.europa.eu/policies/schengen-borders-and-visa/schengen-area/temporary-reintroduction-border-control_en.

to this provision, citizens of member states are recognized as citizens of the Union, granting them the right to free movement and residence within the territories of other member states. However, one of the major criticisms of the EU citizenship is that it does not encompass individuals living within the Union's territories who are not EU citizens. While the Maastricht Treaty facilitated the free movement of member states' citizens, it did not extensively address the asylum applications from third-country nationals.

The adoption of the Treaty of Amsterdam in 1999 boosted the significance of the asylum/migration issues within the political hierarchy of the Union. The Amsterdam Treaty is a significant step towards the supranationalization of the migration issues. The legislation was to be triggered by the Commission. In the European Council's Tampere Summit of 1999, leaders of the member states recognized the necessity for creating a common migration and asylum policy. Moreover, they agreed to manage irregular migration in a more effective manner while improving the regular migration options. These decisions were reflected in the Lisbon Agreement of 1999, whose entry into force offered new opportunities, particularly in terms of labour migration within the EU. The rules of procedure for all types of migration, regular and irregular, were then left up to the European Parliament and the Council of Ministers'; decisions were to be taken by qualified majority.

The 2001 Laeken Summit demonstrated the insufficiency of the efforts for the creation of a common asylum and migration policy. The Hague Programme, adopted in 2004, is seen as a continuation of the Tampere Summit, aimed at advancing the objectives of common security, freedom, and justice.[129] This programme sets goals such as building a common asylum system, enhancing the contributions of regular migration to the EU, combating undocumented employment, establishing partnerships with countries of origin and transit, defining return and readmission policies, increasing border controls, combating irregular migration, establishing biometric and information data systems, determining visa policies, and improving information exchange.[130]

In 2005, the European Council adopted the Global Approach to Migration, which outlined the European Union's cooperation with source countries

129 Council of the European Union, 'The Hague Programme: Strengthening Freedom, Security and Justice in the European Union', 2005/C 53/01 § (2005), https://eur-lex.europa.eu/legal-content/EN/ALL/?uri=CELEX%3A52005XG0303%2801%29.

130 European Commission, 'The Hague Programme: 10 Priorities for the Next Five Years', accessed 2 February 2023, https://eur-lex.europa.eu/EN/legal-content/summary/the-hague-programme-10-priorities-for-the-next-five-years.html.

through economic support, and supported safe third country and readmission agreements. Additionally, during this period, the European Border and Coast Guard Agency (Frontex) was established, tasked with protecting the Union's external borders and conducting operational activities.

The Treaty of Lisbon came into effect in 2009 to revise the three-pillar structure established by the Maastricht Treaty into a new two-pillar framework. According to this restructuring, the Treaty on European Union addresses the structure and organization of the EU, while the Treaty on the Functioning of the European Union outlines the operations of the Union, including the roles and powers of its institutions. Under the freedom, security, and justice section of the latter, issues related to migration and asylum are discussed, and the distribution of powers between the EU institutions and member states is specified. Other innovations introduced by the Treaty include the integrated management of external borders and internal security, and the enhancement of recognized types of protection for asylum applications (refugee, subsidiary protection, temporary protection). While the changes under the Lisbon Treaty can be viewed as efforts to progress by referencing fundamental rights in response to critiques, they have not remedied the instances of rights violations.

In 2009, the European Parliament adopted the Stockholm Programme, which indicated that 'the external dimension of the Union's migration policy focuses on dialogue and partnerships with third countries, based on mutual interests'.[131] The second chapter of the Consolidated Version of the Treaty on the Functioning of the European Union, as accommodated in 2012, that covers articles 77 to 80, is regulating the common policies on border checks, asylum, and immigration.[132] The Union recognizes its duties under the global migration regime by article 78, which states:

> [T]he Union shall develop a common policy on asylum, subsidiary protection and temporary protection with a view of offering appropriate status to any third-country national requiring international protection and ensuring compliance with the principle of non-refoulement. This policy must be in accordance with the Geneva [Refugee] Convention of

131 European Council, 'The Stockholm Programme', *Official Journal of the European Union* 2010/C 115/01 § (2010), 4, https://eur-lex.europa.eu/LexUriServ/LexUriServ.do?uri=OJ:C:2010:115:0001:0038:en:PDF.

132 European Union, 'Consolidated Version of the Treaty on the Functioning of the European Union', Pub. L. no. *Official Journal of the European Union* C 326 (2012), https://eur-lex.europa.eu/legal-content/EN/TXT/?uri=celex%3A12012E%2FTXT.

> 28 July 1951 and the Protocol of 31 January 1967 relating to the status of refugees and other relevant treaties.[133]

Article 79 of the Agreement regulates 'the efficient management of migration flows, fair treatment of third-country nationals residing legally in member states, and the prevention of, and enhanced measures to combat, illegal immigration and trafficking in human beings'.[134] Article 80 underlines the necessity for solidarity and fair responsibility sharing, including the financial dimension, between the member states.

The Dublin Regulations represent a significant phase in the legal framework concerning asylum within Europe. These regulations establish which member state is responsible for examining an asylum application based on several criteria. These include whether the applicant has family members who have previously been granted refugee status under the Refugee Convention (1951), whether a member state has granted them residency or a visa, or the member state through which the applicant has entered illegally unless they are a third-country national not subject to a visa requirement. Additionally, the member state responsible for border checks, or the state through which the applicant has transited by air, becomes the state obligated to examine the asylum application. The Dublin Regulation stipulates that asylum applications to European countries are assessed by a designated member state, as determined by the community, eliminating the need for separate evaluations by each member state. This mechanism prevents abuse of the asylum system by prohibiting applicants from submitting asylum claims in multiple member states. However, the implementation of the asylum system as specified in the regulation has caused dissatisfaction due to its execution and a lack of solidarity among the member states. Dublin II (2003), like its predecessor, primarily addresses the determination of the member state responsible for assessing an asylum claim. Taking into account the challenges encountered during the application of the Dublin Agreement, the European Union decided to create Eurodac (European Dactyloscopy), a fingerprint database to facilitate the comparison of fingerprints for asylum applicants aged fourteen and above, aiding in identifying illegal entries into a member state and determining the state responsible for examining an asylum claim as initially intended by Dublin I. In essence, the Dublin Regulations aim to prevent asylum seekers from choosing where they apply within the EU, which could lead to an uneven distribution of the responsibilities

133 Ibid.
134 Ibid.

among member states, leading to tensions between countries. To reshape Dublin II, Dublin III was prepared in 2013, taking into consideration the rights of refugees, the obligations of member states, international law, and rulings from the European Court of Human Rights and the Court of Justice of the European Union. Dublin III introduced several innovations, including allowing any member state to examine an asylum application even if it is not initially responsible for doing so, thus emphasizing humanitarian reasons based on cultural considerations before making a final decision on the member state responsible.[135]

In 2016, the European Commission presented a series of proposals to reform the common European asylum and migration system.[136] The Council adopted the EU asylum agency regulation in 2021. This regulation recognized the European Asylum Support Office (EASO) as a fully fledged agency, which would improve the implementation of the common asylum and migration policy within the Union. EASO's responsibility was to provide operational and technical assistance to member states and create a common denominator for the refugee status determination procedure.[137]

On 23 September 2020, the European Commission launched the new Pact on Migration and Asylum after extensive consultation with the European Parliament, member states, and various stakeholders. This comprehensive framework was designed to manage migration through a holistic approach that incorporated and enhanced existing policies on migration, asylum, border management, and integration. It introduced a set of new regulations aimed at ensuring equitable responsibility among member states and embodying the core European values of solidarity and shared responsibility. The pact established robust procedures for managing migration, promising a balanced approach that respected individual rights

135 European Commission, 'Country Responsible for Asylum Application (Dublin Regulation)', accessed 3 February 2023, https://home-affairs.ec.europa.eu/policies/migration-and-asylum/common-european-asylum-system/country-responsible-asylum-application-dublin-regulation_en.

136 European Commission, 'Enhancing Legal Channels: Commission Proposes to Create Common EU Resettlement Framework', 13 July 2016, https://ec.europa.eu/commission/presscorner/detail/en/ip_16_2434; European Commission, 'Towards a Sustainable and Fair Common European Asylum System', 4 May 2016, https://ec.europa.eu/commission/presscorner/detail/en/ip_16_1620; European Commission, 'Completing the Reform of the Common European Asylum System: Towards an Efficient, Fair and Humane Asylum Policy', 13 July 2016, https://ec.europa.eu/commission/presscorner/detail/en/ip_16_2433.

137 Council of the European Union, 'Migration and Asylum Pact: Council Adopts EU Asylum Agency Regulation', 9 December 2021, https://www.consilium.europa.eu/en/press/press-releases/2021/12/09/migration-and-asylum-pact-council-adopts-eu-asylum-agency-regulation/.

while ensuring the security of external borders. Key features included a robust screening process, where individuals who do not meet the entry criteria are registered and undergo identification, security, and health checks. Additionally, the enhanced Eurodac system transformed the existing database into a comprehensive asylum and migration database for clear identification purposes. Critical to the pact were the border procedures and return protocols, mandating a border procedure for asylum seekers who likely do not qualify for protection, have misled authorities, or pose a security threat. Efficient return processes, accompanied by reintegration support, are stipulated for those not eligible for international protection. Moreover, the pact provided for crisis protocols and measures against the instrumentalization of migration, ensuring rapid response capabilities with operational support and funding in emergency situations. Following its endorsement by the European Parliament and Council, the new migration rules were implemented on 11 June 2024, with applications phased in over two years, reinforcing the commitment to a system that was fair, robust, and reflective of EU solidarity.[138]

In 2023 the Council of Ministers and the European Parliament reached a deal on the core political elements of five key regulations for refurbishing the EU's legal framework on asylum and migration. The aim was to establish a common procedure that members would follow for the protection of people of concern. A mandatory border procedure was introduced, by which asylum applications could be rapidly assessed, whether unfounded or inadmissible. Member states were expected to ensure there was adequate capacity and human resources available, which is proportional to the number of irregular border crossings and entry refusals over three years. A strict criterion was introduced for safe third countries, where rejected applicants would be referred to. Prevention of abuse is an important priority of the Union in the implementation of the common asylum and migration policy.[139]

### *Institutional Actors in EU Asylum and Migration Policy*

The institutions and instruments devised to regulate the asylum and migration *acquis* in the Union are primarily the Schengen Information System, Frontex, Eurodac, Eurosur, and readmission agreements. These

138 European Commission, 'Pact on Migration and Asylum', 21 May 2024, https://home-affairs.ec.europa.eu/policies/migration-and-asylum/pact-migration-and-asylum_en.

139 Council of the European Union, 'The Council and the European Parliament Reach Breakthrough in Reform of EU Asylum and Migration System', 20 December 2023, https://www.consilium.europa.eu/en/press/press-releases/2023/12/20/the-council-and-the-european-parliament-reach-breakthrough-in-reform-of-eu-asylum-and-migration-system/.

institutions are heavily established to maintain border security and to collect information of migrants to share with the member states.

The European Asylum Support Office (EASO) is an agency of the European Union tasked with three primary responsibilities: contributing to the coherent implementation and development of the Common European Asylum System (CEAS), fostering and enhancing practical cooperation among EU member states on asylum matters, and providing or coordinating operational support for member states facing significant pressure on their asylum and reception systems. The European Union Agency for Asylum promotes diplomacy with non-EU countries and establishes cooperation between the law enforcement units of the EU, which is Europol, and non-EU countries to cope with common challenges, such as cross-border crimes and terrorism.

The European Union Agency for Asylum (EUAA) is an agency of the European Union mandated with supporting EU member states in applying the package of EU laws collectively referred to as the Common European Asylum System (CEAS), which governs asylum procedures, international protection standards, and reception conditions. The national reception and asylum authorities are the sole bodies responsible for their procedures and the role of the EUAA is to provide them with assistance. The assistance can be is various forms, from legal counselling, to technical and operational assistance formats. Thus, the EUAA is deemed to be a resource for EU member states. The overall mandate of the agency is to harmonize the reception conditions, obligations, and procedures among the EU member states.

The Schengen Information System (SIS) was established in 1995 to serve as an information-sharing system for security and border management across Europe. The Council highlighted that member states had been failing to implement identity verifications at border crossing points. The Council had also criticized the member states for failing to effectively monitor border and inter-border areas. Additionally, they failed to assess threats that could compromise the security of external borders, as well as internal security. Thus, the necessity emerged for establishing common and clear rules for border management.

In 2013 SIS-II was introduced with additional features, and in 2023 the latest version entered into force. SIS is a component of central border management cooperation, which ensures the security of the internal borders, where no controls are conducted. The collaboration under SIS unites the border police and customs and judicial authorities, as well as the immigration conduct of EU members and the Schengen associate states (Switzerland, Norway, Liechtenstein, and Iceland). The competent authorities, such as the law enforcement units, are able to enter the system to consult alerts on people and objects in one common database, where fingerprints, photographs, palm prints, fingermarks, palm marks, and DNA records (for missing persons only) can also be added. These data are used for biometric searches through the SIS. For terrorism-related activities, the authorities can add additional data on the given persons for the prevention of crimes and terrorism.

Since 2014 the European Union Agency for Law Enforcement Cooperation (Europol) and SIS have cooperated at different levels; and since 2021 Europol has had access to all alert categories in SIS to match searches for enhancing security. The European Commission conducts the general supervision. Hence, the EC monitors and evaluates the system as well as implements and delegates on how SIS works. Because the system is largely based on an information network, the EU Agency for the Operational Management of Large-Scale IT Systems (eu-LISA) is responsible for the operational management of the network.

Frontex is another significant institutional element of European asylum management. The European Union created a number of initiatives to prevent the entry of migrants into member states. One of them is the European Border and Coast Guard Agency, Frontex. It is an outcome of the discussions in the late 1990s regarding the further strengthening of cooperation among asylum migration areas. These matters were initially handled by the External Border Practitioners Common Unit, which was composed of members of the Strategic Committee on Immigration, Frontiers and Asylum (SCIFA) and the heads of national border control services. Frontex was established in 2004 by Council Regulation (EC) 2007/2004 as an advancement of the methods and procedures of the Common Unit.[140]

Frontex is the European Union's first uniformed law enforcement service, Frontex has transformed into an operational arm of the EU. It is referred to as the centre of excellence for border control activities at the EU's external borders. Through Frontex, EU member countries and Schengen-associated countries share intelligence and expertise. Frontex also collaborates with the neighbouring (non-EU) countries that are also affected by migratory trends and/or cross-border crime. The Frontex officers, in collaboration with national authorities (national police and border and coast guards), perform a variety of tasks such as operations, fighting cross-border crime,

140 Council of the European Union, 'Establishing a European Agency for the Management of Operational Cooperation at the External Borders of the Member States of the European Union', L 349/1 Council Regulation (EC) no 2007/2004 § (2004), https://eur-lex.europa.eu/legal-content/EN/TXT/?qid=1513171334865&uri=CELEX:32004R2007.

monitoring and risk analysis, border surveillance even beyond the EU borders, assisting in return operations, and the European Travel Information and Authorisation System (ETIAS).

Migration movements towards Europe occur along specific maritime routes, such as the Western Mediterranean, the Central Mediterranean, the Eastern Mediterranean, the West African, the Western Balkan, and the Eastern Borders routes. Periodically, some routes experience higher traffic than others. Among them, the Eastern Mediterranean route, corresponding to the Greek border, has been the most frequently used by irregular migrants.

To tackle the waves of migration on these routes, Frontex carries out maritime operations. The duty of Frontex is to detect irregular migrants attempting to reach the European Union via sea, to prevent migrant smuggling, and to enhance collaboration with member states. Authorities are also granted the power to intervene in situations involving vessels carrying migrants. Air operations, which are less frequent compared to other domains, primarily focus on tracking fake visas and passports. On land borders, member states engage in both customs' cooperation and the combat against irregular migration and cross-border crime.

The partner institutions of Frontex within the EU are the European Commission, the European Parliament, the Council of the European Union, and the European External Action Service, plus one EU agency, the Justice and Home Affairs Agencies' Network. Frontex also collaborates with international organizations such as the IOM, UNHCR, OSCE, COE, and Interpol.

According to the SIS, the European Commission is the supervisory and monitoring body over Frontex for the implementation of EU treaties and legislation. The parent institution of Frontex is the Directorate-General for Migration and Home Affairs (DG HOME) of the European Commission. The Commission delegates relevant powers to Frontex and provides prior approval to proposed working arrangements. It proposes Council decisions requiring a member state to cooperate with Frontex as well as decisions on Frontex border management. The DG HOME coordinates the activities of the migration management support teams.

One of the most common criticisms of Frontex is about the pushbacks. In April 2022, a study was released documenting the participation of Frontex in the pushback of at least 957 refugees between March 2020 and September 2021.[141] The human rights organization 11.11.11 published in its

141 Lighthouse Reports, 'Frontex, the EU Pushback Agency', accessed 4 March 2024, https://www.lighthousereports.com/investigation/frontex-the-eu-pushback-agency/.

pushback report in 2023 that there were 346,004 illegal pushbacks of people migrating to Europe in 2023. The NGO asked EU member states

> to advocate within the European Council for effective and independent monitoring that ensures respect for fundamental rights. This entails [...] their capacity as a member of the Frontex management board advocate the immediate scale back of Frontex activities and limit them to monitoring in member states that systematically break the rules. This is in line with Frontex regulation. This is definitely the case for Greece.

The member states were also asked to 'play a pioneering role in further internal reforms of Frontex, with a stronger role for the Fundamental Rights Officer' and to 'make their participation in Frontex operations dependent on independent assessments of the human rights situation and suspend the deployment of means and personnel in case of violations by Frontex or the host country of the operation'.[142]

In a resolution dated December 2023 the European Parliament expressed severe concerns regarding the pushback allegations against Greece and said it was 'convinced that respect for the principles and values of the Union must be the condition sine qua non for Frontex to commit to a joint operation with a Member State' and that

> the Agency [Frontex] should scale down and repurpose its operations towards monitoring activities in the light of Article 46 of its mandate, while maintaining its presence on the ground in order not to leave a vacuum; regrets that the Agency [Frontex] has so far refrained from scaling down or repurposing its operations in Greece.[143]

In conclusion, while Frontex has played a pivotal role in managing the European Union's external borders, its operations have not been without controversy. The agency, tasked with coordinating border surveillance and combating cross-border crime, has faced significant scrutiny over allegations of involvement in migrant pushbacks. These accusations highlight potential conflicts between the agency's border security mandate and the EU's human

142 11.11.11, *Illegality without Borders: Pushback Report 2023* (Belgium: 11.11.11, 2024), https://11.be/sites/default/files/2024-02/20240214-Pushback-Report-2023-eng.pdf.

143 European Parliament, 'European Parliament Resolution of 14 December 2023 on Frontex Building on the Fact-Finding Investigation of the LIBE Working Group for Frontex Scrutiny', 14 December 2023, https://www.europarl.europa.eu/doceo/document/TA-9-2023-0483_EN.html.

rights obligations. Such issues underscore the necessity for reforms within Frontex to ensure that its activities fully comply with international law and the fundamental values of the Union. Ensuring effective oversight and accountability mechanisms within Frontex operations could help restore confidence in the agency's commitment to upholding the rights and dignity of individuals at Europe's borders.

European Dactyloscopy (Eurodac) is the fingerprint database of the European Union for identifying irregular border crossings and asylum seekers. The system is an outcome of the Dublin System and it was established to assist member states in determining which EU member state will be responsible for the evaluation of the refugee status determination of an asylum applicant.

The European Border Surveillance System (Eurosur) is a framework designed to prevent cross-border crimes, address irregular migration, and protect migrants' lives by preventing deaths of irregular migrants during their dangerous journeys. The technical capabilities of Eurosur enable member states and Frontex to exchange information and cooperate on these issue areas.

### *Readmission Agreements: The EU's Externalization Strategy*

The European Union has been concluding readmission agreements in a bilateral manner (one EU member state and one non-EU) or across the EU (the EU and one non-EU state). The aim of these agreements is to facilitate the return of irregular migrants to their country of origin or to the country where they were found in transit. Until today, the EU has concluded several readmission agreements with third states. In particular, due to the increase in migration in the 2010s, the EU covered readmission agreements with third states, with whom EU member states already had bilateral agreements – Albania, Armenia, Georgia, Serbia, Moldova, Belarus, Turkey, etc.[144]

The readmission agreements are widely criticized because they have the potential to violate the non-refoulement principle that is protecting people of concern from being forcibly sent back to the country of origin, where persecution awaits them. This criticism is voiced within and by the European Parliament, too.[145] Another criticism point is related to the

144 For detailed information, see European Commission, 'Bilateral Readmission Agreements', *Home Affairs*, September 2022, https://home-affairs.ec.europa.eu/system/files/2022-10/EMN_INFORM_bilateral_readmission.pdf.

145 Jean-Pierre Cassarino, 'Dealing with Unbalanced Reciprocities: Cooperation on Readmission and Implications', in *Unbalanced Reciprocities: Cooperation on Readmission in the*

domino effect that can be triggered from the EU borders outwards. The removal of persons from one country to another one may end up returning the person to the country of origin or a country where their human rights will not be properly guaranteed. The readmission agreements concluded by the EU do not include any provision to prevent the aforesaid domino effect. The third criticism is related to the term 'illegal immigration'. The readmission agreements underline that the parties are 'determined to strengthen their co-operation in order to combat illegal immigration more effectively'.[146] The employment of the term 'illegal' is criminalizing the irregular or undocumented migrants. Although this was a widely used term until 1975, the UN recommended that the term be avoided and replaced with 'undocumented' or 'irregular' to forestall securitization.[147]

In 2013 one readmission agreement was concluded between the EU and Turkey.[148] By this agreement, Turkey agreed to readmit its own nationals

> who do not, or who no longer, fulfil the conditions in force under the law of that Member State or under the law of the Union for entry to, presence in, or residence on, the territory of the requesting Member State.[149]

Turkey also agreed to readmit third-country nationals and stateless persons

> upon application by a Member State and without further formalities to be undertaken by that Member State other than those provided for in this Agreement, all third-country nationals or stateless persons who do not, or who no longer, fulfil the conditions in force for entry to, presence in, or residence on, the territory of the requesting Member State.[150]

In the case of third-country nationals (aliens) and stateless persons, those will be readmitted who 'illegally and directly entered the territory of the

*Euro-Mediterranean Area*, ed. Jean-Pierre Cassarino (Middle East Institute Special Edition Viewpoints, 2010), 1–29.

146 See European Council, 'Agreement between the European Union and the Republic of Turkey on the Readmission of Persons Residing without Authorisation', L 134/3 § (2013), https://eur-lex.europa.eu/legal-content/EN/ALL/?uri=celex%3A22014A0507%2801%29.

147 Tuğba Bayar, 'The Sheep That God Lost: "Legally" Circumventing the Human Rights of Undocumented Migrants', *Southeast European and Black Sea Studies* 25, no. 2 (2023): 249–67, at 2.

148 European Council, 'Agreement between the European Union and the Republic of Turkey on the Readmission of Persons Residing without Authorisation'.

149 Ibid., article 3(1).

150 Ibid., article 4(1).

Member States after having stayed on, or transited through, the territory of Turkey'.[151] According to article 7 of the Readmission Agreement, they will be returned to their country of origin. This provision can be seen in the light of the second criticism mentioned above, according to which the return may possibly cause the violation of the non-refoulement principle. Considering the fact that most of those transiting Turkey to reach one of the EU member states are coming from countries like Afghanistan, Iran, Pakistan, Iraq, or Syria, the probability increases that they would face persecution when on the soil of their country of origin.

The Arab Spring uprisings triggered significant migratory flows from the Middle East, Africa, and Central Asia towards Europe, reshaping how migration is perceived across the continent. These movements sparked divergent views among EU member states regarding migration's impact on social cohesion, political dynamics, economic stability, and cultural identity. Initially, these challenges led to fragmented, national-level responses. Over time, the growing pressures underscored the need for collective measures to address irregular migration. However, due to member states' reluctance to cede sovereignty over migration policies, the European Union has yet to establish a fully harmonized migration framework. Instead, the EU sought to manage migration flows externally by forging agreements with neighbouring countries, such as readmission agreements and the EU–Turkey deal of 18 March 2016. The deal tasked Ankara with preventing irregular migrants from reaching Europe. In return, the EU provided financial assistance and other incentives. As a part of this arrangement, Turkey adopted a temporary protection status specifically for Syrian nationals, ensuring their legal stay within its borders while relieving pressure on EU member states. This decentralized and externalized approach highlights both the limitations of the EU's migration governance and the growing importance of temporary protection mechanisms in addressing humanitarian needs.

### *Temporary Protection Policy in Comparative Perspective*

The temporary protection policy is followed as an emergency response to influx conditions. It is a palliative migration solution instead of a permanent one. The temporary protection status represents a gap in international migration regulations. It is devised as a comprehensive approach to protect persons fleeing armed conflict, whether or not they satisfy the definition given in the Refugee Convention (1951) or the Refugee Protocol (1967). Following the dissolution of Yugoslavia and the genocide of Bosnia, multiple migrant

151 Ibid., article 4(1.c).

flows in the 1990s towards Europe stimulated the necessity to respond the problem of burden sharing and to formulate a common migration policy.

As a sub-organ of the UN, the United Nations High Commissioner for Refugees (UNHCR) questioned the usefulness of temporary protection status, not specifically for the case of Yugoslavia, but in general. The UNHCR concluded in 1994 that it could be a method to meet protection needs in mass outflows. The basic elements of temporary protection are (i) admission to the country of refuge; (ii) respect for the principle of non-refoulement and basic human rights; and (iii) repatriation when conditions in the country of origin so allows.[152] The entire basic needs of the people under temporary protection are covered by the host country.

The European Council adopted a programme on 30 November 1993 to carry out a detailed examination of the admission and residence of refugees arriving in Western Europe and the burden-sharing problem. The Council agreed to issue a document allowing a temporary suspension of deportation (called a *Duldung* in German) to people whose lives or health were under threat as a result of armed conflict or civil war in the future and so could not return to their country of origin.[153] The criteria for the temporary status protection was then determined by the Treaty of Amsterdam.

A conference was held in March 1996 in Turin, Italy, to refine the European approach to temporary refugee status. As a result, the Treaty of Amsterdam was adopted, in 1999, amending the Maastricht Treaty on European Union. The Treaty of Amsterdam was a reaction to the difficulties experienced under the structures of the Schengen regime, the Dublin Regulations, and the Third Pillar. These structures assumed that members had the same or almost similar national asylum and migration regimes; thus, they commonly established a trust-based interdependence through inter-governmental communication and cooperation. However, the national systems varied to a great extent, from criminal law to refugee status determination (RSD), and were not equivalents of each other. Moreover, the lack of judicial monitoring was shown to be a significant failure. In particular, the Third Pillar (article L of the TEU) became a focus for improvement due to a loophole demonstrating that politics at the EU level and the national level were more contradictory than supplementary. The Treaty of Amsterdam upgraded

152 UNHCR, 'Note on Temporary Protection in a Broader Context', 1 January 1994, https://www.refworld.org/policy/legalguidance/unhcr/1994/en/13438.

153 Official Journal of the European Communities, 'Council Resolution on Burden-Sharing with Regard to the Admission and Residence of Displaced Persons on a Temporary Basis', Pub. L. no. 95/C 262/01 (1995), https://eur-lex.europa.eu/legal-content/EN/TXT/PDF/?uri=CELEX:31995Y1007(01).

asylum and migration to the First Pillar, moving them to the supranational level from the intra-governmental level by entitling the Commission to legislate on these issues. The Amsterdam Treaty introduced these topics to the jurisdiction of the Court of Justice of the EU.

Today, the EU defines temporary protection as 'an exceptional measure for providing immediate and temporary protection in the event of a mass influx or imminent mass influx of displaced persons from non-EU countries who are unable to return to their country of origin'.[154] The status is regulated under the 2001 Temporary Protection Directive, according to which displaced persons are those 'who have had to leave their country or region of origin, or have been evacuated, in particular, in response to an appeal by international organizations, and are unable to return'.[155] The directive is valid for all EU member states, which creates a burden-sharing situation and an equal policy and implementation for non-EU citizens who are displaced. According to article 2 of the Council directive, 'displaced persons' means third-country nationals or stateless persons who have had to leave their country or region of origin, or have been evacuated, in particular, in response to an appeal by international organizations, and are unable to return in safe and durable conditions because of (i) armed conflict or endemic violence; or (ii) systemic or generalized violations of human rights that victimize people and put them under serious risk. Article 8 obliges member states to adopt the necessary measures to ease the provision of residence permits for the duration of the protection. Article 9 requires the member state to provide information about the scope of the protection in the language of the protected. The protected can unite with family members if they enjoy protection in other member states (article 15, para. 2). The directive (article 14) grants access to the education system to all underage protected persons. The directive (article 11) also allows the member state to take back the protection status if the said person remains on, or seeks to enter without authorization onto, the territory of another member state. For the duration of the protection the member state allows persons engaging in employed or self-employed activities. When the temporary protection ends, the general laws on protection and on aliens apply (article 20) and the member states take the necessary measures to make possible the voluntary

154 European Commission, Directorate-General for Migration and Home Affairs, 'Temporary Protection', accessed 9 November 2023, https://home-affairs.ec.europa.eu/policies/migration-and-asylum/common-european-asylum-system/temporary-protection_en.

155 European Council, '2001 Temporary Protection Directive', Pub. L. no. 2001/55/EC, *Official Journal* L 212, 07/08/2001 P. 0012-0023 (2001), https://eur-lex.europa.eu/legal-content/EN/TXT/?uri=CELEX%3A32001L0055&qid=1648223587338.

return of persons enjoying temporary protection (article 21). Temporarily protected persons can always apply for asylum (article 17). The member states may exclude a person from temporary protection (article 28) if there are serious reasons for considering that; and/or if they have committed a crime against peace, a war crime, or a crime against humanity; or if they have committed a serious non-political crime outside the member state of reception.

After the temporary protection status was employed for sheltering Bosniacs, it was activated for the second time by the EU due to the eruption of the Russian invasion of Ukraine on 24 February 2022, as a response to the mass arrivals of people fleeing Ukraine. The Council unanimously adopted the resolution to grant fleeing Ukrainians temporary refugee status.[156] The current implementation of the temporary protection status is observable in the decision of the Council dated 4 March 2022. The decision was published as a response to the 'mass influx of displaced persons from Ukraine within the meaning of Article 5 of Directive 2001/55/EC'.[157]

Denmark has been employing temporary protection as a transition status for asylum seekers and the subjects of family reunification. Currently, a proposal seeks to amend the relevant law on providing persons displaced from Ukraine with extended temporary residence permits. The UNHCR welcomed the extension proposal, which permits residence permits to last until March 2026.[158] Sweden is another country that gives de facto refugees a residence permit with temporary protection, in line with the EU's Temporary Protection Directive. This is actively retained for those fleeing the war in Ukraine.[159]

Similarly, Germany has been issuing a permits for a temporary suspension of deportation (*Duldung*) to those who fled their country of origin but for

156 European Commission, 'Mass Influx of Displaced Persons from Ukraine', Pub. L. no. (EU) 2022/38, *Official Journal of the European Union,* L 71/1 (2022), https://eur-lex.europa.eu/legal-content/EN/TXT/?uri=uriserv%3AOJ.L_.2022.071.01.0001.01.ENG&toc=OJ%3AL%3A2022%3A071%3ATOC.

157 Ibid.

158 UNHCR Nordic and Baltic Countries, 'UNHCR Observations on the Danish Proposal for Law on Amendments to the Law on Temporary Residence Permits for Persons Displaced from Ukraine', 24 October 2024, https://www.unhcr.org/neu/129429-unhcr-observations-on-the-danish-proposal-for-law-on-amendments-to-the-law-on-temporary-residence-permits-for-persons-displaced-from-ukraine.html.

159 Migrationsverket, 'Apply for Protection under the Temporary Protection Directive for the First Time', 28 May 2024, https://www.migrationsverket.se/English/Private-individuals/Protection-under-the-Temporary-Protection-Directive/Apply-for-protection-for-the-first-time.html.

whom temporary refugee status is not possible. The *Duldung* prevents their deportation. It 'does not make the stay legal, but the offence of illegal residence does not apply'.[160] This is almost the case for Netherlands, as well, where the Temporary Protection Directive is reserved for incomers from Ukraine and it entitles the person a residence, a work permit, healthcare, and education for minor children, until 4 March 2026.[161]

The European Union and the Council of Europe are the two prominent international organizations that set laws, rules, and norms on asylum and migration in Europe. While the EU directly implements the process, the COE provides the legal protection framework in relation to abuses and violations in cases of pushback, detention conditions in the transit zones, and detention centres in border areas. Cracks in the global and regional infrastructure developed when widespread violations and abuses occurred during the massive inflows of the 2010s, resulting in the dismantling of the Dublin System.[162] A new approach emerged, based on reducing the incentives that pull irregular migration, protecting the borders, and externalizing the controls, and it involved the formulation of a new common asylum and migration policy. Currently, the member states seem to have distanced themselves from the creation of a common policy. Due to geographical realities, members that represent the outermost borders of the EU face the highest migration burden and the countries within the continent react to influxes by suspending the Schengen system temporarily, from time to time. To diminish the burden of the outermost EU member states and to prevent a Schengen crisis – which could take place, for example, if inland states seek to protect public goods that serve as pull factors to potential migrants – the common EU policy evolved towards deterrence of migration. In order to maintain the stability of the Schengen system by preventing irregular migration and also by putting up obstacles to terrorist activity, some EU states started to protect their outer borders with physical barriers, such as walls and fences. Physical border protection emerged in the early 1990s, when Spain built fences in Ceuta and Melilla, which border northern

160 München.de, 'Temporary Suspension of Deportation (Tolerated Stay)', accessed 11 October 2024, https://stadt.muenchen.de/service/en-GB/info/hauptabteilung-ii-buergerangelegenheiten/10413124/.

161 Immigratie- en Naturalisatiedienst, 'Temporary Protection Directive Ukraine', Ministerie van Asiel en Migratie, accessed 10 November 2024, https://ind.nl/en/ukraine/temporary-protection-directive-ukraine#requirements-temporary-protection-directive.

162 Violeta Moreno-Lax, 'Dismantling the Dublin System: MSS v. Belgium and Greece', *European Journal of Migration and Law* 14, no. 1 (2012): 1–31.

Morocco. These barriers now exceed 2,000 kilometres in length.[163] The European Parliament stressed that the protection of EU external borders must be carried out in line with the Charter of Fundamental Rights of the European Union and relevant international and EU law.[164]

The EU's combat against irregular migration does not include resistance against overall migration. The EU produces policies to attract quantities of (regular) migrants who have desirable qualities. The EU *acquis* on regular migration controls the procedures related to the entry, residence, and work processes of third-country citizens. The *acquis* is designed to reduce the dangers inherent in migration and at the same time foster the benefits and opportunities for both the EU and the third-country citizens that migration entails. This framework is designed to involve the entry and residence of foreigners, who are referred to as 'third-country nationals'. They are characterized as follows: highly qualified migrants and their families (EC Directive 2009/50); seasonal workers (EU Directive 2014/36); intra-corporate transferees (ICTs) (EU Directive 2014/66); those who arrive for the purposes of research, studies, training, voluntary service, pupil exchange schemes, or educational projects and au pairing (EU Directive 2016/801); those who arrive within international agreements concluded by the EU (such as the Association Agreement with Turkey in 1963, a series of joint agreements concluded between the EU and Switzerland, or association agreements with the Maghreb countries: Morocco, Tunisia, and Algeria).[165]

### *Asylum Governance in Turkey and the EU's Role*

Syrians started to arrive in Turkey in April 2011 after civil war erupted in Syria due to the violent response of the Syrian president Bashar al-Assad to anti-regime demonstrations. Turkey immediately announced an open-door policy so as not to turn a blind eye to the humanitarian tragedy ongoing within the neighbouring country. The Disaster and Emergency Management Presidency (AFAD) was appointed as the responsible institution to manage the conditions of the migrants coming from Syria. Soon, the number of incomers climbed dramatically, raising the necessity of establishing new shelters in the border provinces for them. It was understood that covering

163 European Parliament, 'Walls and Fences at EU Borders', October 2022, https://www.europarl.europa.eu/RegData/etudes/BRIE/2022/733692/EPRS_BRI(2022)733692_EN.pdf.
164 Ibid.
165 Dora Kostakopoulou and Daniel Thym, *Research Handbook on European Union Citizenship Law and Policy: Navigating Challenges and Crises* (Northampton, MA: Edward Elgar Publishing, 2022), 349–63.

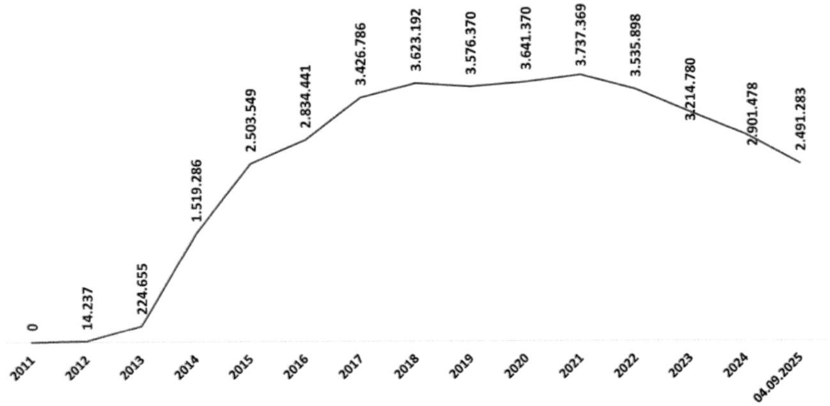


Figure 3. The number of Syrians under temporary protection in Turkey from 2011 to 2024. Source: Ministry of the Interior, General Directorate of Migration.[166]

the entire basic needs of the migrants – nutrition, shelter, healthcare, and education – could not be easily realized within shelters and camps. On the other hand, problems of residence, travel, education, and the right to work in Turkey arose, as well as issues around the asylum applications that were being handled by the UNHCR, registered by the Turkish authorities, and requiring passports from the embassy. In October 2011, the Turkish government shared that the Syrians would fall under 'temporary protection' status while they remained in Turkey.

Turkish leaders did not expect an increase in the migration volume of the inflow of Syrians. When 8,000 Syrians registered in Turkey in 2012, Prime Minister Ahmet Davutoğlu declared that 100,000 incomers would be the psychological threshold.[167] In 2015, nearly one million migrants arrived in Europe, mostly by sea. The majority of them (856,723) landed in Greece after transiting through Turkey.[168]

By 31 October 2024, the number of Syrians residing in Turkey under temporary protection status was 2,935,742 (see fig. 3). The number decreased since 2022, when there were 3,535,898, and 2023, when there were 3,214,780.

166 Göç İdaresi Başkanlığı, 'Geçici Koruma', 7 November 2024, https://www.goc.gov.tr/gecici-koruma5638.

167 Burcu Çalık, 'Mülteci Sayısı Psikolojik Sınırı Aştı', *Sabah Gazetesi*, 16 October 2012, https://www.sabah.com.tr/gundem/2012/10/16/multeci-sayisi-psikolojik-siniri-asti.

168 European Commission, 'Annual Policy Report 2015 on Asylum and Migration' (Athens: European Migration Network, and Greek Ministry of Interior and Administrative Reconstruction, 2016), 7, https://migrant-integration.ec.europa.eu/sites/default/files/2018-07/annual-policy-12a_greece_apr_part2_english.pdf.

Considering the age and gender distribution of the Syrians under temporary protection status, 1,515,339 were males and 1,420,403 were females. The age range of zero to five was the most crowded, with 495,613 members. There were 2,101,118 Syrians below the age of thirty. The age distribution demonstrates a decreasing trend from thirty upwards; 834,660 of the Syrians under temporary protection are older than thirty years old. As for the district distribution of the Syrians under temporary protection, 511,645 of them reside in Istanbul.[169] Among the cities where the smallest Syrian population under temporary protection reside are Hakkari (eleven Syrians), Tunceli (twenty-nine), Bayburt (twenty-nine), Artvin (sixty-nine), and Iğdır (seventy-two). The nationality distribution of irregular migrants apprehended in Turkey varies (see fig. 4). Afghans, Syrians, Palestinians, Turkmenis, and Moroccans are the top five nationalities on this list.

Besides approximately three million Syrians under temporary protection, roughly 60,000 people coming from Syria are living in temporary protection shelters, according to the numbers shared by the Ministry of the Interior. Turkey currently hosts more people of concern than any other county in the world. This is mainly based on the demand of the European Union, which led to the conclusion of a readmission agreement with Turkey in 2013, which was then followed by the EU–Turkey deal of 2016.

The right to seek and enjoy asylum is found in article 14 of the Universal Declaration of Human Rights and Turkey acknowledged the provision. The right to seek asylum is regulated by the Refugee Convention (1951) and the Refugee Protocol (1967), to which Turkey is a party, but with geographical reservations.[170] Accordingly, in Turkey, the definition of a refugee encompasses Europeans only. In this context, 'European' means the citizen of a member country in the Council of Europe. Turkey's commitment, therefore, does not cover Syrians. Nationals of non-European countries can only reside in Turkey for a temporary period, until they find

169 Ibid.

170 The other international treaties related to asylum and migration that Turkey is a party to are (i) the European Convention on Human Rights (ECHR), which safeguards the rights of all persons living in the member countries of the Council of Europe; (ii) the Convention Relating to the Status of Stateless Persons (1954), which acknowledges the equal rights of all individuals, including the stateless; (iii) the Convention on the Reduction of Statelessness (1961), which was adopted to ensure the right of all individuals to choose their nationality in order to be protected from statelessness; (iv) the International Covenant on Civil and Political Rights (1966), which acknowledges the dignity of all persons and obliges the signatory states to ensure the civil and human rights of their subjects.

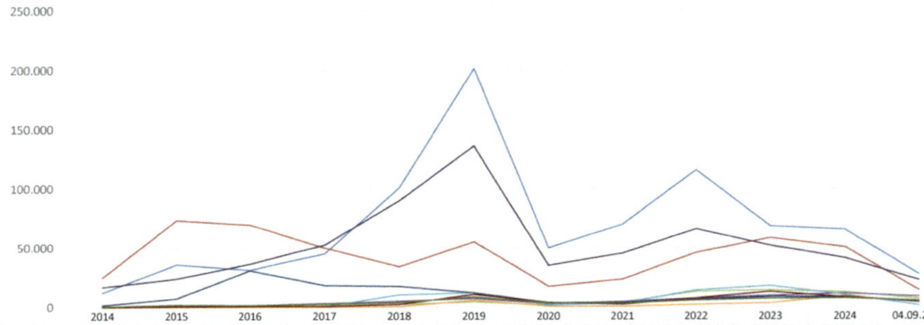


| | 2014 | 2015 | 2016 | 2017 | 2018 | 2019 | 2020 | 2021 | 2022 | 2023 | 2024 | 04.09.2025 |
|---|---|---|---|---|---|---|---|---|---|---|---|---|
| AFGHANISTAN | 12.248 | 35.921 | 31.360 | 45.259 | 100.841 | 201.437 | 50.161 | 70.237 | 115.775 | 68.687 | 65.815 | 27.710 |
| SYRIA | 24.984 | 73.422 | 69.755 | 50.217 | 34.053 | 55.236 | 17.562 | 23.468 | 45.909 | 58.621 | 50.641 | 14.336 |
| TURKMENISTAN | 817 | 1.241 | 1.034 | 1.302 | 2.580 | 4.484 | 1.882 | 4.343 | 13.083 | 14.328 | 12.571 | 7.124 |
| UZBEKISTAN | 503 | 1.393 | 1.648 | 3.321 | 5.203 | 7.478 | 3.030 | 4.819 | 7.553 | 9.649 | 11.521 | 8.923 |
| PALASTINE | 508 | 615 | 365 | 832 | 10.545 | 12.210 | 2.059 | 3.497 | 14.270 | 18.113 | 10.285 | 1.554 |
| EGYPT | 53 | 170 | 130 | 119 | 552 | 5.951 | 939 | 728 | 2.158 | 3.478 | 9.361 | 3.881 |
| IRAQ | 1.728 | 7.247 | 30.947 | 18.488 | 17.629 | 12.097 | 3.836 | 4.404 | 6.628 | 8.803 | 8.535 | 4.335 |
| MOROCCO | 204 | 525 | 905 | 821 | 2.496 | 10.836 | 4.073 | 2.453 | 7.523 | 13.040 | 8.297 | 5.259 |
| IRAN | 626 | 1.978 | 1.817 | 2.707 | 4.066 | 8.753 | 3.562 | 3.505 | 5.849 | 7.295 | 7.614 | 5.504 |
| OTHER | 16.976 | 23.973 | 36.505 | 52.686 | 90.038 | 136.180 | 35.198 | 45.542 | 66.279 | 51.994 | 41.191 | 22.783 |

Figure 4. Nationality distribution of irregular migrants in Turkey, 2014–24. Source: Ministry of the Interior, General Directorate of Migration.[171]

refuge in a third country. Then they are resettled. The solution Turkey offered to migrants coming from Syria was temporary protection status. The Refugee Convention and the Refugee Protocol do not feature temporary protection status.[171]

Temporary protection status is formulated to fill the gap in the international infrastructure where it falls short in providing protection for a limited time period to a large group of fleeing people. When non-European nationals arrive in Turkey seeking asylum, they used to lodge an asylum application by the UNHCR.

Since 10 September 2018, refugee status determination has been carried out by the Presidency for Migration Management (Göç İdaresi Başkanlığı, GİB) only. It was the sole authority responsible for processing asylum applications and refugee registration in Turkey. Since then, the UNHCR has continued to provide protection in terms of legal counselling for people of concern. It has also collaborated with the GİB to identify refugees in the most vulnerable situations to see if the individuals concerned are eligible for resettlement processing.

According to Turkish regulations, temporary protection is a legal status reserved only for people arriving from Syria, thus including Syrian nationals

171 Göç İdaresi Başkanlığı, 'Düzensiz Göç', 11 July 2024, https://www.goc.gov.tr/duzensiz-goc-istatistikler.

as well as others, such as Palestinian refugees or stateless people arriving in Turkey from Syria. This status was established by the Temporary Protection Regulation dated 22 October 2014. Under this regime, Syrians were shielded by the non-refoulement principle. Voluntary return to Syria was possible and it was considered to be grounds for the cessation of temporary protection. They were granted residence permits. Their fundamental rights were preserved, and they had access to social benefits such as the healthcare system, the education system, the judiciary, and social aid. The regulation determined in article 1 that temporary protection was provided to foreigners who were forced to leave their counties, were unable to return to the countries they left, arrived at or crossed Turkish borders en masse or individually, and did not have their international protection needs adjudicated under an individual procedure.[172] Moreover, the amendment dated 7 April 2016 held that Syrian nationals who were not previously beneficiaries of temporary protection and irregularly crossed to Greece could be granted temporary protection status upon their return to Turkey. This development is a supplementary act to the EU–Turkey deal of 18 March 2016.

The EU–Turkey deal that was reached on 18 March 2016 is the statement of cooperation between the two parties for stopping the migration flow towards the EU. The elements of the deal were: (i) as of 20 March 2016 all new irregular migrants crossing to Greek islands from Turkey will be returned to Turkey; (ii) for every Syrian being returned to Turkey from Greek islands, another Syrian will be resettled in the EU according to the UN vulnerability criteria (see fig. 5); (iii) Turkey will take any necessary measures to prevent new sea or land routes for illegal migration opening from Turkey to the EU; (iv) a voluntary humanitarian admission scheme will be activated upon the ending (or substantial reduction) of irregular crossings; (v) the visa liberalization road map will be accelerated vis-à-vis all participating member states with a view to lifting the visa requirements for Turkish citizens; (vi) the EU[173] will speed up the disbursement of the initially allocated €3 billion under the Facility for Refugees in Turkey and ensure funding of further projects for persons under temporary protection – once these resources

172 European Commission, 'Commission Staff Working Document Accompanying the Document Report from the Commission to the European Parliament and the Council Third Report on Progress by Turkey in Fulfilling the Requirements of its Visa Liberalisation Roadmap', Pub. L. no. SWD (2016) 161 final, COM(2016) 278 final (2016), https://home-affairs.ec.europa.eu/document/download/1cbb2e5d-5a42-4d7e-af8c-0f884d6f39c8_en.

173 Göç İdaresi Başkanlığı, 'Geçici Koruma'.

| Country | Total |
|---|---|
| Total | 69,818 |
| USA | 7,501 |
| Germany | 19,494 |
| Australia | 919 |
| Austria | 219 |
| Belgium | 1,909 |
| Bulgaria | 94 |
| Denmark | 31 |
| Estonia | 59 |
| Finland | 2,975 |
| France | 6,304 |
| Croatia | 250 |
| Netherlands | 5,852 |
| U.K. | 2,741 |
| Spain | 1,213 |
| Sweden | 3,174 |
| Switzerland | 220 |
| Italy | 399 |
| Iceland | 0 |
| Canada | 13,562 |
| Latvia | 46 |
| Lichtenstein | 0 |
| Lithuanian | 102 |
| Luxemburg | 206 |
| Malta | 17 |
| Norway | 1,742 |
| Portugal | 463 |
| Romania | 254 |
| Slovenia | 57 |
| New Zealand | 15 |

Figure 5. Resettlement of Syrians to third countries between 2016 and 2024. Source: Ministry of the Interior, General Directorate of Migration.[173]

were nearly used up and provided the above commitments were met, the EU was to mobilize an additional €3 billion in funding for the facility up to the end of 2018; (vii) the EU and Turkey agreed to continue the upgrading of the Customs Union; (viii) the EU and Turkey reconfirmed their commitment to re-energize the accession process; and (ix) the EU and its member states will work with Turkey in any joint endeavour to improve humanitarian conditions inside Syria.

Under the EU–Turkey deal, Turkey was designated as a safe third country for undocumented migrants returned from Greek islands. This is problematic considering the five criteria used to determine whether a third country was safe, as mentioned in the EU's Asylum Procedures Directive.[174] Offering asylum seekers the possibility of refugee status was one of the criteria, however, Turkey's geographical reservations in the Refugee Convention (1951) and the Refugee Protocol (1967) prevented non-Europeans from attaining refugee status there.

## The EU–Turkey Deal

Although a dramatic drop happened in the number of irregular migrants crossing the Aegean Sea from Turkey to Greece (see fig. 6), it is important to bear in mind that in that year the Balkan states built walls and fences to prevent entry.

| Year | Sea Arrivals | Land Arrivals |
|---|---|---|
| **2024*** | 48.984 | 7.014 |
| **2023** | 41.561 | 7.16 |
| **2022** | 12.758 | 6.022 |
| **2021** | 4.331 | 4.826 |
| **2020** | 9.714 | 5.982 |
| **2019** | 59.726 | 14.887 |
| **2018** | 32.494 | 18.014 |
| **2017** | 29.718 | 6.592 |
| **2016** | 173.45 | 3.784 |
| **2015** | 856.723 | 4.907 |
| **2014** | 41.038 | 2.28 |

Figure 6. Sea and land arrivals to Greece from 2014 to 2024. Source: UNHCR Operational Data Portal.[175]

In 2020, following the 28 February Idlib attack, Turkish president Erdoğan declared that Turkey could not contain the new wave of migration and so Turkey would no longer prevent migrants from travelling on to Europe. He stopped the EU–Turkey deal unilaterally and opened the border to migrants who wished to leave Turkey. As an immediate response to the

174 European Parliament and Council of the European Union, 'Directive on Common Procedures for Granting and Withdrawing International Protection, 2013/32/EU, 26 June 2013', Refworld, accessed 7 February 2021, https://www.refworld.org/docid/51d29b224.html.

175 UNHCR Operational Data Portal, 'Europe Sea Arrivals/Greece', accessed 29 November 2024, https://data.unhcr.org/en/situations/europe-sea-arrivals/location/24489.

announcement, migrants flooded the Pazarkule Border Gate between Turkey and Greece. However, Greece did not open its borders to the thousands of migrants (mostly Pakistanis, Afghans, and East Africans) heading towards the EU.[176] Greek border security used violence and inhumane methods to prevent the crossings. Failures of both the EU and Turkey to comply with the agreement led to tragic chaos across the borders, leaving many migrants with injuries. The outbreak of the COVID-19 pandemic in 2020 resulted in a decrease in the volume of migrant crossings. The global closure of borders, interruption in international travel, and imposition of harsh sanitary measures almost completely halted the migration deal, as for example, Germany also decided not to hold the one-to-one resettlement scheme with Turkey.

After the conclusion of the EU–Turkey deal in 2016 and the adoption of the amendment to the temporary protection regulation, Turkey sent letters to the European Commission in April 2016 to guarantee that all the Syrians returned from Greece to Turkey will be granted temporary protection status upon their return. Moreover, by 29 April 2016, the UNHCR had been guaranteed access to the removal centres and to speak with migrants detained for fulfilling its protection mandate.

As of 10 September 2018, the UNHCR stopped registering international protection applicants, and it also stopped carrying out mandate refugee status determination procedures. Today, the main body responsible for the registration of all foreigners, including irregular migrants and also those seek international protection, is the Directorate General of Migration Management (DGMM) and its provincial branches. The registration is key to enabling people to remain legally in Turkey. The holder of temporary protection status has the right to family reunification. The claim includes the spouse and minor or dependent children of any age. The family reunification applications are also done through the DGMM.

The temporary protection regulation is granted on the basis of the Law on Foreigners and International Protection (LFIP, Law no. 6458) of 4 April 2013. The LFIP is formulated to govern all aspects of migration- and asylum-related matters in Turkey. In accordance with Turkey's geographical reservations in the Refugee Convention (1951) and the Refugee Protocol (1967), Turkey is not obligated to grant refugee status to asylum

176 Ayşe Dicle Ergin, 'What Happened at the Greece–Turkey Border in Early 2020?', *Verfassungsblog*, 30 September 2020, https://verfassungsblog.de/what-happened-at-the-greece-turkey-border-in-early-2020/.

seekers coming from countries other than Europe. The LFIP retains these reservations.

The LFIP offers four types of protection: (i) refugee status; (ii) conditional refugee status; (iii) subsidiary protection status; and (iv) temporary protection status. Any European who satisfies the definition provided by the Refugee Convention (1951) can acquire refugee status in Turkey.[177]

The conditional refugee is a person who satisfies the aforementioned definition by fulfilling the elements of being outside of the country of origin, fled the country of origin owing to a well-founded fear of persecution, the country of origin is other than a European country, and the person is unable or unwilling to return owing to the given fear. These persons are then accepted as conditional refugees and they receive a residence permit from the Turkish state for one year. They have to be resettled to third countries for the full enjoyment of their refugee status. Until resettlement they do not have the right to family reunification. They are allowed to benefit from public services such as healthcare and education. The conditional refugees are mostly people fleeing Iraq, Afghanistan, and Pakistan who arrive in Turkey and lodge an asylum application (see fig. 4). The refugee status determination (RSD) process is currently carried out by Turkish authorities. Until 2018, the UNHCR was in charge of the process. They are allowed to receive a work permit only after six months from their application for asylum.

The subsidiary protection is reflecting chapter 5 and chapter 6 of the Council Directive 2011/95/EU.[178] The definition of the beneficiary of the subsidiary protection is very similar to that found in the EU directive (article 2, para. f) and in the Turkish law (LFIP, article 63). In both of the, the beneficiary is a foreigner or a stateless person, they do not qualify as a refugee or as a conditional refugee, but they are people of concern because they are subject to a death penalty; or torture or inhuman or degrading treatment or punishment; or indiscriminate violence (armed conflict).

177 Article 1, para. 2, of the Refugee Convention (1951) states that a refugee is 'owing to well-founded fear of being persecuted for reasons of race, religion, nationality, membership of a particular social group or political opinion, is outside the country of his nationality and is unable or, owing to such fear, is unwilling to avail himself of the protection of that country'.

178 European Parliament and Council of the European Union, 'Council Directive on Standards for the Qualification of Third-Country Nationals or Stateless Persons as Beneficiaries of International Protection, for a Uniform Status for Refugees or for Persons Eligible for Subsidiary Protection, and for the Content of the Protection Granted', Pub. L. no. 2011/95/E, L 337/9 (2011), https://eur-lex.europa.eu/eli/dir/2011/95/oj.

The definition in the Council Directive 2011/95/EU, article 2, para. (f):

> 'person eligible for subsidiary protection' means a third-country national or a stateless person who does not qualify as a refugee but in respect of whom substantial grounds have been shown for believing that the person concerned, if returned to his or her country of origin, or in the case of a stateless person, to his or her country of former habitual residence, would face a real risk of suffering serious harm as defined in Article 15 [according to which serious harm consists of: (a) the death penalty or execution; or (b) torture or inhuman or degrading treatment or punishment of an applicant in the country of origin; or (c) serious and individual threat to a civilian's life or person by reason of indiscriminate violence in situations of international or internal armed conflict], and to whom Article 17(1) and (2) does not apply, and is unable, or, owing to such risk, unwilling to avail himself or herself of the protection of that country.

The definition in the LFIP, article 63:

> A foreigner or a stateless person, who neither could be qualified as a refugee nor as a conditional refugee, shall nevertheless be granted subsidiary protection upon the status determination because if returned to the country of origin or country of [former] habitual residence would: (a) be sentenced to death or face the execution of the death penalty; (b) face torture or inhuman or degrading treatment or punishment; (c) face serious threat to himself or herself by reason of indiscriminate violence in situations of international or nationwide armed conflict; and therefore is unable or for the reason of such threat is unwilling, to avail himself or herself of the protection of his country of origin or country of [former] habitual residence.

The LFIP (article 64, para. 5) excludes from subsidiary protection those who pose a serious threat to public order or public security and those who left their country of origin to avoid punishment for a serious crime (a crime for which imprisonment would have been ordered if committed in Turkey). The protection terminates when the circumstances upon which the status has been granted no longer apply (article 85, para. 3). As in article 82 of the LFIP, the Directorate General may require the beneficiary to reside at a given province and report to authorities in accordance with determined procedures and periods. The beneficiary receives identity papers valid for a year. The identity papers are a substitute for a work permit. They may work independently or be employed. Their access to the labour market is restricted to the given period. The restrictions do not apply once the person has been residing in Turkey for three years (article 89, paras. b and c).

## Conclusion

Turkey is home to approximately 3.5 million Syrians under temporary protection and approximately 5.5 million migrants of other nationalities under diverse statuses of international protection, those with residence permits. This status of Turkey is bound to continue due to three reasons. The first is due to Turkey's strategic location, which has been designating it as a transit country. The second pertains to the region's ongoing or emerging armed conflicts and political unrest. For example, recently, due to the events between Israel and Lebanon, a wave of Lebanese migrants headed towards Syria and Turkey. The third reason is the securitized approach of the European Union towards the migration issue. The closure of the borders of European states, entry prevention policies, construction of walls and fences, and violation of the international asylum regime by expulsions via misleading voluntary return petitions and the mass rejections of asylum applications which were supposed to be evaluated on a case-by-case basis has been increasing the burden of the non-EU neighbours of the EU, as well as Turkey.

While Turkey hosts millions of people, the human rights of these individuals are not adequately guaranteed. This shortfall stems from both Turkey's domestic challenges and the European Union's policies. As already mentioned above, within Turkey, the temporary protection status granted to those coming from Syria lacks a defined timeline, creating significant uncertainty for both parties, the state and the protected. This loophole prevents the Turkish government from developing long-term integration or removal strategies and leaves Syrians without a clear vision for their future. Moreover, the designation of Turkey as a 'safe third country' by the EU adds to this complexity, a classification that contradicts the EU's own criteria and undermines the rights of asylum seekers. Additionally, Turkey's ongoing economic and political instability further exacerbates these issues, limiting its capacity to ensure adequate protection and support for those seeking refuge within its borders.

The conditions for migrants and asylum seekers in Turkey remain precarious due to gaps in implementation, resource limitations, and the broader securitized approach to migration adopted by the EU. Although Turkey has taken steps to align its asylum and migration laws with EU standards to establish the rights of the migrants and guarantee them before the national courts, such as the legislation of the Law on Foreigners and International Protection (LFIP), these measures often create limitations on the rights of the protected ones. This alignment was guided by the EU, particularly during the drafting of the Turkish National Action Plan for the Adoption of the EU Acquis in the Field of Asylum and Migration (2005). However, these legal advancements are undermined by the EU's failure to form a cohesive and centralized migration policy. As member states prioritize their national interests, Turkey is left bearing a disproportionate burden as a buffer zone.

The EU's fragmented approach to migration management is emblematic of broader issues within the Union. Member states' reluctance to surrender sovereignty over asylum and migration policy has prevented the development of a fully harmonized framework. For instance, the absence of shared responsibility in managing migration pressures has been a significant driver behind events like Brexit. The EU's externalization of migration control, as seen in its agreements with Turkey, shifts the responsibility to its neighbours without addressing the root causes or providing sustainable solutions. This approach not only fails to meet international human rights standards but also risks destabilizing the very countries it relies on to manage migration flows.

The asymmetric integration of the European Union is characterized by a division between economic integration and political integration. The disparity has led to the uneven Europeanization of various policies, especially the asylum policy. While the Schengen system has Europeanized certain aspects of asylum policy, such as eliminating physical controls at internal borders, other substantive elements, such as setting eligibility criteria, adjudicating individual cases, and organizing the reception of migrants, remain under the control of individual member states.[179]

At the same time, the power asymmetry between the EU and Turkey is another source of instability in terms of migration. The two perspectives that blame Turkey and the EU are based on the power asymmetry approach. Those who blame Turkey for the migration chaos hold that Turkey takes advantage of Europe's securitization of migration and threatens the Union by opening the gates and not stopping the migrants in Turkey anymore. By doing so, Turkish officials create economic and political benefits for Turkey. On the other side, those who blame the Union for the mounting of

179 Agustín José Menéndez, 'The Refugee Crisis: Between Human Tragedy and Symptom of the Structural Crisis of European Integration', *European Law Journal* 22 (2016): 388–416.

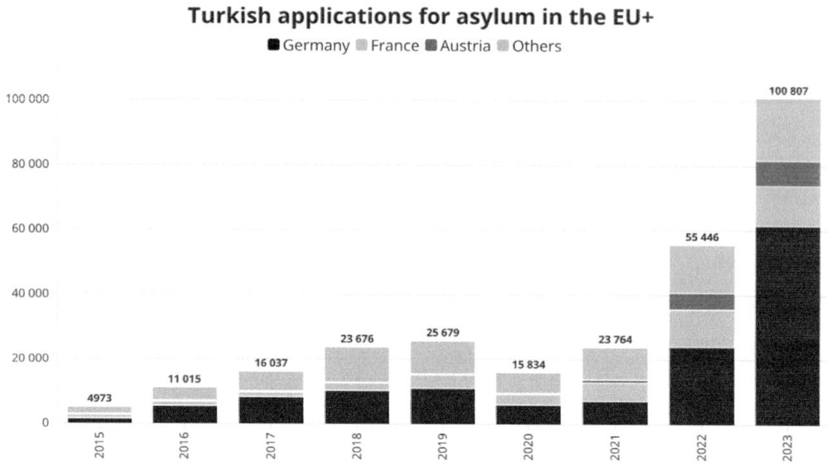


Figure 7. Turkish applications for asylum in the EU+ countries from 2015 to 2023. Source: European Union Agency for Asylum.[180]

migrants in Turkey hold that the Union offered carrots to Turkey, such as visa liberalization negotiations and €6 billion to cover the needs of migrants. By doing so, the EU enabled Turkey to shelter migrants. However, Turkey is not capable of providing a safe home to guarantee their rights. Moreover, the worsening political and economic conditions in Turkey has been functioning as a push factor for Turkish citizens. Since 2022, the number of Turkish citizens seeking asylum in Europe increased dramatically (see fig. 7).[180]

The political decline in Turkey is marked by democratic backsliding and severe restrictions on liberties and freedoms, including internet freedom, freedom of expression, and press freedom. Economically, the situation is equally dire, with inflation steadily rising since 2016, peaking at 73.31 per cent in 2022 before falling to 53.86 per cent in 2023, a decline of 18.45 per cent annually, yet still significantly high.[181] Under these conditions, life in Turkey is challenging even for its own citizens, let alone for people of concern. The legal framework for their protection is riddled with gaps, the indefinite nature of the temporary protection status being a notable example. In such an environment, the EU's designation of Turkey as a 'safe third country' for migrants is deeply inconsistent with regional and international human rights standards.

180 European Union Agency for Asylum, 'Turkish applications for asylum in the EU+', https://public.flourish.studio/visualisation/16693152/

181 Macrotrends, 'Turkey Inflation Rate 1960–2024', 2024, https://www.macrotrends.net/global-metrics/countries/TUR/turkey/inflation-rate-cpi.

Despite formal commitments to asylum and migration regimes, the real-world compliance with international, regional, and national standards is alarmingly low. Properly conducted refugee status determination (RSD) procedures remain an exception rather than the rule. Factors such as the unwillingness and incapacity of states to protect people of concern, the lack of effective monitoring over asylum regimes, and the inherently nationalized nature of RSD processes undermine the system's integrity. Additionally, the voluntary return option for refugees and asylum seekers is frequently abused, as authorities often present voluntary return petitions in languages the individuals do not understand. Refugees, unaware of the petition's content, sign it and are subsequently deported, rendering the process a likely violation of the principle of non-refoulement. While the signature may provide a veneer of legality, the practice undermines fundamental human rights protections and exposes serious flaws in asylum procedures. Other violations also occur, such as mass rejections of asylum applications that disregard the rule of case-by-case examination, and entrance prevention measures, ranging from maritime blockades to walls, fences, and extensive use of law enforcement and private security, actively prevent asylum seekers from lodging their claims. These failures result in suffering for refugees and asylum seekers at the hands of both Turkey and the EU, revealing a humanitarian crisis perpetuated by policies on both sides.

The measures the EU takes only address the symptoms of migration, not its root causes. Both Turkey and the EU must shift their focus towards addressing the push factors driving forced migration. Neither has offered meaningful solutions to improve conditions in countries like Syria, Pakistan, or Afghanistan. Instead, all other measures remain palliative, failing to stem the growing trends of migration. As armed conflicts continue to expand, exemplified by the escalation of violence from Israel and Gaza to Israel and Lebanon, with subsequent attacks on Syria and the resurgence of jihadist activity in Aleppo, millions remain displaced. The EU agenda has been also focusing on the outbreak of the Russo-Ukrainian War, the EU has also started hosting millions of Ukrainian refugees who were forced to leave their country. Similarly, after the Taliban seized control of Afghanistan in September 2021, the fleeing Afghans became a central issue for Turkey.

Compounding these issues are environmental factors, as climate change increasingly renders regions uninhabitable, forcing people to migrate in search of safety and survival. Without collaborative and comprehensive efforts to address these underlying drivers, migration pressures will persist and intensify, further exposing the fragility of existing asylum systems.

Lastly, despite the Lisbon Treaty's efforts to supranationalize asylum policy and the EU's regulatory attempts to harmonize asylum standards and procedures, significant decision-making authority regarding asylum matters, i.e., the application of laws to individual cases, remains firmly within the executive discretion of member states.[182] As a result, the EU has yet to establish a truly uniform asylum system.

Despite formal commitments to asylum and migration regimes, real-world compliance with international, regional, and national standards remains alarmingly low. This reflects a broader pattern of passive revolution and externalization. Turkey's legal reforms, encouraged by the EU, have produced a superficial alignment with European standards without fundamentally strengthening human rights protections. Simultaneously, the EU's hegemonic position allows it to shape migration governance externally, while itself retreating from its proclaimed normative commitments. Voluntary return procedures, mass rejections of asylum claims, and physical border defences exemplify a broader strategy of managing, rather than protecting, forced migrants. In this configuration, migration management serves to stabilize the hegemonic order without resolving the systemic injustices that produce displacement.

182 Galina Cornelisse, 'What's Wrong with Schengen? Border Disputes and the Nature of Integration in the Area without Internal Borders', *Common Market Law Review* 51, no. 3 (2014).

# 6. Current Challenges

**Abstract:** This chapter examines the deepening challenges in EU–Turkey relations, focusing on the erosion of democratic governance, judicial independence, and the rule of law in Turkey. Despite continued cooperation on migration and regional stability, systemic human rights violations and authoritarian drift dominate the relationship. The chapter details political interference in the judiciary, lack of transparency in judicial appointments, and non-compliance with ECtHR rulings. It also highlights repression of legal professionals and structural corruption enabled by weak oversight. Framed within the EU's human rights architecture, the chapter argues that the widening normative gap undermines both the EU's credibility and the effectiveness of conditionality, raising pressing questions about the future of rights-based engagement and normative influence in EU–Turkey relations.

**Keywords:** judicial independence, the rule of law, human rights governance, corruption and accountability, gender justice

The current landscape of EU–Turkey relations and human rights governance is defined by a paradoxical interplay of challenges and opportunities. As Turkey continues to navigate a trajectory marked by democratic backsliding, constrained freedoms, and a politicized judiciary, its relationship with the European Union reflects a mixture of contention and cooperation. This chapter explores the contemporary dynamics shaping this relationship, with a particular focus on how evolving political, legal, and social contexts create obstacles to progress while simultaneously opening avenues for transformative change. At the heart of these challenges are questions surrounding Turkey's willingness and readiness to align with European human rights standards, juxtaposed against the EU's capacity to uphold its normative commitments amid increasing internal and external pressures. Against this backdrop, opportunities emerge through shared concerns, such as migration governance and regional stability, which offer potential

Bayar, Tuğba. *The Rise and Relapse of European Human Rights in Turkey: The AKP Era, 2002–2024.* Amsterdam University Press/Central European University Press, 2025.
DOI 10.5117/9789048573813_CH06

for renewed dialogue and collaboration. By analysing the intersections of political motivations, legal frameworks, and societal aspirations, this chapter aims to provide a comprehensive understanding of the delicate balance between obstacles and possibilities in the evolving EU–Turkey partnership.

The functioning of Turkey's judiciary continues to face critical challenges, particularly in terms of independence, impartiality, and adherence to the principles of separation of powers. Although these principles are nominally enshrined in Turkey's constitution and legislative framework, the persistent politicization of the judiciary undermines their implementation. High-level government officials frequently make public statements on ongoing cases, exerting undue pressure on judges and prosecutors. Public attacks against defendants further compromise the integrity of judicial proceedings. This politicized environment deters members of the judiciary from discharging their duties in line with EU standards, resulting in a judiciary increasingly influenced by external pressures.

A particularly striking example is the case of Member of Parliament Can Atalay in October 2023. The Constitutional Court ruled that Atalay's rights to liberty, security, and electoral participation had been violated. However, instead of complying with this decision, the lower court escalated the matter to the Court of Cassation. The Court of Cassation not only failed to implement the ruling but also sought to strip Atalay of parliamentary immunity and initiated a criminal complaint against the Constitutional Court judges who supported Atalay's release. Such actions highlight a troubling trend of lower courts disregarding or delaying the implementation of Constitutional Court decisions, further undermining the rule of law.

Structural deficiencies in the judiciary exacerbate these issues. The selection, recruitment, and promotion of judges and prosecutors lack transparency, with the Ministry of Justice maintaining significant control over selection boards. Annual evaluations are conducted by the Council of Judges and Prosecutors (HSK), whose members are appointed without input from peer judges, raising concerns about accountability and impartiality. Furthermore, no reforms have been introduced to prevent the arbitrary transfer of judges without their consent, a practice that weakens judicial independence.

The judiciary also suffers from inadequate oversight and accountability. While judges and prosecutors are required to declare their assets every five years, no evidence exists of sanctions being imposed for non-compliance. Allegations of judicial corruption frequently emerge in the media, yet there is little transparency regarding investigations into these claims. The Ministry of Justice oversees judicial services through inspectors and internal auditors, raising concerns about the independence of such supervisory mechanisms.

The quality of judicial decisions and indictments remains substandard, often characterized by insufficient legal reasoning and a lack of factual evidence. These deficiencies are particularly evident in political and terrorism-related cases. Defence lawyers frequently encounter restricted access to case files, with confidentiality orders routinely invoked to impede their work. This practice violates the defendants' rights to a fair trial and effective legal representation, further undermining confidence in the judiciary. The use of secret or uncorroborated witness testimony in terrorism-related cases also contravenes European Court of Human Rights jurisprudence, posing significant challenges to procedural fairness.

International rulings continue to spotlight these systemic issues. For instance, the ECtHR Grand Chamber ruled in September 2023 that Turkey had violated the rights to a fair trial, freedom of association, and the principle of legality in the case of Yüksel Yalçınkaya. The court emphasized that these violations were systemic and called on Turkey to undertake remedial measures. However, no significant steps have been taken to address these concerns, including opening cases for retrial.

Lawyers, judges, and prosecutors often face distress and carry out their professional duties under intimidation, interference, hindrance, and harassment. A recent example of interference and harassment targeting lawyers in the course of their professional duties is the case of Dilek Ekmekçi. Ekmekçi claims to be imprisoned because of her fight against the sexual exploitation of children under state care.[1] After her first detention she was released on 22 October 2024 and was immediately detained once again. Following her release, she was forcibly confined to a mental hospital, upon which Ekmekçi announced the beginning of an indefinite hunger strike. The urge to capture her after each release already reflects the ongoing repression of the government over the legal professionals in Turkey.

The judiciary in Turkey remains beset by profound structural and procedural challenges that hinder its independence, impartiality, and efficiency. These issues not only contravene international legal standards but also erode public confidence in the justice system, further complicating Turkey's alignment with European human rights norms.

The fight against corruption in Turkey faces significant systemic and structural challenges, revealing critical gaps in prevention, enforcement,

1 Bianet, 'Arrested Lawyer Dilek Ekmekçi Begins Hunger Strike', 18 November 2024, https://bianet.org/haber/arrested-lawyer-dilek-ekmekci-begins-hunger-strike-301911.

and accountability. Despite formal commitments to international conventions such as the United Nations Convention against Corruption, Turkey's anti-corruption framework remains insufficiently robust, failing to meet international and EU standards. Investigations, prosecutions, and convictions in corruption cases have been notably weak, reflecting the passive stance of prosecution authorities and the lack of collaboration between audit and inspection units and prosecution offices. This inertia undermines the effectiveness of oversight mechanisms and allows corruption to persist unchecked. Public procurement processes are particularly vulnerable, with frequent exemptions that compromise their transparency and integrity. Similarly, political party financing, judiciary operations, public administration, municipal governance, land administration, and zoning and construction activities remain areas prone to corruption. These systemic vulnerabilities highlight the inadequacy of current measures to ensure accountability and governance.

Turkey continues to lack a permanent, functionally independent body dedicated to preventing corruption. The State Supervisory Council, tasked with leading anti-corruption efforts, operates without functional independence, limiting its capacity to act as an effective anti-corruption agency. The absence of specialized law enforcement authorities, prosecution services, and courts focused on corruption cases further weakens enforcement. Additionally, undue political influence over the judicial police hinders impartiality in investigations, while inter-agency coordination, including collaboration with the Financial Crimes Investigation Board (Mali Suçları Araştırma Kurulu, MASAK), remains underdeveloped.

The legal framework for combating corruption also exhibits critical deficiencies. Provisions in the Penal Code, including the definition of active bribery, fail to align with international standards, particularly in addressing bribery within the private sector. Public procurement legislation does not meet EU *acquis* requirements, and privileges granted to public officials, such as requiring prior authorization from superiors before investigating alleged misconduct, effectively obstruct accountability. Whistle-blower protections, conflict-of-interest regulations, and asset declaration laws are similarly inadequate, leaving significant gaps in preventive measures. Furthermore, the lack of legislation regulating lobbying and the absence of financial oversight for political parties exacerbate the structural weaknesses in Turkey's anti-corruption framework.

Efforts to raise awareness about transparency and corruption remain insufficient, with a notable absence of regular campaigns aimed at fostering a culture of accountability. Moreover, the legal and institutional frameworks to combat corruption in the private sector are underdeveloped, further highlighting the need for comprehensive reform.

Overall, the fight against corruption in Turkey is undermined by a combination of systemic weaknesses, legislative gaps, and insufficient enforcement. To address these challenges, Turkey must establish an independent anti-corruption body, strengthen inter-agency coordination, and align its legal and institutional frameworks with international and EU standards. Without these reforms, corruption will continue to erode public trust, compromise governance, and hinder Turkey's ability to meet its international commitments.

The protection and promotion of fundamental rights in Turkey continue to face significant challenges, despite its formal commitments as a party to most international human rights instruments. Aligning national legislation and its implementation with the European Convention on Human Rights and the case law of the European Court of Human Rights remains a pressing concern. The lack of progress in addressing these deficiencies has drawn criticism, including from the Parliamentary Assembly of the Council of Europe, which has maintained its full monitoring procedure for Turkey. Persistent non-compliance with ECtHR rulings and related judgements by Turkey's own Constitutional Court highlights systemic shortcomings in the enforcement of human rights.

Numerous violations of the ECHR were identified by the ECtHR during the reporting period, including breaches of the right to respect for private and family life, freedom of assembly and association, the right to liberty and security, and the right to a fair trial. Excessive use of force by security forces and unjustified detentions further underscores ongoing structural issues. Currently, 185 cases against Turkey remain under enhanced supervision by the Committee of Ministers, reflecting systemic deficiencies that require urgent resolution. High-profile cases, such as those involving former HDP co-chair Selahattin Demirtaş and human rights defender Osman Kavala, continue to exemplify Turkey's disregard for ECtHR judgements, despite repeated calls for their release by the Council of Europe.

The AKP's Human Rights Action Plan, introduced in March 2021, has proven inadequate in addressing these deep-seated issues. The limited operational, structural, and financial independence of key institutions such as the Human Rights and Equality Institution of Turkey (Türkiye İnsan Hakları ve Eşitlik Kurumu, HREI) and the ombudsman severely undermine their effectiveness. Reports of torture and ill-treatment persist in detention centres, prisons, and other locations, compounded by the disproportionate use of force by security forces and inadequate administrative measures against perpetrators. Overcrowding in prisons, widespread impunity for officials, and differential treatment of political inmates further exacerbate human rights violations within the penal system.

Turkey faces critical challenges in ensuring the protection of fundamental rights. Systemic deficiencies in judicial independence, enforcement of ECtHR judgements, and institutional accountability must be urgently addressed. Strengthening compliance with international standards, improving the independence of human rights bodies, and ensuring equitable treatment within the criminal justice system are essential steps towards rectifying these persistent issues and safeguarding fundamental freedoms.

The protection of personal data in Turkey remains an area of significant concern, despite recent legislative updates. The adoption of the Eighth Judicial Reform Package in March 2024 introduced changes to the conditions governing the processing of sensitive categories of personal data and the transfer of such data to third countries. While these updates represent a step towards addressing existing gaps, they fall short of aligning Turkey's framework with the stringent requirements of the EU *acquis*.

The 2016 Personal Data Protection Act, which serves as the cornerstone of Turkey's data protection regime, lacks key provisions necessary to meet EU standards. Moreover, the Personal Data Protection Authority, established to oversee compliance and safeguard personal data, operates with structural and functional deficiencies that hinder its effectiveness. The authority's framework and practices remain inadequately aligned with EU benchmarks, limiting its capacity to provide robust oversight and enforcement.

Particularly concerning are the rights of individuals whose personal data are processed for law enforcement purposes. These rights are not sufficiently protected under Turkey's current legal framework, diverging significantly from EU standards. This discrepancy underscores the need for comprehensive reforms to ensure the protection of personal data in all contexts, including law enforcement, where risks of misuse and overreach are especially high.

Although recent reforms signal a recognition of the importance of personal data protection, substantial efforts are required to harmonize Turkey's legal and institutional framework with EU standards. Strengthening the independence and capacity of the Personal Data Protection Authority, enhancing legal safeguards for individuals, and ensuring robust compliance mechanisms are critical steps towards fostering a data protection regime that upholds privacy and aligns with international best practices.

A significant data breach exposed the personal information of approximately 108 million individuals registered with Turkish official institutions, including sensitive details such as names, ID numbers, birth information, addresses, marital status, and phone numbers. Transport and Infrastructure Minister Abdulkadir Uraloğlu acknowledged the breach, stating that the leak originated from the health system and could not be prevented at the time.

The breach also encompassed data belonging to refugees and foreign residents. The National Cyber Incident Response Centre (Ulusal Siber Olaylara Müdahale Merkezi, USOM) took swift action, notifying Google of the uploaded files containing the stolen data, which totalled 42.18 GB. The files included 108.57 million Turkish ID numbers, 82.32 million residential addresses, and 134.82 million mobile phone numbers. USOM requested the immediate removal of these files and the identification of the uploaders, emphasizing the urgency of the matter to protect affected users.[2]

This incident has sparked sharp criticism, with opposition figures denouncing the lack of accountability and expressing concerns over the handling of personal data security in Turkey. The breach highlights the urgent need for robust cybersecurity measures and a more effective framework for protecting personal data in line with international standards.

The freedoms of journalists, writers, lawyers, academics, human rights defenders, opposition politicians, and other critical voices continued to be severely curtailed through arrests, detentions, prosecutions, and convictions. These restrictive practices have perpetuated a climate of fear, leading to widespread self-censorship. As of June 2024, fifty-four journalists and media workers remained imprisoned, either awaiting trial or serving sentences, reflecting a persistent trend from the previous year when fifty-nine were similarly detained.[3]

Recently, on 16 December 2024, a well-known Turkish freelance journalist, Nevşin Mengü, who runs her own YouTube channel was detained for an interview released on her channel. The interview was with the co-leader of the Syrian pro-Kurdish Democratic Union Party (Partiya Yekîtiya Demokrat, PYD), Salih Müslim. Mengü was convicted for statements praising the terrorist organization and its actions. She was then released and a ban on international travel was implemented.[4] The Turkish court sentenced her

2 Duvar English, 'Turkish Minister Confirms Vast Personal Data Breach of Millions', 9 December 2024, https://www.duvarenglish.com/turkish-minister-confirms-vast-personal-data-breach-of-millions-news-64941.

3 European Commission, 'Turkey 2024 Progress Report', 30 October 2024, https://www.ab.gov.tr/siteimages/birimler/kpb/trkiye_report_2024.pdf.

4 Medyascope, 'Journalist Nevşin Mengu Detained Following Interview with PYD Leader Salih Müslim', 16 December 2024, https://medyascope.tv/2024/12/16/nevsin-mengu-detained-following-interview-with-pyd/.

to one year and three months in prison. However, the court suspended the sentence.[5]

The gender justice is a real weakness of the AKP. Since Erdoğan withdrew Turkey from the Council of Europe's Istanbul Convention in 2021, Turkey's policies have failed to align with the EU directive on combating violence against women and domestic violence. Despite the introduction of strategies and action plans, such as the Twelfth National Development Plan (2024–28), the Women's Empowerment Strategy Document and Action Plan (2024–28), and the Vision Document and Action Plan for the Protection and Strengthening of the Family (2024–28), these measures have yet to yield credible and effective results. Violence against women persists at alarming levels due to weak enforcement of legislation, lenient sentencing, and inadequate support services. The prevalence of femicides, with at least 315 recorded in 2023 and 32 in April 2024 alone, underscores the severity of the issue. Furthermore, the absence of a comprehensive data collection system, coupled with entrenched cultural norms and persistent gender stereotypes, continues to impede progress towards gender equality.

Regarding the rights of children, implementation remains insufficient here, too, and it fails to meet international standards or EU *acquis* requirements. While national legislation recognizes the principle of the best interests of the child, its application often depends on subjective interpretations. The protection of children's rights is undermined by inadequate resources, insufficient budgetary allocations, and limited tailored services for child victims of crime. Despite some efforts, such as developing an emergency foster care system, progress remains stagnant in critical areas like deinstitutionalization and independent living. The education system continues to grapple with challenges in integrating a large number of migrant children, while economic pressures, exacerbated by high inflation, have increased the risk of school dropouts among vulnerable families. Comprehensive training and certification programmes for professionals working with children in contact with the law are urgently needed to address these deficiencies and safeguard the rights and welfare of children effectively.

Other minority groups that face challenges are Roma, LGBTIQ (lesbian, gay, bisexual, transgender, intersex, and queer) people, and disabled people.

5 MLSA, 'Journalist Nevşin Mengü sentenced to 1 year and 3 months in "propaganda" case', 27 February 2025, https://www.mlsaturkey.com/en/journalist-nevsin-mengu-sentenced-to-1-year-and-3-months-in-propaganda-case

# 7. Conclusion: EU–Turkey Relations and the Contestation of Hegemony in an Age of Normative Crisis

**Abstract:** This concluding chapter revisits the book's core puzzle: how and why the EU's normative power over Turkey deteriorated, giving way to transactionalism, migration securitization, and authoritarian resilience. Using a neo-Gramscian lens, it traces a three-phase evolution in EU–Turkey relations – from early consent and reform, to stagnation, and finally counter-hegemonic confrontation. The chapter argues that the EU's shift to material bargaining, especially after the 2016 migration deal, hastened Turkey's authoritarian turn and revealed the EU's normative contradictions. It reframes norm diffusion as cyclical and contested, shaped by shifting hegemonic structures. Turkey is positioned as a case of post-hegemonic order, where hybrid regional identities challenge Western integration models. The chapter calls for rethinking regime theory, human rights governance, and normative power under multipolarity.

**Keywords:** normative power, neo-Gramscian theory, EU–Turkey relations, hegemonic decline, counter-hegemony, post-Western order

This book set out to explore a fundamental and pressing puzzle: How and why did the European Union's normative influence over Turkey, once a major driver of domestic reforms, erode over time, giving way to a relationship increasingly defined by strategic transactions, securitized migration management, and authoritarian resilience?

Framed within the broader field of international relations and grounded in a neo-Gramscian perspective, this inquiry addressed critical sub-questions such as: What explains the initial receptiveness of Turkey to EU human rights norms? How did the interplay between EU conditionality and Turkey's domestic political transformations evolve over two decades? To what extent

Bayar, Tuğba. *The Rise and Relapse of European Human Rights in Turkey: The AKP Era, 2002–2024.* Amsterdam University Press/Central European University Press, 2025.
DOI 10.5117/9789048573813_CH07

can the EU still act as a normative power vis-à-vis Turkey? What does this imply for the future of EU–Turkey relations and the global normative order?

At its core, the central puzzle revolved around the paradox of normative power asking how an actor founded on the promise of advancing human rights and democracy abroad could, over time, become complicit in practices undermining those very norms, especially when confronted with internal crises and external challenges. Turkey, as a strategic candidate country and crucial migration partner, embodied the clearest and most consequential site for this paradox to unfold.

The analytical lens adopted throughout the book was neo-Gramscianism. Conventional rationalist models, whether liberal institutionalism or realist bargaining theories, were insufficient to capture the depth and complexity of EU–Turkey relations. A neo-Gramscian approach allowed for a richer understanding by situating this relationship within broader hegemonic structures, emphasizing the interconnections between consent, coercion, material interests, and normative claims.

This framework highlighted not just strategic bargaining, but the deeper contest over the meaning of legitimate order, both within Turkey and between Turkey and Europe. It also enabled the tracing of Turkey's counter-hegemonic evolution, from an initially reform-oriented aspirant to a self-assertive regional actor resistant to externally imposed norms.

The EU–Turkey relationship unfolded in three distinct phases. Between 2002 and 2007, Turkey engaged in substantial reforms, aligning with EU standards as a strategy to consolidate domestic power and legitimacy. From 2008 to 2013, this momentum stalled amid the EU's credibility crisis driven by hypocrisy over Cyprus, the rise of 'privileged partnership' discourse, and Turkey's growing domestic majoritarianism. After 2013, a clear turn occurred, the Gezi Park protests, the collapse of accession negotiations, and the EU–Turkey migration deal all marked a transition from reform to resistance. Turkey constructed a counter-hegemonic narrative and defied EU norms while the Union shifted to a policy of material containment.

This trajectory reveals the mutual erosion of legitimacy. Turkey abandoned consent-based engagement in favour of sovereign defiance; the EU retreated from its normative posture, replacing conditionality with coercion through migration deals, visa regimes, and securitized aid. The result was not merely stalled accession, but a deeper rupture in the normative architecture of the relationship.

Theoretically, this book critiques dominant approaches in IR. It questions the linearity of norm diffusion, exposing how hegemonic credibility is central to sustaining normative regimes. It refines regime theory by highlighting how alternative counter-hegemonies emerge when normative cores decay. And it advances neo-Gramscian international relations by showing how passive revolutions can give way to active resistance once material and ideological alignments shift. Turkey, once a model periphery aspiring to join the Western core, has repositioned itself as a hybrid regional actor which is strategic, transactional, and norm resistant. Its trajectory reflects global trends such as the erosion of Western liberal hegemony, the rise of multipolarity, and the assertion of regional powers promoting alternative visions of order and legitimacy.

The implications extend far beyond Turkey. Authoritarian resilience in the Global South, the decline of enlargement credibility, and the EU's internal contradictions suggest that the normative international order is not just weakening, it is fragmenting. Restoring EU credibility will require more than rhetoric; it demands consistency across internal and external policies, renewed democratic incentives, and a clear break from migration-focused pragmatism.

Turkey is not an outlier, it is a bellwether. Understanding its turn is not only key to salvaging EU–Turkey relations but also to reimagining the foundations of international order in a post-hegemonic world. This book offers a radical rethinking of key theoretical frameworks in international relations. It challenges the idealized vision of the normative power Europe by demonstrating how material interests, particularly in migration governance, have hollowed out the EU's normative claims. It refines international regime theory by emphasizing the fragility of norm-based regimes when hegemonic credibility erodes and alternative counter-hegemonies arise. It advances neo-Gramscianism in international relations by demonstrating how a passive revolution can initially co-opt external norms, only to later morph into counter-hegemonic resistance when material and ideological alignments shift.

Rather than viewing norm diffusion as a linear or irreversible process, this research reveals the cyclical, contested, and contingent nature of hegemonic projects. It shows how a 'decaying hegemon', such as the EU, can become a vector of its own decline when it sacrifices normative consistency for short-term strategic gains. Thus, the findings not only critique dominant theories but also offer a new conceptual model for understanding norm diffusion under conditions of multipolarity and hegemonic decline. Looking forward, the future of EU–Turkey relations will likely continue to oscillate between strategic necessity and normative estrangement.

From the perspective of compliance and conditionality literature, the Turkish case suggests that coercive conditionality without credible rewards (e.g., membership prospects) accelerates norm rejection rather than compliance. From the perspective of EU enlargement studies, it highlights the consequences of enlargement fatigue and the death of enlargement credibility as key drivers of authoritarian entrenchment in candidate states. From the perspective of the hegemony theory, it exemplifies a moment where neo-Gramscian dynamics such as consent, passive revolution, coercion, counter-hegemony play out visibly and with profound global consequences. Future efforts to restore normative leverage will require the EU to rebuild credibility through the consistency between internal and external policies; through offering genuine incentives linked to democratic reforms; and moving beyond migration-focused transactionalism.

In this context I propose international relations colleagues seek answers to the following questions: Under what conditions can a decaying hegemon reinvent its normative appeal? Can human rights regain primacy under multipolarity, or will pragmatic transactionalism dominate? How does authoritarian resilience in the Global South relate to the weakening of Western hegemony? Turkey stands as an early test case of this new era, where global fragmentation, regional assertion, and normative contestation define international relations. Understanding Turkey's trajectory is thus critical not only for EU–Turkey relations but for grasping the future of the international order itself.

# Bibliography


11.11.11. *Illegality without Borders: Pushback Report 2023*. Belgium: 11.11.11, 2024. https://11.be/sites/default/files/2024-02/20240214-Pushback-Report-2023-eng.pdf.

'3686 Sayılı İnsan Haklarını İnceleme Komisyonu Kanunu', 20719 3686 § Tertip 5, Sayı 20719 (1990). https://www.mevzuat.gov.tr/mevzuat?MevzuatNo=3686&MevzuatTur=1&MevzuatTertip=5.

Adalet Bakanlığı. 'Yargı Reformu Stratejisi, 2009', 2009. https://sgb.adalet.gov.tr/Resimler/SayfaDokuman/23122019163043Yargi-Reformu-Stratejisi.pdf.

Akça, İsmet, Süreyya Algül, Hülya Dinçer, and Erhan Keleşoğlu. *Olağanlaşan OHAL: Khk'larin Yasal Mevzuat Üzerindeki Etkileri*. Heinrich Böll Stiftung, 2018. https://tr.boell.org/tr/2018/01/10/olaganlasan-ohal-khklarin-yasal-mevzuat-uezerindeki-etkileri.

Akça, İsmet, Süreyya Algül, Hülya Dinçer, Erhan Keleşoğlu, and Barış Alp Özden. *When the State of Emergency Becomes the Norm: The Impact of Executive Decrees on Turkish Legislation*. Heinrich Böll Stiftung, 2018. https://tr.boell.org/sites/default/files/ohal_rapor_ing.final_version.pdf.

Akgün, Mert Hüseyin. 'Başörtüsü Özgürlüğü ve Anayasal Güvence Arayışı'. SETA, January 2023. https://www.setav.org/assets/uploads/2023/01/R214.pdf.

Akkaş, Simge. 'Cumhurbaşkanına Hakaretten Kaç Kişi Yargılanıyor?' *Doğruluk Payı*, 16 October 2019. https://www.dogrulukpayi.com/bulten/2018-yilinda-cumhurbaskanina-hakaretten-kac-kisi-sanik-oldu.

Altıok, Zeynep. 'OHAL Bilançosu Hak Ihlalleri Raporu'. Ankara: CHP, 12 January 2018. https://content.chp.org.tr/file/33743.pdf.

Amnesty International. *Gezi Park Protests: Brutal Denial of the Right to Peaceful Assembly in Turkey*. London: Amnesty International, 2013. https://www.amnesty.org/en/documents/EUR44/022/2013/en/.

Amnesty International. 'Turkey: No Security without Human Rights', 30 September 1996. EUR/44/84/96. https://www.amnesty.org/en/documents/eur44/084/1996/en/.

Anka Hukuk. 'Kenan Evren'in 1980 Anayasası'nı Tanıtma Konuşmaları', 5 September 2023. http://www.ankahukuk.com/kenan-evrenin-1980-anayasasini-tanitma-konusmalari/.

Arslan, Zühtü. 'The Status of the International Law in the Turkish Constitution'. Constitutional Court of the Republic of Türkiye, 23 November 2022. https://www.anayasa.gov.tr/en/president/former-presidents-speeches/zuhtu-arslan/speeches/the-status-of-the-international-law-in-the-turkish-constitution/.

Assembly of the Western European Union. 'Proceedings: Fortieth Ordinary Session Third Part', June 1995. http://aei.pitt.edu/66919/1/WEU148.pdf.

Aydın Düzgit, Senem, and Ruşen Çakır. 'Turkey: A Sustainable Case of de-Radicalisation?' In *Islamist Radicalisation: The Challenge for Euro-Mediterranean Relations*, edited by Michael Emerson, Kristina Kausch, and Richard Youngs, 87–108. Brussels: Centre for European Policy Studies, 2009.

Bayar, Tuğba. 'The Sheep That God Lost: "Legally" Circumventing the Human Rights of Undocumented Migrants'. *Southeast European and Black Sea Studies* 25, no. 2 (2023): 249–67.

Bayar, Tuğba. 'Turkey's Withdrawal from Istanbul Convention: International Human Rights Regime vis-à-vis Authoritarian Survival'. *Turkish Studies* 25, no. 1 (2024): 22–42.

Bayulgen, Oksan, Ekim Arbatli, and Sercan Canbolat. 'Elite Survival Strategies and Authoritarian Reversal in Turkey'. *Polity* 50, no. 3 (2018): 333–65.

BBC. 'Andrew Brunson: Trump Meets US Pastor Freed by Turkey'. 13 October 2018. https://www.bbc.com/news/world-europe-45842735.

BBC. 'Erdoğan: AYM'nin Kararına Saygı Duymuyorum'. 28 February 2016. https://www.bbc.com/turkce/haberler/2016/02/160228_erdogan_dundar_aym.

BBC. 'Erdoğan'dan Yargıtay'ın AYM kararıyla ilgili açıklama: "Bu tartışmada taraf değil hakem konumundayız"'. 10 November 2023. https://www.bbc.com/turkce/articles/cjrp8xgr79lo.

BBC. 'Ergenekon Davasında Karar Açıklandı: Hüküm Sonrası Kim Ne Dedi?' 1 July 2019. https://www.bbc.com/turkce/haberler-turkiye-48830230.

BBC. 'Türkiye'de Olağanüstü Hâllerin Tarihi'. 21 July 2016. https://www.bbc.com/turkce/haberler-turkiye-36852284.

Bermeo, Nancy. 'On Democratic Backsliding'. *Journal of Democracy* 27, no. 1 (2016): 5–19.

Bianet. 'Arrested Lawyer Dilek Ekmekçi Begins Hunger Strike', 18 November 2024. https://bianet.org/haber/arrested-lawyer-dilek-ekmekci-begins-hunger-strike-301911.

Bianet. 'Bahçeli: AKP İdama Hazırsa Biz de Varız'. 19 July 2016. https://bianet.org/haber/bahceli-akp-idama-hazirsa-biz-de-variz-176885.

Bianet. 'Erdoğan: Afedersin Ermeni Diyen Oldu'. 6 August 2014. https://bianet.org/haber/erdogan-afedersin-ermeni-diyen-oldu-157616.

Bianet. 'Orhan Pamuk'un 301 Davası Ortadan Kalktı', 3 August 2007. https://bianet.org/haber/orhan-pamukun-301-davasi-ortadan-kalkti-100513.

Bila, Fikret. 'Yüreğim Yanıyor Vicdanım Sızlıyor'. *Hürriyet*, 8 December 2016. https://www.hurriyet.com.tr/yazarlar/fikret-bila/yuregim-yaniyor-vicdanim-sizliyor-40190131.

Bizzotto, Mara. 'Consolidation of the Islamic Gülen Movement within the EU'. European Parliament, Parliamentary Question, 22 September 2011. https://www.europarl.europa.eu/doceo/document/E-7-2011-008665_EN.html.

Bora, Tanıl. *Demirel*. İstanbul: İletişim Yayınları, 2023.

Bull, Hedley. 'Civilian power Europe: a contradiction in terms', Journal of Common Market Studies. (1982): 21-149.

Brown, Chris, and Kirsten Ainley. *Understanding International Relations*. Springer, 2009.

Brumberg, Daniel. 'Rhetoric and Strategy: Islamic Movements and Democracy in the Middle East'. In *The Islamism Debate*, edited by Martin S. Kramer, 11–33. Syracuse, NY: Syracuse University Press, 1997.

Brzezinski, Zbigniew. *Out of Control: Global Turmoil on the Eve of the 21st Century*. New York: Simon and Schuster, 2010.

Çalık, Burcu. 'Mülteci Sayısı Psikolojik Sınırı Aştı'. *Sabah Gazetesi*, 16 October 2012. https://www.sabah.com.tr/gundem/2012/10/16/multeci-sayisi-psikolojik-siniri-asti.

Can, Osman. 'The Motion before Turkey's Constitutional Court to Ban the Pro-Kurdish HDP'. *Stiftung Wissenschaft und Politik*, 17 June 2021. https://www.swp-berlin.org/en/publication/the-motion-before-turkeys-constitutional-court-to-ban-the-pro-kurdish-hdp.

Cassarino, Jean-Pierre. 'Dealing with Unbalanced Reciprocities: Cooperation on Readmission and Implications'. In *Unbalanced Reciprocities: Cooperation on Readmission in the Euro-Mediterranean Area*, edited by Jean-Pierre Cassarino, 1–29. Middle East Institute Special Edition Viewpoints, 2010.

Chayes, Abram, and Antonia Handler Chayes. 'On Compliance'. *International Organization* 47, no. 2 (1993): 175–205.

Chrona, Stavroula, and Cristiano Bee. 'Right to Public Space and Right to Democracy: The Role of Social Media in Gezi Park'. *Research and Policy on Turkey* 2, no. 1 (2017): 49–61.

Churchill, Winston. 'Winston Churchill, Speech Delivered at the University of Zurich, 19 September 1946'. https://rm.coe.int/16806981f3.

COE Parliamentary Assembly. 'Humanitarian Situation of the Kurdish Refugees and Displaced Persons in South-East Turkey and North Iraq'. Assembly debate on 25 June 1998

(22nd Sitting), 25 June 1998. https://assembly.coe.int/nw/xml/XRef/Xref-XML2HTML-en.asp?fileid=16638&lang=en.

Cole, Wade M. 'Sovereignty Relinquished? Explaining Commitment to the International Human Rights Covenants, 1966–1999'. *American Sociological Review* 70, no. 3 (2005): 472–95.

Commission of the European Communities. 'Commission Opinion on Turkey's Request for Accession to the Community'. 20 December 1989. http://aei.pitt.edu/4475/1/4475.pdf.

Congress of Europe. 'Cultural Resolution of the Hague Congress (7–10 May 1948)'. 1948. https://www.cvce.eu/en/recherche/unit-content/-/unit/04bfa990-86bc-402f-a633-11f39c9247c4/4ab19baa-6d0e-4de8-9d9c-6391612bf22a/Resources.

Congress of Europe. 'Political Resolution of the Hague Congress (7–10 May 1948)'. 1948. https://www.cvce.eu/obj/political_resolution_of_the_hague_congress_7_10_may_1948-en-15869906-97dd-4c54-ad85-a19f2115728b.html.

Cornelisse, Galina. 'What's Wrong with Schengen? Border Disputes and the Nature of Integration in the Area without Internal Borders'. *Common Market Law Review* 51, no. 3 (2014).

Coşkun, Vahap. 'Demirel (II): "Ben Devlet Fikrinin Adamıyım"'. *Perspektif*, 18 August 2023. https://www.perspektif.online/demirel-ii-ben-devlet-fikrinin-adamiyim/.

Council of Europe. European Convention on Human Rights (1950). https://www.echr.coe.int/documents/d/echr/convention_ENG.

Council of Europe Newsroom. 'Joint Statement on Death Penalty', 9 October 2024. https://www.coe.int/en/web/portal/-/european-and-world-day-against-the-death-penalty-10-october-2024.

Council of the European Union. 'The Council and the European Parliament Reach Breakthrough in Reform of EU Asylum and Migration System', 20 December 2023. https://www.consilium.europa.eu/en/press/press-releases/2023/12/20/the-council-and-the-european-parliament-reach-breakthrough-in-reform-of-eu-asylum-and-migration-system/.

Council of the European Union. 'Establishing a European Agency for the Management of Operational Cooperation at the External Borders of the Member States of the European Union', L 349/1 Council Regulation (EC) No 2007/2004 § (2004). https://eur-lex.europa.eu/legal-content/EN/TXT/?qid=1513171334865&uri=CELEX:32004R2007.

Council of the European Union. 'The Hague Programme: Strengthening Freedom, Security and Justice in the European Union', 2005/C 53/01 § (2005). https://eur-lex.europa.eu/legal-content/EN/ALL/?uri=CELEX%3A52005XG0303%2801%29.

Council of the European Union. 'Migration and Asylum Pact: Council Adopts EU Asylum Agency Regulation', 9 December 2021. https://www.consilium.europa.eu/en/press/press-releases/2021/12/09/migration-and-asylum-pact-council-adopts-eu-asylum-agency-regulation/.

Cox, Robert W. 'Gramsci, Hegemony and International Relations: An Essay in Method'. In *Gramsci, Historical Materialism and International Relations*, edited by Stephen Gill, 49–66. Cambridge: Cambridge University Press, 1993. https://doi.org/10.1017/CBO9780511558993.003.

Cox, Robert W. 'Social Forces, States and World Orders: Beyond International Relations Theory'. *Millennium* 10, no. 2 (1981): 126–55.

Daily Sabah. 'Fight against FETÖ Prevails 7 Years after Coup Attempt in Türkiye'. 13 July 2023. https://www.dailysabah.com/politics/fight-against-feto-prevails-7-years-after-coup-attempt-in-turkiye/news.

Daily Telegraph. 'Snubbed Turks Set to Withdraw EU Application'. 18 December 1997. http://www.telegraph.co.uk/et?ac=000142848523311&pg=/et/97/12/18/wtur18.html.

Death Penalty Information Center. 'The Death Penalty in 2023: Year End Report', 1 December 2023. https://deathpenaltyinfo.org/facts-and-research/dpic-reports/dpic-year-end-reports/the-death-penalty-in-2023-year-end-report.

Diken. 'Erdoğan'a Hakarette Üç Yıl: 68 Bin 817 Kişiye Soruşturma, 3 Bin 414 Kişiye Hapis'. 12 November 2018. https://www.diken.com.tr/erdogana-hakarette-uc-yil-68-bin-817-sorusturma-3-bin-414-ceza/.

Diken. 'Erdoğan Tutuklu Die Welt Muhabiri İçin "Ant İçti": Ben Olduğum Sürece Asla İade Yok', 14 April 2017. https://www.diken.com.tr/erdogan-tutuklu-die-welt-muhabiri-icin-ant-icti-ben-oldugum-surece-asla-iade-yok/.

Donnelly, Jack. 'International Human Rights: A Regime Analysis'. *International Organization* 40, no. 3 (1986): 599–642.

Duchêne, François, 'The European Community and the uncertainties of interdependence', in A nation writ large? Foreign-policy problems before the European community eds. M. Kohnstamm and W. Hagner (London: Routledge, 1973), 1-21.

Duvar English. 'Turkish Court Arrests Former Rescue Association Chair for "Spreading Disinformation"'. 21 November 2024. https://www.duvarenglish.com/turkish-court-arrests-former-rescue-association-chair-for-spreading-disinformation-news-65284.

Duvar English. 'Turkish Minister Confirms Vast Personal Data Breach of Millions'. 9 December 2024. https://www.duvarenglish.com/turkish-minister-confirms-vast-personal-data-breach-of-millions-news-64941.

ECHR. 'Statistical Reports – Pending Applications', 31 October 2024. https://www.echr.coe.int/statistical-reports.

ECOSOC. 'Safeguards Guaranteeing Protection of the Rights of Those Facing the Death Penalty', Pub. L. no. 1984/50 (1984). https://www.unodc.org/documents/commissions/CCPCJ/Crime_Resolutions/1980-1989/1984/ECOSOC_Resolution_1984-50.pdf.

ECtHR. *Abdullah Altun v. Turkey*, no. 24561/94. 19 January 2007.

ECtHR. *Kavala v. Turkey*, no. 28749/18. 5 November 2020.

ECtHR. *Opuz v. Turkey*, no. 33401/02. 9 June 2009.

ECtHR. *Refah Partisi (the Welfare Party) and Others v. Turkey*, no. 41340/98, 41342/98, 41343/98, and 41344/98. 13 February 2003.

ECtHR. *Sadak and Others v. Turkey*, no. 29900/96, 29901/96, 29902/96, and 29903/96. 11 June 2002.

ECtHR. *Selahattin Demirtaş v. Turkey (no. 2)*, no. 14305/17. 22 December 2020.

ECtHR. *United Communist Party of Turkey and Others v. Turkey*, no. 133/1996/752/95. 30 January 1998.

Erem, Onur. 'OHAL Sona Erdi: İki Yıllık Sürecin Bilançosu'. *BBC*, 19 July 2018. https://www.bbc.com/turkce/haberler-turkiye-44799489.

Ergin, Ayşe Dicle. 'What Happened at the Greece–Turkey Border in Early 2020?' *Verfassungsblog*, 30 September 2020. https://verfassungsblog.de/what-happened-at-the-greece-turkey-border-in-early-2020/.

Erkoc, Taptuk. 'Taksim Gezi Park Protests: Birth and Backlash of a Political Sphere'. *Journal of Global Faultlines* 1, no. 2 (2013): 43–46.

Esen, Berk, and Sebnem Gumuscu. 'Why Did Turkish Democracy Collapse? A Political Economy Account of AKP's Authoritarianism'. *Party Politics* 27, no. 6 (2021): 1075–91.

EuroNews. 'Bahçeli: Anayasa Mahkemesi Ya Kapatılmalı Ya Da Yeniden Yapılandırılmalı'. 14 November 2023. https://tr.euronews.com/2023/11/14/bahceli-anayasa-mahkemesi-ya-kapatilmali-ya-da-yeniden-yapilandirilmali.

EuroNews. 'Erdoğan'dan Osman Kavala Açıklaması: Bizim Mahkeme Kararlarımızı Tanımayanı Biz de Tanımayız'. 2 March 2022. https://tr.euronews.com/2022/02/03/erdogan-dan-osman-kavala-ac-klamas-bizim-mahkeme-kararlar-m-z-tan-mayan-biz-de-tan-may-z.

EuroNews. 'Turkey Re-evaluating Death Penalty after Erdogan's Wildfires Comment – Minister'. 26 June 2022. https://www.euronews.com/2022/06/26/uk-climate-wildfires-turkey.

European Commission. 'Accession Criteria'. Accessed 29 December 2023. https://neighbourhood-enlargement.ec.europa.eu/enlargement-policy/glossary/accession-criteria_en.

European Commission. 'Annual Policy Report 2015 on Asylum and Migration'. Athens: European Migration Network, and Greek Ministry of the Interior and Administrative Reconstruction, 2016. https://migrant-integration.ec.europa.eu/sites/default/files/2018-07/annual-policy-12a_greece_apr_part2_english.pdf.

European Commission. 'Bilateral Readmission Agreements'. *Home Affairs*, September 2022. https://home-affairs.ec.europa.eu/system/files/2022-10/EMN_INFORM_bilateral_readmission.pdf.

European Commission. 'Commission Staff Working Document Accompanying the Document Report from the Commission to the European Parliament and the Council Third Report on Progress by Turkey in Fulfilling the Requirements of its Visa Liberalisation Roadmap', Pub. L. no. SWD (2016) 161 final, COM(2016) 278 final (2016). https://home-affairs.ec.europa.eu/document/download/1cbb2e5d-5a42-4d7e-af8c-0f884d6f39c8_en.

European Commission. 'Completing the Reform of the Common European Asylum System: Towards an Efficient, Fair and Humane Asylum Policy'. 13 July 2016. https://ec.europa.eu/commission/presscorner/detail/en/ip_16_2433.

European Commission. 'Country Responsible for Asylum Application (Dublin Regulation)'. Accessed 3 February 2023. https://home-affairs.ec.europa.eu/policies/migration-and-asylum/common-european-asylum-system/country-responsible-asylum-application-dublin-regulation_en.

European Commission. 'Enhancing Legal Channels: Commission Proposes to Create Common EU Resettlement Framework'. 13 July 2016. https://ec.europa.eu/commission/presscorner/detail/en/ip_16_2434.

European Commission. 'The Hague Programme: 10 Priorities for the Next Five Years'. Accessed 2 February 2023. https://eur-lex.europa.eu/EN/legal-content/summary/the-hague-programme-10-priorities-for-the-next-five-years.html.

European Commission. 'Human Rights'. Accessed 16 November 2023. https://policy.trade.ec.europa.eu/development-and-sustainability/sustainable-development/human-rights_en.

European Commission. 'Mass Influx of Displaced Persons from Ukraine', Pub. L. no. (EU) 2022/38, *Official Journal of the European Union*, L 71/1 (2022). https://eur-lex.europa.eu/legal-content/EN/TXT/?uri=uriserv%3AOJ.L_.2022.071.01.0001.01.ENG&toc=OJ%3AL%3A2022%3A071%3ATOC.

European Commission. 'Pact on Migration and Asylum'. 21 May 2024. https://home-affairs.ec.europa.eu/policies/migration-and-asylum/pact-migration-and-asylum_en.

European Commission. 'Temporary Reintroduction of Border Control'. *Live, Work, Travel in the EU.* Accessed 13 November 2023. https://home-affairs.ec.europa.eu/policies/schengen-borders-and-visa/schengen-area/temporary-reintroduction-border-control_en.

European Commission. 'Towards a Sustainable and Fair Common European Asylum System'. 4 May 2016. https://ec.europa.eu/commission/presscorner/detail/en/ip_16_1620.

European Commission. 'Turkey 1998 Regular Report'. 27 November 1998. https://neighbourhood-enlargement.ec.europa.eu/turkey-regular-report-1998_en.

European Commission. 'Turkey 1999 Regular Report'. 13 October 1999. https://op.europa.eu/en/publication-detail/-/publication/bbe56597-782f-42d2-b16e-90ed9dbd28c9.

European Commission. 'Turkey 2001 Progress Report'. 13 November 2001. https://www.ab.gov.tr/siteimages/birimler/kpb/tr_rep_20061998/2001_tr_rap.pdf.

European Commission. 'Turkey 2002 Progress Report'. 10 September 2002. https://www.ab.gov.tr/siteimages/birimler/kpb/tr_rep_20061998/2002_tr_rap.pdf.

European Commission. 'Turkey 2003 Progress Report'. 19 May 2003. https://www.ab.gov.tr/siteimages/birimler/kpb/tr_rep_20061998/2003_tr_rap.pdf.

European Commission. 'Turkey 2004 Progress Report'. 10 June 2004. https://www.ab.gov.tr/siteimages/birimler/kpb/tr_rep_20061998/2004_tr_rap.pdf.

European Commission. 'Turkey 2014 Progress Report'. 8 October 2014. https://www.ab.gov.tr/files/IlerlemeRaporlari/2014_progress_report.pdf.

European Commission. 'Turkey 2016 Progress Report'. 11 September 2016. https://www.ab.gov.tr/files/pub/2016_progress_report_en.pdf.

European Commission. 'Turkey 2018 Progress Report'. 17 April 2018. https://www.ab.gov.tr/siteimages/kapbtablolar/20180417-turkey-report.pdf.

European Commission. 'Turkey 2019 Progress Report'. 29 May 2019. https://www.ab.gov.tr/siteimages/resimler/20190529-turkey-report(1).pdf.

European Commission. 'Turkey 2024 Progress Report'. 30 October 2024. https://www.ab.gov.tr/siteimages/birimler/kpb/trkiye_report_2024.pdf.

European Commission. 'Turkey: Supporting Fundamental Rights in Turkey'. Instrument for Pre-Accession Assistance (IPA II) 2014–20. Accessed 1 September 2023. https://neighbourhood-enlargement.ec.europa.eu/document/download/8f5bf356-1fed-4c95-8110-ccd1436f3c2c_en?filename=ad_fr.pdf.

European Commission, Directorate-General for Migration and Home Affairs. 'Temporary Protection'. Accessed 9 November 2023. https://home-affairs.ec.europa.eu/policies/migration-and-asylum/common-european-asylum-system/temporary-protection_en.

European Council. '2001 Temporary Protection Directive', Pub. L. no. 2001/55/EC, Official Journal L 212, 07/08/2001 P. 0012-0023 (2001). https://eur-lex.europa.eu/legal-content/EN/TXT/?uri=CELEX%3A32001L0055&qid=1648223587338.

European Council. 'Agreement between the European Union and the Republic of Turkey on the Readmission of Persons Residing without Authorisation', L 134/3 § (2013). https://eur-lex.europa.eu/legal-content/EN/ALL/?uri=celex%3A22014A0507%2801%29.

European Council. 'Helsinki Meeting'. Presidency Conclusions. Helsinki, 10 December 1999. https://www.europarl.europa.eu/summits/hel1_en.htm#:~:text=The%20European%20Council%20met%20in,stage%20in%20the%20enlargement%20process.

European Council. 'The Stockholm Programme'. *Official Journal of the European Union* 2010/C 115/01 § (2010). https://eur-lex.europa.eu/LexUriServ/LexUriServ.do?uri=OJ:C:2010:115:0001:0038:en:PDF.

European Parliament. 'Cardiff European Council Presidency Conclusions'. 15 June 1998. https://www.europarl.europa.eu/summits/car1_en.htm.

European Parliament. 'Democracy and Respect for Human Rights in the Enlargement Process of the European Union'. Accessed 16 November 2024. https://www.europarl.europa.eu/enlargement/briefings/20a2_en.htm.

European Parliament. 'European Parliament Resolution of 14 December 2023 on Frontex Building on the Fact-Finding Investigation of the LIBE Working Group for Frontex Scrutiny', 14 December 2023. https://www.europarl.europa.eu/doceo/document/TA-9-2023-0483_EN.html.

European Parliament. 'EU–Turkey Association Agreement (the "Ankara Agreement")'. Accessed 15 October 2023. https://www.europarl.europa.eu/delegations/en/d-tr/documents/eu-texts.

European Parliament. 'Luxembourg European Council 12 and 13 December 1997 Presidency Conclusions'. Accessed 4 March 2024. https://www.europarl.europa.eu/summits/lux1_en.htm#:~:text=The%20European%20Council%20meeting%20in,the%20divisions%20of%20the%20past.

European Parliament. 'Report Drawn on Behalf of the Political Affairs Committee on the Human Rights Situation in Turkey'. Working Documents. A Series, 9 October 1985. http://aei.pitt.edu/49213/.

European Parliament. 'Report of the Committee on Foreign Affairs and Security on EC–Turkey Relations', 22 May 1992. http://aei.pitt.edu/48471/1/A9400.pdf.

European Parliament. 'Walls and Fences at EU Borders', October 2022. https://www.europarl.europa.eu/RegData/etudes/BRIE/2022/733692/EPRS_BRI(2022)733692_EN.pdf.

European Parliament and Council of the European Union. 'Council Directive on Standards for the Qualification of Third-Country Nationals or Stateless Persons as Beneficiaries of International Protection, for a Uniform Status for Refugees or for Persons Eligible for Subsidiary Protection, and for the Content of the Protection Granted', Pub. L. no. 2011/95/E, L 337/9 (2011). https://eur-lex.europa.eu/eli/dir/2011/95/oj.

European Parliament and Council of the European Union. 'Directive on Common Procedures for Granting and Withdrawing International Protection, 2013/32/EU, 26 June 2013'. Refworld. Accessed 7 February 2021. https://www.refworld.org/docid/51d29b224.html.

European Parliament and European Commission. 'Proposal on: Information Exchange between Law Enforcement Authorities of Member States', Pub. L. no. COM (2021) 782 final, 2021/0411(COD). Accessed 12 November 2024. https://eur-lex.europa.eu/legal-content/EN/TXT/HTML/?uri=CELEX%3A52021PC0782.

European Union. 'Consolidated Version of the Treaty on the Functioning of the European Union', Pub. L. no. Official Journal of the European Union C 326 (2012). https://eur-lex.europa.eu/legal-content/EN/TXT/?uri=celex%3A12012E%2FTXT.

European Union Agency for Asylum, 'Turkish applications for asylum in the EU+', https://public.flourish.studio/visualisation/16693152/

Fendoğlu, H. Tahsin. '2001 Anayasa Değişikliği Bağlamında Temel Hak ve Özgürlüklerin Sınırlanması AY. Md 13'. *Anayasa Yargısı* 18, no. 1 (2002): 111–49.

Finnemore, Martha. *National Interests in International Society.* Ithaca, NY: Cornell University Press, 1996.

Font, Nuria. 'Why the European Union Gave Turkey the Green Light'. *Journal of Contemporary European Studies* 14, no. 2 (2006): 197–212.

Galtung, Johan. The European Community: A Superpower in the Making. London: George Allen & Unwin, 1973.

Garriga, Ana Carolina. 'Human Rights Regimes, Reputation, and Foreign Direct Investment'. *International Studies Quarterly* 60, no. 1 (2016): 160–72.

Gazete Duvar. 'Turhan Çömez ve Mustafa Yeneroğlu Arasında "Balyoz-Ergenekon" Polemiği'. 20 April 2023. https://www.gazeteduvar.com.tr/turhan-comez-ve-mustafa-yeneroglu-arasinda-balyoz-ergenekon-polemigi-haber-1614506.

Gill, Stephen. *Gramsci, Historical Materialism and International Relations.* Cambridge: Cambridge University Press, 1993.

Gill, Stephen R., and David Law. 'Global Hegemony and the Structural Power of Capital'. *International Studies Quarterly* 33, no. 4 (1989): 475–99.

Gilpin, Robert. *War and Change in World Politics.* Cambridge: Cambridge University Press, 1981.

Göç İdaresi Başkanlığı. 'Düzensiz Göç', 11 July 2024. https://www.goc.gov.tr/duzensiz-goc-istatistikler.

Göç İdaresi Başkanlığı. 'Geçici Koruma', 7 November 2024. https://www.goc.gov.tr/gecici-koruma5638.

Goodman, Ryan, and Derek Jinks. 'How to Influence States: Socialization and International Human Rights Law'. *Duke Law Journal* 54, no. 3 (2004): 621–703.

Gözler, Kemal. '3 Ekim 2001 Tarihli Anayasa Değişikliği: Bir Abesle İştigal Örneği'. *Anayasa Yargısı* 18, no. 1 (3AD).

Güney, Aylin, and Petek Karatekelioğlu. 'Turkey's EU Candidacy and Civil–Military Relations: Challenges and Prospects'. *Armed Forces & Society* 31, no. 3 (2005): 439–62.

Hafner-Burton, Emilie M. 'The Power Politics of Regime Complexity: Human Rights Trade Conditionality in Europe'. *Perspectives on Politics* 7, no. 1 (2009): 33–37.

Hafner-Burton, Emilie M., Edward D. Mansfield, and Jon C.W. Pevehouse. 'Human Rights Institutions, Sovereignty Costs and Democratization'. *British Journal of Political Science* 45, no. 1 (2015): 1–27.

Hafner-Burton, Emilie M., Kiyoteru Tsutsui, and John W. Meyer. 'Human Rights in a Globalizing World: The Paradox of Empty Promises'. *American Journal of Sociology* 110, no. 5 (2005): 1373–1411.

Harvey, David. 'The "New" Imperialism: Accumulation by Dispossession'. In *Karl Marx*, edited by Bertell Ollman and Kevin B. Anderson, 213–37. London: Routledge, 2017.

Hathaway, Oona A. 'Do Human Rights Treaties Make a Difference?' *The Yale Law Journal* 111, no. 8 (2002): 1935–2042.

Hathaway, Oona A. 'Why Do Countries Commit to Human Rights Treaties?' *Journal of Conflict Resolution* 51, no. 4 (2007): 588–621.

Helsinki Watch Report. 'Denying Human Rights and Ethnic Identity: The Greeks of Turkey'. Human Rights Watch, March 2022. https://www.hrw.org/sites/default/files/reports/TURKEY923.PDF.

Hill, Christopher. 'Cheques and Balances: The European Union's soft power strategy' in *Soft power and hegemony in US foreign affairs*. eds. M. Cox and I. Parmar (London: Routledge, 2010), 194-210.

Human Rights Association. 'İHD: No to Coups!', 11 September 2023. https://ihd.org.tr/en/ihd-no-to-coups/.

Human Rights Watch. 'Iran: Flurry of New Death Sentences', 14 September 2024. https://www.hrw.org/news/2024/11/20/iran-flurry-new-death-sentences.

Huntington, Samuel P., and Joan M. Nelson. *No Easy Choice: Political Participation in Developing Countries*. Cambridge, MA: Harvard University Press, 1976.

Hürriyet. 'DGM Yerine Ağır Ceza'. 12 May 2004. https://www.hurriyet.com.tr/gundem/dgm-yerine-agir-ceza-38603002.

Immigratie- en Naturalisatiedienst. 'Temporary Protection Directive Ukraine'. Ministerie van Asiel en Migratie. Accessed 10 November 2024. https://ind.nl/en/ukraine/temporary-protection-directive-ukraine#requirements-temporary-protection-directive.

International Commission of Jurists. 'Turkey: End Abuse of Criminal Proceedings against Selahattin Demirtaş'. Accessed 23 February 2024. https://www.icj.org/resource/turkey-end-abuse-of-criminal-proceedings-against-selahattin-demirtas/.

Jenkins, Gareth. *Political Islam in Turkey: Running West, Heading East?* New York: Palgrave Macmillan, 2008.

Kabasakal Arat, Zehra F. 'Collisions and Crossroads: Introducing Human Rights in Turkey'. In *Human Rights in Turkey*, edited by Zehra F. Kabasakal Arat, 1–16. Philadelphia: University of Pennsylvania Press, 2007. https://doi.org/10.9783/9780812201147.

Kahn, Paul W. 'Lessons for International Law from the Gulf War'. *Stanford Law Review* 45 (1992): 425–41.

Kahraman, Selçuk, and Önder Kutlu. 'International Organisations on National Politics: Council of Europe Effects on Political Party in Turkiye'. *Otoritas: Jurnal Ilmu Pemerintahan* 14, no. 2 (2024): 429–49.

Keohane, Robert O. *After Hegemony: Cooperation and Discord in the World Political Economy.* Princeton: Princeton University Press, 2005.

Keohane, Robert O. *International Institutions and State Power: Essays in International Relations Theory.* New York: Routledge, 2008.

Keohane, Robert O. 'International Institutions: Can Interdependence Work?' *Foreign Policy,* 110 (1998): 82–194.

Keohane, Robert O. 'The Demand for International Regimes'. *International Organization* 36, no. 2 (1982): 325–55.

Keohane, Robert O., and Joseph S. Nye. *Power and Independence.* Boston: Little, Brown, 1977.

Keyman, E. Fuat, and Senem Aydın Düzgit. 'Europeanization, Democratization and Human Rights in Turkey'. In *Turkey and the European Union: Prospects for a Difficult Encounter,* edited by E. LaGro and K.E. Jørgensen, 69–89. London: Palgrave Macmillan, 2007.

Kindleberger, Charles P. *The World in Depression, 1929–1939.* Berkeley: University of California Press, 1986.

Koh, Harold Hongju. 'The 1998 Frankel Lecture: Bringing International Law Home'. *Houston Law Review* 35 (1998): 623–81.

Koh, Harold Hongju. 'Why Do Nations Obey International Law?'. *Yale Law Journal* 106 (1996): 2599–2660.

Köse, Türey. '"Türk Tipi Başkanlık" TBMM Genel Kurulu'nda'. *BBC Türkçe,* 8 January 2017. https://www.bbc.com/turkce/haberler-turkiye-38529200.

Kostakopoulou, Dora, and Daniel Thym. *Research Handbook on European Union Citizenship Law and Policy: Navigating Challenges and Crises.* Northampton, MA: Edward Elgar Publishing, 2022.

Krasner, Stephen D. 'Structural Causes and Regime Consequences: Regimes as Intervening Variables'. *International Organization* 36, no. 2 (1982): 185–205.

Krisch, Nico. 'The Open Architecture of European Human Rights Law'. *The Modern Law Review* 71, no. 2 (2008): 183–216.

Kubicek, Paul. 'Debating the Merits of the "Turkish Model" for Democratization in the Middle East'. *Alternatives: Turkish Journal of International Relations* 12, no. 3 (2013): 66–80.

Levitsky, Steven. *Competitive Authoritarianism: Hybrid Regimes after the Cold War.* Cambridge: Cambridge University Press, 2010.

Lighthouse Reports. 'Frontex, the EU Pushback Agency'. Accessed 4 March 2024. https://www.lighthousereports.com/investigation/frontex-the-eu-pushback-agency/.

Macrotrends. 'Turkey Inflation Rate 1960–2024', 2024. https://www.macrotrends.net/global-metrics/countries/TUR/turkey/inflation-rate-cpi.

Manners, Ian. 'Normative Power Europe: A Contradiction in Terms?' *JCMS: Journal of* Common Market Studies 40, no. 2 (2002): 235–58.

Maull, Hanns W. 'Germany and Japan: The New Civilian Powers', Foreign Affairs 69, no. 5 (1990): 91-106.

McGonagle, Tarlach, Bethany Davis Noll, and Monroe Price, eds. *Minority-Language Related Broadcasting and Legislation in the OSCE.* Vienna: OSCE, 2003.

Mckelvey, Tara. 'US–Turkey Row: Pastor a "Pawn in Personal Feud"'. *BBC,* 19 August 2018. https://www.bbc.com/news/world-us-canada-45237372.

Mearsheimer, John J. 'Structural Realism'. In *International Relations Theories: Discipline and Diversity,* edited by Tim Dunne, Milja Kurki, and Steve Smith, 5th ed., 51–67. Oxford: Oxford University Press, 2021.

Mearsheimer, John J. *The Tragedy of Great Power Politics,* updated ed. New York: W.W. Norton & Company, 2003.

Medyascope. 'Journalist Nevşin Mengu Detained Following Interview with PYD Leader Salih Müslim', 16 December 2024. https://medyascope.tv/2024/12/16/nevsin-mengu-detained-following-interview-with-pyd/.

Menéndez, Agustín José. 'The Refugee Crisis: Between Human Tragedy and Symptom of the Structural Crisis of European Integration'. *European Law Journal* 22 (2016): 388–416.

MERIP. 'Document: Forced Evictions and Destruction in Villages in Turkish Kurdistan'. *Middle East Report* 199 (Summer 1996). https://merip.org/1999/06/forced-evictions-and-destruction-in-villages-in-turkish-kurdistan/.

MFA Turkey. '"Turkish Accession Partnership" Prepared by EU Commission', 2 November 2000. https://www.mfa.gov.tr/_turkish-accession-partnership_-prepared-by-eu-commission-_br__unofficial-translation__br_no_211-_november-8_-2000.en.mfa.

Migrationsverket. 'Apply for Protection under the Temporary Protection Directive for the First Time', 28 May 2024. https://www.migrationsverket.se/English/Private-individuals/Protection-under-the-Temporary-Protection-Directive/Apply-for-protection-for-the-first-time.html.

Milliyet. 'Tartışılan Iftar Yemeği'. 11 January 1997. https://www.milliyet.com.tr/siyaset/tartisilan-iftar-yemegi-5389678.

Ministry of Foreign Affairs of the Turkish Republic. 'Human Rights', 2023. https://www.mfa.gov.tr/İnsan-hakları.en.mfa.

MLSA, 'Journalist Nevşin Mengü sentenced to 1 year and 3 months in "propaganda" case', 27 February 2025, https://www.mlsaturkey.com/en/journalist-nevsin-mengu-sentenced-to-1-year-and-3-months-in-propaganda-case

Moravcsik, Andrew. 'Explaining the Emergence of Human Rights Regimes: Liberal Democracy and Political Uncertainty in Postwar Europe'. Working Paper Series 98-17, Weatherhead Center for International Affairs, Harvard University, 1998.

Moravcsik, Andrew. 'The Origins of Human Rights Regimes: Democratic Delegation in Postwar Europe'. *International Organization* 54, no. 2 (2000): 217–52.

Moreno-Lax, Violeta. 'Dismantling the Dublin System: MSS v. Belgium and Greece'. *European Journal of Migration and Law* 14, no. 1 (2012): 1–31.

Müftüler Baç, Meltem. 'Backsliding in Judicial Reforms: Domestic Political Costs as Limits to EU's Political Conditionality in Turkey'. *Journal of Contemporary European Studies* 27, no. 1 (2019): 61–76.

Müftüler Baç, Meltem. 'The Never-ending Story: Turkey and the European Union'. *Middle Eastern Studies* 34, no. 4 (1998): 240–58.

Müftüler Baç, Meltem. 'Turkey's Political Reforms and the Impact of the European Union'. *South European Society and Politics* 10, no. 1 (2005): 17–31.

München.de. 'Temporary Suspension of Deportation (Tolerated Stay)'. Accessed 11 October 2024. https://stadt.muenchen.de/service/en-GB/info/hauptabteilung-ii-buergerangelegenheiten/10413124/.

Norrlof, Carla. 'Hegemony'. In *Oxford Bibliographies in International Relations*, 2015. https://www.oxfordbibliographies.com/display/document/obo-9780199743292/obo-9780199743292-0122.xml.

NTV. 'Gezi Olayları MGK'da', 26 June 2013. https://www.ntv.com.tr/turkiye/gezi-olaylari-mgkda,xKVaowHyJEix_byG9LwAYg.

NTV. 'YAŞ Kararlarına Yargı Yolu Açılıyor'. 9 April 2010. https://www.ntv.com.tr/turkiye/yas-kararlarina-yargi-yolu-aciliyor,IRIrqxd5PU6EOO10WFLhDQ.

O'Donnell, Guillermo A. 'Horizontal Accountability in New Democracies'. *Journal of Democracy* 9, no. 3 (1998): 112–26.

Official Journal of the European Communities. 'Council Resolution on Burden-Sharing with Regard to the Admission and Residence of Displaced Persons on a Temporary Basis', Pub. L. no. 95/C 262/01 (1995). https://eur-lex.europa.eu/legal-content/EN/TXT/PDF/?uri=CELEX:31995Y1007(01).

Official Journal of the European Communities. 'Decision on the EC–Turkey Association Council', L 35/1 96/142/EC § (1995).

OHCHR. 'Status of Ratification Interactive Dashboard'. Accessed 10 March 2024. https://indicators.ohchr.org.

'Olağanüstü Hal Kapsaminda Bazı Düzenlemeler Yapılması Hakkında Kanun Hükmünde Kararname', KHK/696 § (2017). https://www.resmigazete.gov.tr/eskiler/2017/12/20171224-22.htm.

Önderoğlu, Erol. 'Pamuks File at the Justice Ministry's Door'. *Bianet*, 14 December 2005. https://bianet.org/haber/pamuks-file-at-the-justice-ministrys-door-71569.

Oran, Baskın. 'Dönemin Bilançosu'. In *Türk Dış Politikası: Kurtuluş Savaşı'ndan Bugüne Olgular, Belgeler, Yorumlar,* edited by Baskın Oran, 655–81. İstanbul: İletişim Yayınları, 2011.

OSCE. 'Document of the Copenhagen Meeting of the Conference on the Human Dimension of the CSCE', 29 June 1990. https://www.osce.org/odihr/elections/14304.

OSCE. 'Istanbul Document 1999'. 1999. https://www.osce.org/files/f/documents/6/5/39569.pdf.

Özbudun, Ergun. *The Constitutional System of Turkey: 1876 to the Present.* New York: Palgrave Macmillan, 2011.

Özbudun, Ergun, and Füsun Türkmen. 'Impact of the ECtHR Rulings on Turkey's Democratization: An Evaluation'. *Human Rights Quarterly* 35 (2013): 985–1008.

Parliamentary Assembly. 'Abolition of Capital Punishment', Recommendation 1246 (1994). https://pace.coe.int/en/files/16455.

Parliamentary Assembly. '"The Death Penalty Does Not Make Society Safer", Says General Rapporteur', 10 September 2024. https://pace.coe.int/en/news/9638.

Parliamentary Assembly of the Council of Europe. 'Opinion 302: Application by Kosovo for Membership of the Council of Europe', 15 April 2024. https://pace.coe.int/en/files/33496.

Pass, Jonathan. 'What Neo-Gramscians Get Right (and Wrong) about the World'. *Medium*, 23 January 2024. https://medium.com/international-affairs-blog/what-neo-gramscians-get-right-and-wrong-about-the-world-74c8349a8bb9.

Paul, Amanda. 'Turkey–EU Relations: Forever Engaged, Never to Be Married?' Heinrich Böll Stiftung, 8 July 2015. https://eu.boell.org/en/2015/07/08/turkey-eu-relations-forever-engaged-never-be-married.

Republic of Turkey. 'The Constitution of the Turkish Republic (November 7, 1982)'. https://www.anayasa.gen.tr/1982Constitution-EYasar.htm.

Reuters. 'EU Reminds Turkey It Bound by Treaty Not to Use Death Penalty'. 18 July 2016. https://www.reuters.com/article/world/eu-reminds-turkey-it-bound-by-treaty-not-to-use-death-penalty-idUSKCN0ZY10F/.

Reuters. 'EU, Turkey Seek to Tone Down Membership'. 18 December 1997. http://www.infoseek.com/Content?arn=a0972LBY655reulb-19971218&col=NW.

Reuters. 'Turkey's Erdogan Links Fate of Detained U.S. Pastor to Wanted Cleric Gulen'. 29 September 2017. https://www.reuters.com/article/world/turkeys-erdogan-links-fate-of-detained-us-pastor-to-wanted-cleric-gulen-idUSKCN1C31IJ/.

Rosenau, James N. 'Governing the Ungovernable: The Challenge of a Global Disaggregation of Authority'. *Regulation & Governance* 1, no. 1 (2007): 88–97.

Sade, Gizem. '15 Temmuz Darbe Girişimi Sonrasında Kaç Kişi Görevinden Ihraç Edildi, Kaç Kişi Tutuklandı?' *EuroNews*, 15 July 2020. https://tr.euronews.com/2020/07/15/verilerle-15-temmuz-sonras-ve-ohal-sureci.

Saraç, Ahmet. 'Türkiye'de İnsan Hakları Resmi Örgütlenmesi'. *Türk İdare Dergisi*, no. 435 (2002): 157–76.

Sayın, Ayşe. 'Ekrem İmamoğlu'na Ceza Onanırsa CHP'de Hangi Adımlar Atılacak?' *BBC Türkçe*, 10 October 2024. https://www.bbc.com/turkce/articles/c5yov2z5r78o.

Schabas, William A. *The Customary International Law of Human Rights*. Oxford: Oxford University Press, 2021.

Schimmelfennig, Frank, Stefan Engert, and Heiko Knobel. 'Costs, Commitment and Compliance: The Impact of EU Democratic Conditionality on Latvia, Slovakia and Turkey'. *JCMS: Journal of Common Market Studies* 41, no. 3 (2003): 495–518.

Secretariat General for EU Affairs. 'Political Reforms in Turkey'. Ankara, 2007. https://www.ab.gov.tr/files/pub/prt.pdf.

Simmons, Beth A. 'Mobilizing for Human Rights: International Law in Domestic Politics'. In *Leading Works in International Law*, edited by Donna Lyons, 177–88. Routledge, 2024.

Simmons, Beth A. 'Should States Ratify? Process and Consequences of the Optional Protocol to the ICESCR'. *Nordic Journal of Human Rights* 27, no. 1 (2009): 65–82.

Snidal, Duncan. 'Coordination versus Prisoners' Dilemma: Implications for International Cooperation and Regimes'. *American Political Science Review* 79, no. 4 (1985): 923–42.

Strategic Communications. 'About Us: EU Special Representatives'. The Diplomatic Service of the European Union, 15 November 2024. https://www.eeas.europa.eu/eeas/eu-special-representatives_en.

T24. 'Cumhurbaşkanı, "Bu Kardeşinize Yetkiyi Verin, Şunla Bunla Nasıl Uğraşılır Göreceksiniz" Demişti; TL, 50 Günde Yüzde 25 Değer Kaybetti'. Ağustos 2018. https://t24.com.tr/haber/cumhurbaskani-bu-kardesinize-yetkiyi-verin-sunla-bunla-nasil-ugrasilir-goreceksiniz-demisti-tl-50-gunde-yuzde-25-deger-kaybetti,675523.

TBMM. 'Başbakan Sayın Turgut Özal'ın Anavatan Partisi TBMM Grubunda Yaptığı Konuşma'. In *Başbakan Turgut Özal'ın Konuşma, Mesaj, Beyanat ve Mülakatları: 13.12.1986–12.12.1987*, Nisan 1987. https://acikerisim.tbmm.gov.tr/items/893ad1e3-bd59-4f45-a407-1dad9903f9a2/full.

TBMM. *Başbakan Turgut Özal'ın Konuşma, Mesaj, Beyanat ve Mülakatları: 13.12.1986–12.12.1987*. Nisan 1987. https://acikerisim.tbmm.gov.tr/items/893ad1e3-bd59-4f45-a407-1dad9903f9a2/full.

TBMM. 'I. Özal Hükümeti Bakanlar Kurulu 13.12.1983–21.12.1987'. Accessed 11 November 2023. https://www5.tbmm.gov.tr/hukumetler/old_files/HB45.htm.

T.C. Anayasa Mahkemesi. 'Bireysel Başvuru'. Accessed 7 November 2023. https://www.anayasa.gov.tr/tr/mahkeme/gorev-ve-yetkileri/bireysel-basvuru/.

T.C. Dışişleri Bakanlığı. 'Türkiye Cumhuriyeti Dışişleri Bakanlığının AB Lüksemburg Kararı İle İlgili Açıklaması', 14 December 1997. https://www.mfa.gov.tr/turkiye-cumhuriyeti-_disisleri-bakanliginin_-ab-luksemburg-karari-ile-ilgili-aciklamasi_-14-aralik-1997.tr.mfa.

T.C. Milli Güvenlik Kurulu Genel Sekreterliği. 'Milli Güvenlik Kurulu ve Milli Güvenlik Kurulu Genel Sekreterliği Hakkında Genel Bilgi', 2018. https://www.mgk.gov.tr/index.php/kurumsal/hakkimizda.

T.C. Resmi Gazete. Avrupa Birliği Müktesebatının Üstlenilmesine İlişkin Türkiye Ulusal Programının Uygulanması, Koordinasyonu ve İzlenmesine Dair Karar, Pub. L. no. 2001/2129 (2001). https://www.resmigazete.gov.tr/eskiler/2001/03/20010324M1-1.pdf.

T.C. Resmi Gazete. İnsan Hakları Evrensel Beyannamesi, 7217 § (1949). https://www.resmigazete.gov.tr/arsiv/7217.pdf.

T.C. Resmi Gazete. Olağanüstü Hal Kapsamında Alınan Tedbirlere İlişkin Kanun Hükmünde Kararname, KHK/667 § (2016). https://www.resmigazete.gov.tr/eskiler/2016/07/20160723-8.htm.

Torelli, Stefano M. 'The Rise and Fall of the Turkish Model for the Middle East'. *Turkey's Relations with the Middle East: Political Encounters after the Arab Spring*, edited by Hüseyin Işıksal and Oğuzhan Göksel, 53–64. Springer, 2018.

Transparency International. 'Our Work in Türkiye: Corruption Perceptions Index'. Accessed 20 October 2024. https://www.transparency.org/en/countries/türkiye.

'Treaty of Guarantee: UK, Greece and Turkey and Cyprus', Pub. L. No. Nicosia (1960). https://peacemaker.un.org/sites/peacemaker.un.org/files/CY%20GR%20TR_600816_Treaty%20of%20Guarantee.pdf.

Trstenjak, Verica. 'Limitations of Fundamental Rights in EU Law: Are Human Rights Absolute?' *European Review* 32, no. 2 (April 2024): 135–49. https://doi.org/10.1017/S1062798723000509.

Türk Anayasa Hukuku Sitesi. 'Türkiye Cumhuriyeti Anayasasının Bazı Maddelerinin Değiştirilmesi Hakkında Kanun', 7 May 2004. https://www.anayasa.gen.tr/5170sk.htm.

Türkeş, Hale. 'Death Penalty Will End Turkey's EU Bid, Says Juncker'. *AA*, 25 July 2016. https://www.aa.com.tr/en/europe/death-penalty-will-end-turkeys-eu-bid-says-juncker/615091.

Türkiye Maarif Vakfı. 'FETÖ'nün Yurt Dışındaki 218 Okulu Maarif Vakfı'nda', 17 July 2019. https://turkiyemaarif.org/news/fetonun-yurt-disindaki-218-okulu-maarif-vakfinda.

Türkmen, Fusun. 'Turkey's Participation in Global and Regional Human Rights Regimes'. In *Human Rights in Turkey*, edited by Zehra F. Kabasakal Arat, 249–61. Philadelphia: University of Pennsylvania Press, 2007.

Tushnet, Mark. 'Authoritarian Constitutionalism'. *Cornell Law Review* 100 (2014): 391–462.

Twitchett, Kenneth J. *Europe and the World: The External Relations of the Common Market*, New York: St. Martin's Press, 1976.

UK Parliament, Lords Chamber. 'Turkey: Human Rights', 18 July 1997. https://api.parliament.uk/historic-hansard/lords/1997/jul/18/turkey-human-rights.

UN. 'Convention on the Elimination of All Forms of Discrimination against Women (Status on 11.11.2023)'. Accessed 11 November 2023. https://treaties.un.org/pages/ViewDetails.aspx?src=TREATY&mtdsg_no=IV-8&chapter=4&clang=_en#EndDec.

UNGA. Convention against Torture and Other Cruel, Inhuman or Degrading Treatment or Punishment, 39/46 § (1984). https://www.ohchr.org/en/instruments-mechanisms/instruments/convention-against-torture-and-other-cruel-inhuman-or-degrading.

UNHCR. 'Note on Temporary Protection in a Broader Context', 1 January 1994. https://www.refworld.org/policy/legalguidance/unhcr/1994/en/13438.

UNHCR Nordic and Baltic Countries. 'UNHCR Observations on the Danish Proposal for Law on Amendments to the Law on Temporary Residence Permits for Persons Displaced from Ukraine', 24 October 2024. https://www.unhcr.org/neu/129429-unhcr-observations-on-the-danish-proposal-for-law-on-amendments-to-the-law-on-temporary-residence-permits-for-persons-displaced-from-ukraine.html.

UNHCR Operational Data Portal. 'Europe Sea Arrivals/Greece'. Accessed 29 November 2024. https://data.unhcr.org/en/situations/europe-sea-arrivals/location/24489.

Uslu, Sinan, Ali Kemal Akan, and Adem Balta. 'TBMM Başkanı Şentop: Taammüden Adam Öldürme ve Cinsel Suçlarla Ilgili Idam Cezasının Düşünülebileceği Kanaatindeyim', 29 September 2023. https://www.aa.com.tr/tr/politika/tbmm-baskani-sentop-taammuden-adam-oldurme-ve-cinsel-suclarla-ilgili-idam-cezasinin-dusunulebilecegi-kanaatindeyim/1989509.

Venice Commission. 'Turkey: Opinion on Emergency Decree Laws Nos. 667–676 Adopted Following the Failed Coup of 15 July 2016'. Opinion (865/2016). Strasbourg: Council of

Europe, 12 December 2016. https://www.venice.coe.int/webforms/documents/default.aspx?pdffile=CDL-ad(2016)037-e.

Veryansın TV. 'Ümit Özdağ ve Muharrem İnce'den Mustafa Yeneroğlu'nun "Ergenekon-Balyoz" Sözlerine Tepki'. 20 April 2023. https://www.veryansintv.com/umit-ozdag-ve-muharrem-inceden-mustafa-yeneroglunun-ergenekon-balyoz-sozlerine-tepki.

Waltz, Kenneth N. 'Realist Thought and Neorealist Theory'. In *The Realism Reader*, edited by Colin Elman and Michael Jensen, 124–28. London: Routledge, 2014.

Waltz, Kenneth N. *Theory of International Politics*. Long Grove, IL: Waveland Press, 2010.

Yıldız, Ali. 'Did Turkey's Recent Emergency Decrees Derogate from the Absolute Rights?' *Verfassungsblog*, 28 September 2019. https://verfassungsblog.de/did-turkeys-recent-emergency-decrees-derogate-from-the-absolute-rights/.

Yıldız, Zehra. '7 Kez Uzatıldı, 2 Yıl Sürdü: OHAL'in Bilançosu'. *EuroNews*, 18 July 2018. https://tr.euronews.com/2018/07/18/7-kez-uzatildi-2-yil-surdu-ohal-in-bilancosu.

Yılmaz, Gözde. 'Europeanisation or De-Europeanisation? Media Freedom in Turkey (1999–2015)'. In *Is Turkey De-Europeanising? Encounters with Europe in a Candidate Country*, edited by Alper Kaliber and Senem Aydin-Düzgit, 147–62. London: Routledge, 2018.

Zontur, Erdoğan Çağatay. 'Turkish President Remembers 1980 Military Coup Victims'. *Anadolu Agency*, 12 September 2019. https://www.aa.com.tr/en/turkey/turkish-president-remembers-1980-military-coup-victims/1580335.

# Index

For Product Safety Concerns and Information please contact our
EU representative GPSR@taylorandfrancis.com Taylor & Francis
Verlag GmbH, Kaufingerstraße 24, 80331 München, Germany